COMPREHENSIVE MENTORING PROGRAMS
for New Teachers

Models of Induction and Support

SECOND EDITION

SUSAN VILLANI
Foreword by Charlotte Danielson

A JOINT PUBLICATION

CORWIN
A SAGE Company

For information:

Corwin
A SAGE Company
2455 Teller Road
Thousand Oaks, California 91320
(800) 233-9936
Fax: (800) 417-2466
www.corwinpress.com

SAGE Ltd.
1 Oliver's Yard
55 City Road
London EC1Y 1SP
United Kingdom

SAGE India Pvt. Ltd.
B 1/I 1 Mohan Cooperative
    Industrial Area
Mathura Road, New Delhi 110 044
India

SAGE Asia-Pacific Pte. Ltd.
33 Pekin Street #02-01
Far East Square
Singapore 048763

Printed in the United States of America

**A Joint Publication of WestEd and Corwin **

Library of Congress Cataloging-in-Publication Data

Villani, Susan. Comprehensive mentoring programs for new teachers: Models of induction and support/Susan Villani. — 2nd ed.
      p. cm.
Rev. ed. of: Mentoring programs for new teachers. c2002.
Includes bibliographical references and index.
ISBN 978-1-4129-6612-2 (cloth)
ISBN 978-1-4129-6613-9 (pbk.)

   1. First-year teachers—Inservice training—United States. 2. Mentoring in education—United States.
I. Villani, Susan. Mentoring programs for new teachers. II. Title.

LB2844.1.N4V55 2009
371.102—dc22   2009002816

This book is printed on acid-free paper.

09 10 11 12 10 9 8 7 6 5 4 3 2 1

Acquisitions Editor:	Debra Stollenwerk
Associate Editor:	Julie McNall
Production Editor:	Libby Larson
Copy Editor:	Rachel Keith
Typesetter:	C&M Digitals (P) Ltd.
Proofreader:	Wendy Jo Dymond
Indexer:	Sheila Bodell
Cover and Graphic Designer:	Michael Dubowe

Contents

Foreword

The Need for Mentoring

The idea that beginning teachers require a structured system to support their entry into the profession has moved from the fringes of the policy landscape to the center; it is now generally recognized as a critical component of a comprehensive approach to teacher development and is mandated in many states. As the education community develops better understanding of the life cycle of a teaching career and of how best to support teachers' professional learning, the first few years of practice are widely acknowledged to be critical steps in the development of expertise.

Teaching is the only career without a recognized apprenticeship stage. Physicians and surgeons are not asked to make diagnoses or perform operations unsupervised at the end of their classroom training; that supervision is the purpose of internships and residencies. Newly licensed architects are not asked to design a major building during their first week on the job, nor are novice attorneys given the full responsibility for a major case. But a new teacher has the same responsibilities as a veteran with 20 years' experience.

Furthermore, in many settings, beginning teachers are presented with more difficult teaching assignments than their more experienced colleagues. They are frequently assigned the most preparations, the most challenging students, and no classroom of their own. Although these practices are unconscionable, they are widespread.

It is small wonder, then, that attrition rates among new teachers are so high. Estimates vary, but most researchers maintain that about 30 percent of teachers leave the profession within the first five years, with a staggering 50 percent in urban and isolated rural areas. This represents a tremendous cost, both human and economic.

The human cost is unmistakable. Most teachers in training begin their education programs filled with optimism and confidence. Many have a strong calling to the profession and expect to be successful. In general, that confidence lasts into their first year of teaching, when they are confronted with the daunting challenges of real students in real situations. They are, in most cases, thrown into the proverbial deep end and expected to sink or swim.

The lack of support for beginning teachers appears to be grounded in the erroneous belief that they have learned in their preparation programs all they need to know to be successful. If they are not successful, it is their own fault; they are not tough enough or unfit in some way for the rigors of teaching. Fortunately, well-conceived mentoring programs have been developed to make a difference in the success rates of beginning teachers, and many of them are described in this book. Attrition rates are dropping, and teachers' skills and confidence in their work are significantly improving. When asked, "If you had the opportunity to make the decision again, would you choose teaching as a career?" far more answer in the affirmative than in the negative.

So, what is a well-conceived, comprehensive mentoring program?

1. The program is far more than a buddy system, in which the buddy is available as a sounding board and a sympathetic ear and shoulder. A buddy is important, and

every well-designed program includes provision for a more experienced colleague to offer moral support. But well-designed programs consist of far more than buddies: they provide help with instruction as well.

2. The program provides more than practical guidance on school policies and procedures, such as how to order supplies or videos and how to conduct back-to-school night. Again, this type of assistance is important but not sufficient.

3. The program includes more than generalized support. Coaching of a novice teacher can assist that individual in clarifying goals and exploring options. But learning to teach is a highly complex undertaking, and the novice's progress is hastened by well-designed activities focused on the improvement of practice. The program should be organized around a vision of good teaching—a common language that serves to structure the professional conversations between beginning teachers and their mentors.

4. The program includes adequate training for mentors and orientation for site administrators so that they can carry out their roles with skill. Ideally, the training for mentors engages them in important professional learning and a heightened awareness of their own practice.

5. The program engages beginning teachers in self-assessment, reflection on practice, and formative assessment—the same ingredients found to enhance everyone's learning, that of students as well as adults.

6. Last, the program is planned and organized, with adequate compensation for mentors, schedule time for mentors and beginning teachers to work together, and support for the mentors (who are, after all, performing a new role). Mentoring of new teachers should not be a haphazard affair; it must be organized for success.

The programs described in this book offer practitioners a valuable tour of the mentoring landscape. They range widely, from those that have been developed by educators in their own settings to others that have been developed nationally and implemented in a range of locations. They vary in the amount and type of training given mentors and in the kinds of activities used by beginning teachers. Those searching for guidance will find much to draw on here.

—*Charlotte Danielson*

Preface

*P*hew! I've finally finished hiring for September. For a while there, it didn't seem as though we would get all the positions filled. It is definitely harder these days to get qualified candidates for all the openings we have. There were predictions that this would happen . . . warnings of a teacher shortage . . . and now it's hitting home. While I'm glad to have the hiring over with, a thought nags at me: we'd better keep all these people, because replacing them and hiring for new positions will be even more of a problem in the next few years.

How are we going to support all our new teachers? They're asking us that question themselves. New teachers need to learn so many things all at once, and those working toward an alternative certification will have even more of a learning curve. Even experienced teachers who are new to our district have a lot to learn. I wonder how our current teaching staff would react to an invitation to become involved in helping the newcomers? I've heard that mentoring can have a big impact on those providing it as well as those receiving it, and some say that it can even make a difference in school culture.

I don't have time to research this idea of mentoring. I want to make an informed decision, and it would help to know what's out there. I'd hate to commit our time, energy, and money to something that doesn't work for us. Where do I begin?

THE PURPOSE OF THIS BOOK

If you're reading this book, you're interested in programmatic ways to support new teachers. Perhaps you have read about the impact induction and mentoring have on new teachers and want to institutionalize that support for your new faculty. Maybe you are in one of the 24 states that require the district or board to implement some form of induction or mentoring program. You may already have a program and want to explore ways to make it better. Many educators see induction and mentoring not only as ways to provide support for new teachers, but also as means for stimulating reflective practice among experienced teachers. Whatever your motivation, there are many programs in this book that may guide you in developing or revising an effective program for your setting.

WHOM THIS BOOK IS FOR

This book is written for everyone who is interested in supporting new teachers and educators, including:

- School building educators, including teacher leaders and principals
- District office administrators, including directors of personnel or human resources, assistant superintendents of curriculum and instruction, and directors of special education
- College and university faculty and directors of teacher preparation and field experience programs
- Directors of regional educational collaboratives
- State department of education staff, including those whose work focuses on teacher credentialing and licensure and teacher quality

- Professional organization leaders, including those representing teachers' unions
- New teachers and educators
- Retired educators

HOW THIS BOOK IS DIFFERENT FROM THE FIRST EDITION

When this book was first published in 2002, mentoring programs were often regarded as the best way to support new teachers. Since that time, many educators have come to realize the need for multi-year orientation and professional development programs for new teachers. I have chosen to refer to these as comprehensive mentoring programs for reasons discussed in Parts I and III of this book.

This second edition presents 18 programs that support new teachers. There are 11 new programs that offer a variety of approaches to inducting new teachers as well as updates on seven programs from the first edition. I have added chapters on supporting teachers in two critical shortage areas, special education and math and science, because these populations of teachers are often the most difficult to recruit and retain in the profession.

In an effort to make the programs even more accessible, I have now organized program descriptions into several categories: district programs; state programs; regional and national programs to support mathematics and science teachers; district and university programs to support new special education teachers; and a collaboration of three institutions to support new teachers through cross-career learning communities. My intention is to assist you as you consider what might be most applicable for your own setting, as well as to help you expand your thinking regarding the needs of specific populations of teachers.

Some of the programs from the first edition are no longer featured; they have been discontinued because of lack of funding, either by the district, university, or state; because a director retired without a successor being named; or because the state's requirement for induction was discontinued. These events provide lessons for future leaders who are trying to design a sustainable program: plan for leadership succession and continued sources of funding to ensure that new teachers remain supported over time, and do so because it is the right thing to do, whether or not is it required by the state.

The beginning chapters have been totally redone. The supporting research has been updated, and changes in thinking in the field are identified. A few seminal pieces of research are highlighted; Ingersoll's 2006 paper on teacher recruitment, retention, and shortage is featured because it is the most complete and understandable study of teacher shortages and retention that I have read.

The last chapter has been significantly expanded to help you get started on developing or revising your programs of support for new teachers. I have included a rubric on seven components of comprehensive mentoring programs, as well as a rubric on coaching skills for mentors and coaches. This chapter gives you tools and ways to think about how to begin or enhance your programs to provide the most effective professional development and support for new teachers.

HOW TO USE THIS BOOK

You may approach this book in a variety of ways, depending on your purposes and interest. You may read from cover to cover. You may look at the Table of Contents, select programs based on whom you serve, and proceed directly to their descriptions. If you like to read with the end in mind, you may choose to go first to Part III for some ideas about how to get started. Or you may scan the charts at the beginning of Part II to find which programs are most similar in demographics to your new teachers and educators.

This book describes programs from states throughout the United States, as well as multi-state initiatives. I have endeavored to offer programs that match urban, suburban, and rural settings as well as districts of differing size and resources. Some programs focus on the needs of specific teaching positions, while others offer ways to approach induction, including electronically and through regional collaboratives. University programs that support new teachers are also included. By identifying like purposes or contexts, you will be able to proceed to descriptions of relevant programs in Part II.

My goal in writing this book is to provide a user-friendly resource with easily accessible research and program descriptions. Perhaps you will find research here that will be helpful in convincing others of the need for mentoring and induction programs. Or you may find that sharing a few program descriptions is a place for a committee to begin.

BOOK LAYOUT

Part I

Chapter 1 identifies the major causes of the shortage of teachers, the impact of high teacher turnover on students, and the fiscal cost of teacher turnover. It defines induction, mentoring, and comprehensive mentoring, explaining ways that they address the needs of new teachers and the five phases experienced by first-year teachers.

Chapter 2 takes a closer look at mentoring. It describes the roles of mentors, the ways mentors support new teachers and educators, and mentor preparation. The stages of mentoring growth are presented. Definitions of comprehensive mentoring programs are offered, as well as the benefits of such programs to members of school communities.

Chapter 3 offers five factors to consider when developing a comprehensive mentoring program: goals, funding, the roles of shareholders, evaluation of new teachers and confidentiality, and the duration of the program.

Part II

Charts that summarize key aspects of induction and mentoring programs are provided at the beginning of this section. These charts may help you identify programs you would like to read about first because they parallel your own situation or because their unique approach intrigues you. The charts organize the programs by:

1. The size of the student population

2. Whether the district is urban, suburban, or rural

3. The district's per-pupil expenditure

4. Whether or not the program is mandated by the state

5. The cost of the program

6. The duration of the program for new teachers

7. Whether the mentors are full-time classroom teachers, part-time teachers and part-time mentors, or full-time mentors

8. Mentor remuneration

9. Unique features of the program

10. Teacher retention data

Each program is presented in the same format. First there is a chart that summarizes key aspects of the program, facilitating easy viewing of highlights. Then each program is described through responses to the same questions. Thus, it will be easy for you to compare programs and notice their similarities and differences. Certain questions do not apply to some programs and have been answered "NA" (not applicable) accordingly.

Chapter 4 provides descriptions of eight district programs from districts in Arizona, Georgia, Iowa, Massachusetts, Michigan, Minnesota, New York, and Ohio, including urban, suburban, and rural districts of varying sizes.

Chapter 5 provides descriptions of state programs along with examples of district implementation of the two long-standing programs for new teachers: California's Beginning Teacher Support and Assessment (BTSA) and Connecticut's Beginning Educator Support and Training (BEST). There is a description of a new plan for the state of New Jersey.

Chapter 6 provides descriptions of regional and national efforts to specifically support new mathematics and science teachers. These three programs combine a variety of methods, including electronic communication, to bring together people who are in different locations throughout a region or the United States.

Chapter 7 provides descriptions of district and university programs in Hawaii, Missouri, and Virginia that support new special education teachers.

Chapter 8 describes a collaboration among three institutions to support new teachers. This program was piloted in Atlanta, Georgia.

Part III

Chapter 9 offers a rubric on seven components of comprehensive mentoring programs for you to use in assessing your own setting and in thinking about which aspects of your program you would like to enhance or develop. A discussion of these components, along with a list of things to do to get started, is provided to help guide you toward what you should do next.

Appendices of resources to use in program development, as well as an extensive **Bibliography** of relevant research and readings, complete this edition.

Appreciations

It is difficult to name all the people who have taught, coached, supported, and inspired me. To my family, friends, former and present colleagues, former students and their families, and instructors, I am most grateful. I especially want to thank:

- Helen Hartzman Villani, for suggesting I become a teacher, and for encouraging me to write when I was very young by telling me to "make believe you're telling it to someone"
- Pat Keohane, for giving me a chance to student-teach in her first-grade classroom, and for modeling caring about students' achievement and well-being
- Lonnie Carton, for inspiring me as a graduate student to do the unconventional if it made learning relevant to students
- Laura Cooper, Julie Nann, and Kevin Harding, for our working together to design, implement, and evaluate a mentoring program in the Concord, Massachusetts, public schools that became a reference point in my thinking
- Kathy Dunne, for becoming my mentor when I joined Learning Innovations at WestEd, nurturing my growth and confidence as a staff developer, and helping me think through key issues in this book. I am particularly appreciative of the graphic she designed for this book to visually represent my work.
- My colleagues at Learning Innovations and director Jan Phlegar, for walking their talk about collaboration, positive presupposition, and mutual support of risk taking to promote growth
- Su. Henry and Rose Feinberg, for giving me feedback and invaluable suggestions to improve my manuscript drafts
- Marlyn Miller, for giving me insights on my first-edition manuscript
- Robb Clouse, for mentoring me into publishing with information, encouragement, enthusiasm, and trust
- Henry Damon, for working with me throughout the writing of this book to clarify concepts, synthesize ideas, and improve the introductory and concluding chapters
- My family, friends, and colleagues, for encouraging me and understanding my absence while I research and write
- Jon Otto, for hours of technical assistance in the final hours of manuscript preparation
- The directors of the programs described in this book, for their time, commitment to this project, enthusiasm, and contribution to the profession

PUBLISHER'S ACKNOWLEDGMENTS

Corwin gratefully acknowledges the contributions of the following reviewers:

Luajean Bryan
Teacher, Secondary Math
USA Today All Star Teacher 2006
Walker Valley High School
Cleveland, TN

Virginia K. Resta
Assistant Dean for Academic Affairs
College of Education
Texas State University - San Marcos
Round Rock Higher Education Center
San Marcos, TX

Gary L. Willhite, PhD
Associate Professor
Department of Educational Studies
University of Wisconsin La Crosse
La Crosse, WI

Cindy Wilson, EdD
Associate Professor of Teacher Education
University of Illinois at Springfield
Springfield, IL

About the Author

**Susan Villani** has been training teachers and administrators to become more effective instructors and leaders for over 30 years.

A member of WestEd's Learning Innovations, Villani specializes in consulting and professional development in the area of mentoring and induction programs for new teachers and principals, and in collaborative coaching training for math and literacy coaches as well as mentors. Villani has worked with thousands of new and experienced teachers and administrators who have reported improvement in their practice and heightened job satisfaction, resulting in improved academic performance of tens of thousands of students.

Villani chaired the Teacher Quality Initiative of the New York Comprehensive Center. Also, as coordinator for Project ACROSS (Alternative Certification Route with Ongoing Support Systems), Villani has worked with over 100 New Hampshire teachers seeking alternative certification and their mentors. She also worked with district educators through two technology support teacher centers that enhance teacher effectiveness for New Hampshire teachers. Villani consulted with and provided professional development for Maine educators to design and implement a statewide new-teacher mentoring program linked to the new Maine Teaching Standards. In collaboration with the New York State Association of Supervision and Curriculum Development, she helped districts and other service providers meet the new state law requiring mentoring programs for new teachers. Such work helps increase teacher retention and quality.

Villani also works with school principals and district administrators throughout the East Coast to help them enrich their practice and heighten their effectiveness with faculty and staff. Embedded in all of Villani's work is a commitment to help all educators be culturally proficient, thereby being sensitive to and addressing the needs of all students and their families, as well as school and consulting staff.

Villani is the author of *Are You Sure You're the Principal? Guiding New and Aspiring Leaders* and *Mentoring and Induction Programs That Support New Principals.* In 2007, Villani coauthored, with Kathy Dunne, *Mentoring New Teachers Through Collaborative Coaching: Linking Teacher and Student Learning* and the accompanying facilitation and training guide. Villani frequently presents at national and regional conferences.

Prior to joining WestEd in 2000, Villani was a school principal for 21 years and served as an adjunct faculty member at Lesley University for more than 10 years. She received a BA in business administration from Harpur College, S.U.N.Y. at Binghamton, an MEd in elementary education from Tufts University, and an EdD in educational administration from Northeastern University.

PART I

Supporting New Teachers to Accelerate Their Effectiveness and Keep Them in the Profession

*C*omprehensive Mentoring Programs for New Teachers is a way to help you get started on planning or revising a program of support for new teachers. It responds to a question many practitioners ask as they face the "revolving door" dynamic of hiring new teachers and replacing exiting teachers year after year: "What programs are out there that effectively support new teachers?"

A total of 18 programs of support for new teachers are presented in this second edition. These programs demonstrate a wide variety of ways school districts, educational collaboratives, institutions of higher education, and state departments of education are supporting new teachers. Readers will gain nuts-and-bolts information about different approaches to support new teachers that affect hiring, orientation, teacher effectiveness, school climate, and teacher retention. All of the programs are described in the same format, making for easy review and comparison. In just a few hours, you may begin to imagine which of these programs might work well in your school, district, or region, or how particular components of programs could be woven together to best serve your setting.

1

Addressing the Needs of New Teachers and Supporting Their Learning

When this book was first published in 2002, teacher supply and demand were already critical issues. In 2007, there were a projected 3.7 million elementary and secondary school teachers in public and private schools, which was 17 percent higher than in 1997 (National Center for Education Statistics, 2008). Recruiting and hiring well-prepared teachers is more a concern than ever. The current projections call for 2.2 million new teachers in the next decade, or 210,000 new teachers per year for the next 10 years (National Center for Education Information, n.d.). Shortages of teachers are reported throughout the country, especially in rural and urban districts. After they graduate, only about 60 percent of students trained as teachers actually enter the profession (Chaika, 2006). It is not clear whether a sufficient number of mathematics and science teachers are being prepared, given the critical shortages of teachers in these content areas throughout the United States.

MAJOR CAUSES OF THE SHORTAGE OF TEACHERS

Teacher retention has been a serious issue for the past two decades. On average, 30 to 50 percent of teachers leave the profession altogether within their first five years (National Conference of State Legislatures, n.d.). This is not a new problem, yet it remains a continual challenge. Richard Ingersoll, who has done considerable research and writing on teacher supply, turnover, and shortage, has contributed to our understanding of the issues and how we must solve them. Ingersoll (2001) charted the cumulative percentage of K–12 public school teachers in the United States who left teaching:

Of teachers with one year of experience or less, 14 percent left teaching

Of teachers with two years of experience or less, 24 percent left teaching

Of teachers with three years of experience or less, 33 percent left teaching

Of teachers with four years of experience or less, 40 percent left teaching

Of teachers with five years of experience or less, 46 percent left teaching

While the aging population of current teachers had caused many to think there would be a teacher shortage due to retirement, Ingersoll (2006) found that only 14 percent of surveyed teachers stated retirement was a reason for leaving. Instead, 50 percent of teachers cited job dissatisfaction as a reason for departure, and 36 percent cited pursuit of another job, family considerations, or personal reasons. Sources of dissatisfaction for teachers who left their schools included too little preparation time, too heavy a teaching load, poor salary or benefits, too large classes, student behavioral problems, lack of faculty influence, too little parental support, no opportunities for professional advancement, and too little collaboration time. Many of these reasons reflect poor working conditions, which we can and must address. In fact, research from the Project on the Next Generation of Teachers, headed by Susan Moore Johnson at Harvard University, found that 56 percent of new teachers reported that no extra assistance was available to them as new teachers (*Harvard University Gazette*, 2003). Susan M. Kardos, researcher in the Next Generation project, advises,

> Once they arrive for their first day in the classroom, new teachers need their schools to support them in an ongoing way. Without the necessary school site support, they will not have success with their students, and they will be frustrated and dissatisfied in their jobs. (Implications section, para. 2)

Studies have suggested that teachers considered the most talented—those who score highest on the SAT, the national teacher exam, and teacher certification tests—are among those who leave (Ingersoll, 2006). It is very disturbing to find that the teaching profession is losing many of its most promising prospects soon after they begin.

How teachers are prepared also matters. The trend toward alternative teacher certification routes is producing a significant number of teachers who have strong content-specific preparation and often lack pedagogical expertise and teaching practicum experience. The intention of alternative teacher preparation routes is to increase the number of teachers who enter the educator pipeline to respond to the high attrition rates and increasing need for new teachers.

There are many reasons why state departments of education have included these alternative paths to teaching. Critical shortages of teachers in the areas of mathematics and science, for example, have made it seemingly necessary to lure mathematicians and scientists into teaching, in the belief that they have the content knowledge and can learn to teach. Some of these career changers are highly effective at teaching, and others are not, which confirms that subject matter knowledge alone does not ensure either good teaching or job satisfaction. Perhaps some teachers who have pursued an alternative certification path are surprised and saddened to realize that their students are not always ready or willing to learn what they want to teach them. Perhaps others were not prepared for the rigors of teaching. All could certainly have benefited from comprehensive mentoring programs to support their unique entry into the profession.

Research findings conflict regarding the risk of leaving for those who are prepared through alternative teacher certification routes. Linda Darling-Hammond, a prolific researcher and author on teacher quality, has written that teachers who begin their career via alternative certification routes have far lower retention rates than colleagues prepared in four- or five-year teacher preparation programs (Darling-Hammond, 2000). In her study of different pathways into teaching, she found that the retention rate after three years for teachers from a five-year teacher preparation program was 84 percent, compared with a retention rate of 53 percent for teachers from a four-year program. Teachers who pursued an alternative route to certification had a 34-percent retention rate. On the other hand, a 2003 report by the Education Commission of the States (ECS) revealed that alternative programs graduate high percentages of effective new teachers with average or higher-than-average rates of teacher retention. Given the increasing number of people seeking alternative certification, we need more research on their rate of retention.

THE IMPACT OF HIGH TEACHER TURNOVER ON STUDENTS

Ingersoll notes that approximately a third of the nation's teachers are entering or leaving their schools each year. This is an astounding realization. Ironically, underserved populations suffer the most. Ingersoll (2006) states that "poverty, size, and urbanicity were among the factors most correlated with teacher turnover" (p. 23).

The instability of the teacher workforce results in many students' not having teachers who are best able to teach them, since we may hypothesize that new teachers are often less effective than teachers who have had several years of experience (Strong, 2006, p. 16). Having less effective teachers several years in a row threatens the achievement of students in devastating ways. William Sanders, whose research on "value added" has impacted the way we measure schools' and teachers' effectiveness, found that students who had less effective teachers three years in a row made achievement gains 54 percent lower than students who had the most effective teachers three years in a row (Sanders & Rivers, 1996).

Compounding the problem of teacher turnover, the National Center for Education Statistics (NCES; as cited in Gewertz, 2002) reported in 2002 that more than half of the nation's middle school students and a quarter of its high school students are learning core academic subjects from teachers who lack certification in those subjects and who did not major in them in college. Frequent teacher turnover, low retention rates, and lack of subject matter knowledge are often crippling blows to struggling students.

Urban and rural districts have the highest percentages of teachers unqualified to teach subjects that they are assigned, and rural schools often don't have the resources to compete with the salaries and benefits of urban districts. Therefore, rural districts often have higher levels of out-of-field teachers than urban districts (Hull, 2004).

THE FINANCIAL COST OF HIGH TEACHER TURNOVER

The cost of teacher attrition, while significant, is difficult to calculate because it depends on many factors. The Texas State Board of Educator Certification commissioned a study entitled *The Cost of Teacher Turnover* (Texas Center for Educational Research, 2000) and found that, using one employee turnover model, the cost could be conservatively estimated to be 20 percent of the leaving teacher's annual salary; using another model, the cost was found to be as high as 200 percent of the leaver's salary. For example, if one third-year teacher earns a salary of $35,000, the cost associated with her leaving the district is estimated at between $7,000 and $70,000, depending on the level of resources the district has invested.

Reasons for differences in estimates of the cost of turnover include the expense incurred for recruiting teachers, the amount of teacher and administrator time devoted to orienting and supporting new teachers, and the amount of professional development new teachers were provided before departing. A principal in a rural district where I consulted remarked that she was doing a great deal of professional development for neighboring districts; her new teachers were highly trained during their first three years in her district before they left for higher salaries elsewhere. Obviously, if one third of the staff turned over in a given year, this represents a significant loss in financial and human capital.

INDUCTION AND MENTORING PROGRAMS IMPROVE TEACHER RETENTION

Many of the induction and mentoring programs presented in the first edition of this book raised teacher retention significantly, sometimes after only one year (Villani, 2002). Retention rates in many of the programs studied continued to be high in the ensuing years. For example, in Glendale, Arizona, teacher retention before 1991 was 47 percent. After the program was implemented, it ranged from 53 to 80 percent, and the average retention rate between 2005 and 2008 was 79 percent. In Rochester City, New York, the retention rate before 1986 (i.e., before the teachers association' and the administration worked together to promote heightened teacher effectiveness and retention) was 65 percent. In the ensuing 15 years, the average retention rate was 87 percent. The retention rate for the 22 years after the Peer Assistance and Review (PAR) program was implemented has averaged 88 percent.

In this second edition, there are other examples of the impact of mentoring programs on teacher retention. For example, the retention rate for special education teachers hired between 2005 and 2008 in Special School District, Saint Louis, Missouri, was 91 percent. These findings are particularly noteworthy because attrition rates for special education, mathematics, and science teachers are approaching 20 percent a year (National Commission on Teaching and America's Future & NCTAF State Partners, 2002). In Stockton Unified, California, an urban district, the Beginning Teacher Support and Assessment (BTSA) program averaged an 89-percent retention rate between 2003 and 2008. The program in Muscatine, Iowa, a rural district, has averaged 89-percent retention for teachers hired between 2004 and 2007.

While retention is important, it is only part of the broader goal of raising student achievement. That goal is much more difficult to measure because there are so many variables that impact student learning. Retaining teachers is a first step. Enhancing teacher efficacy while maintaining a stable teacher workforce moves us closer to impacting student learning and achievement.

DEFINING INDUCTION, MENTORING, AND COMPREHENSIVE MENTORING PROGRAMS

Induction is a multi-year, systemic process specifically designed to orient newly recruited people to their work and support them through ongoing professional development (Public Education Network, 2004). While mentoring is usually part of an induction program, this is not always the case.

Mentoring is historically defined as a relationship between colleagues, usually one to one, often in which an experienced practitioner works to help a novice enter a profession or place of work and become highly proficient. Many districts have formalized mentoring to ensure that it moves beyond a one-to-one relationship and provides new teachers with the comprehensive support and professional development they need. Such *comprehensive mentoring programs* include the practices often identified in induction programs and emphasize the importance of dialogue among colleagues to promote reflection, heightened performance, and retention. One way to think about comprehensive mentoring programs is to understand that they have the following components:

1. Involvement of key shareholders and members of the school community
2. Administrator commitment and support
3. A selection process and criteria for mentor teachers
4. A new teacher and mentor matching method
5. Training and support for new teachers and their mentors
6. Sustaining policies and procedures
7. Evaluation of the mentoring program (Dunne & Villani, 2007)

In this book, I will use the term "comprehensive mentoring program" when referring to an organized approach to providing all of these practices.

Chapter 9 includes a deeper discussion of comprehensive mentoring programs and a rubric to help you assess your own setting and set goals for developing or enhancing a program of support for new teachers that accelerates their effectiveness and heightens their retention in the profession. Whatever the program, and whatever it is named by its planners, it needs to be grounded in the needs and experiences of new teachers.

THE NEEDS OF NEW TEACHERS

We need new teachers to be as effective as possible in their teaching assignments because they have students who are counting on them as soon as classes begin. We also need effective new teachers to remain in their positions so that there isn't a revolving door effect in our schools, particularly in urban and rural districts. Understanding the needs of new teachers is an important first step in providing the support they require and deserve.

"Reality shock" is what Simon Veenman (1984) called the state of mind new teachers often enter when they first deal with the demands of teaching. In an older and still important study of students in teacher education programs, Veenman found that students believed they would experience less difficulty than the "average first year teacher" on a number of different tasks. You can imagine their distress at finding that they, too, felt overwhelmed by all that they were expected to accomplish. It is not surprising that any new teacher would feel inadequate. Parents, principals, and the entire school community expect teachers in their first year to perform as well as teachers with multiple years of experience. This expectation is unrealistic and weighs heavily on any new teacher. Knowledge about reality shock and the likely experiences of new teachers is useful to mentors and other colleagues who work to support them.

Stephen Gordon and Susan Maxey, who write about programmatic ways to support new teachers (2000, p. 6), have identified the following high-priority needs of beginning teachers:

- Managing the classroom
- Acquiring information about the school system

- Obtaining instructional resources and materials
- Planning, organizing, and managing instruction, as well as other professional responsibilities
- Assessing students and evaluating student progress
- Motivating students
- Using effective teaching methods
- Dealing with individual students' needs, interests, abilities, and problems
- Communicating with colleagues, including administrators, supervisors, and other teachers
- Communicating with parents
- Adjusting to the teaching environment and role
- Receiving emotional support

With all of these needs and more, there clearly is a necessity for a well-planned approach to new teacher induction.

FIVE PHASES EXPERIENCED BY FIRST-YEAR TEACHERS

Ellen Moir, executive director of the New Teacher Center at the University of California, Santa Cruz, and her colleagues (Moir, 1999) identified five phases (listed below) that teachers experience in their first year. Knowledge of these phases is important for new teachers to help reduce their feelings of isolation. These phases are also useful for mentors, administrators, and other colleagues to consider while contemplating individual and systemic efforts to support new teachers.

Anticipation Phase

Before teachers start their first assignment, they are idealistic, excited, and anxious.

Survival Phase

During the first month of school, the new teacher is bombarded with a variety of problems and situations he or she had not anticipated. Besides planning and preparing lessons, the new teacher is responsible for organizational tasks like taking lunch counts, announcing PTA fundraising drives, and establishing classroom routines and procedures.

Disillusionment Phase

Around November, new teachers begin to question their commitment and their competence. They are faced with back-to-school night, parent conferences, and observations by their principals. Just when they are running fast to keep pace with all the varied obligations, they need to run even faster to keep up. It is a time of distress. Surviving this phase may be the toughest challenge for new teachers.

Rejuvenation Phase

After winter break, teachers feel rested and rejuvenated. There is a slow rise in their attitude. They come back with renewed hope and a better understanding of the job. They are relieved they have survived the first half of the year.

Reflection Phase

This is the time teachers review their curriculum, management, and teaching strategies. It is a "what worked and what will I do different" stage. The end of the year is approaching, and they start thinking about next year. It is a time of self analysis. (Moir, 1999)

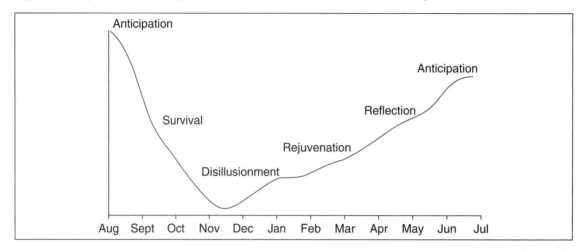

SOURCE: From Moir, E. (1999). The stages of a teacher's first year. In M. Scherer, *A better beginning: Supporting and mentoring new teachers* (pp. 19–23). Alexandria, VA: Association of Supervision and Curriculum Development. Reprinted with permission.

While some teachers with whom I have worked—both new and experienced—find the above phases representative of their experience in their first year as well as in ensuing years, others convey different viewpoints about their first year. Some say that reflection should occur throughout the year as an ongoing spiral. Others question the timing of these phases. For example, a group I worked with in Vermont said that disillusionment doesn't end until after "mud season" is over, usually in April! It is not important that all teachers experience the same phases at the same time, but it is important that we recognize that there are likely to be similarities among the experiences of new teachers and that they know the feelings they are having are not unique to them. If mentors anticipate the possibility of these phases and provide accordingly, and if new teachers are reassured that others before them have had similar feelings and still went on to have satisfying careers in teaching, it may help obviate feelings of desperation that some new teachers endure.

A 2003 report by the Illinois Education Research Council studied teachers who became certified in 1999–2000 and teachers with up to five years of teaching experience at the time of the report (Strong, 2006). Teachers cited "formal mentoring programs" as one of four valuable activities that influenced their decision to remain in the profession. Comprehensive mentoring programs are designed to provide the support these teachers cited as most valuable. In my experience working with districts throughout the country, new teachers affirm that comprehensive mentoring programs make the difference in their initial teaching success as well as their job satisfaction and commitment to remain in their positions.

In Chapter 2, we take a closer look at the important role of mentors, the ways mentors support new teachers, and ways to prepare and support mentors through different stages of their growth. The chapter concludes with a discussion of professional development that addresses the varied needs of new teachers and the benefits of comprehensive mentoring programs to the entire school community.

2

A Closer Look at Mentoring

MENTORS: SUPPORTERS, GUIDES, AND SOMETIMES REFORMERS

The word *mentor* comes from the character Mentor, in Homer's *Odyssey*, who was chosen to educate and support Telemachus while his father was fighting in the Trojan War. The word now means a wise and trusted friend, and the role has expanded to include teacher, supporter, guide, protector, and sponsor.

Who should be mentored? Typically, new teachers are assigned mentors. New teachers may be first-year teachers who just graduated from a teacher preparation program, teachers who came through an alternative route to certification, or people who changed careers to become teachers. In addition, mentors may be assigned to experienced teachers who are new to the school or district, returning after an extended leave from teaching, or teaching a different grade level or subject.

Many studies of the partnerships between mentors and new teachers provide evidence that these relationships have a positive influence on new teachers' orientation to the school system. Through comprehensive mentoring programs, new teachers are socialized to the school culture and improve their effectiveness in promoting student learning. Socialization, however, is not limited to promoting conventional norms, warned Sharon Feiman-Nemser, a noted teacher-educator and researcher, more than a decade ago. She suggested "pairing new teachers with mentors 'who are already reformers in their schools and classrooms' or developing 'collaborative contexts where mentors and novices can explore new approaches together'" (Brewster & Railsback, 2001, para. 2).

Michael Fullan, a Canadian researcher who studies school change, wrote nearly two decades ago, "As proactive change agents, mentors function as the sponsors of actions to reform education. They empower others to rethink obsolete routines and be accountable for continued improvement" (as cited in Bey, 1995, p. 15). The challenge for mentors to improve education as well as to acculturate new teachers had clearly been issued, and it continues to make the difference between a "buddy" system and a comprehensive approach to school reform. Mentoring done well is a catalyst for school improvement through its direct influence on new teachers' effectiveness and retention. Additionally, because experienced mentors reflect on their craft with new staff, mentoring can improve the practice of experienced teachers, a school's culture, and professional development practices.

Within comprehensive mentoring programs, mentors have multiple roles, including those of colleague, confidant, supporter, model, and coach. Mentors are typically full-time classroom teachers who work with one new teacher or educator, sometimes referred to as a "mentee." As the number of new teachers is increasing, mentors are sometimes assigned to work with more then one mentee, and sometimes they work with them in small groups. Some programs have created part-time or full-time positions for mentors so that they may focus their time and attention on supporting new teachers.

Although mentors originally worked with new classroom teachers, it soon became apparent that many other new educators would also benefit from mentoring. These individuals include school psychologists, special education teachers, speech and language therapists, physical and occupational therapists, reading specialists, instructional coaches, and guidance counselors. For clarity and smooth flow of language, all these educators will be referred to as teachers from here on. Please include their roles in your thinking about comprehensive mentoring programs, because there may be times when it will be helpful, in considering mentor matching or materials used, to differentiate mentoring support based on the varying roles of those in the program. In addition, mentors may be very helpful to experienced teachers who are new to a school or district. Therefore, please consider the range of experience of teachers new to a setting when planning for new-teacher mentoring and induction.

THE MENTOR'S ROLE

New teachers have a number of high-priority needs. Mentors can support new teachers in many different ways, depending on their time, resources, and the parameters of their role. Consider the following analogous scenario:

Suppose you are studying the reintroduction of wolves into the continental United States, and you want to learn more about it at Yellowstone National Park. You make plans to visit the park and seek out a ranger when you arrive. Since you have never visited the park before, the ranger orients you to the park's layout, including the location of park headquarters, food, and facilities; the rules for being in the park; and the opening and closing times. As you describe your interests, the ranger asks you several questions: "Have you ever been here before?" "How much time and money do you have to support your stay?" "What specifically do you want to learn?" Your answers will help the ranger know the breadth and depth of the support she may provide to you.

What you want to learn about the wolves and how much time you have will affect the ranger's recommendations, including whether it would be wise to have a park service guide accompany you during your study. If you want a guide, the experience will be different depending on whether you have only an hour and want a quick walk around the perimeter of the habitat or if you can stay longer. Perhaps you could become part of a small group that will spend four hours walking through the area of the park you want to see. If you say that you have several days to devote to your observations, you might arrange for a ranger who is very knowledgeable to join you each day and share his knowledge, assisting you while you make your observations and answering your questions along the way. Your priorities and resources will determine the course of action of the ranger who is introducing you to the park.

Designing a mentoring program for new teachers is similar to your visiting the park. Just as there were different levels of support the ranger could provide for you, your school district must decide what it wants mentors to provide for new teachers and what resources are available to support those interactions. The extent and depth of interactions between mentors and new teachers are determined by decisions about goals, resource allocation, and structural supports that are made when the program is created or revised.

For example, the district may want mentors to orient new teachers to the school and provide information about routines and practices. Providing new teachers with this information is helpful. If mentors have additional time to interact with new teachers, they can discuss the state teaching standards and curriculum frameworks. If the district is able to provide professional development for mentors before and while they assume the role as well as released time for them to work with new teachers, then mentors might do collaborative coaching on a regular basis throughout the school year, working side by side with new teachers as they become even better instructors.

Similar to the different levels of support provided in the Yellowstone example, there are different levels of guidance and support that a mentor may provide for a new teacher. Typical levels of support provided for new teachers include:

Essential Beginnings

1. Contacting the new teacher right after hiring to set up a time to meet

2. Helping the new teacher with classroom setup and ensuring that there are adequate furnishings and teaching materials

3. Familiarizing the new teacher with school culture, events, and tacit agreements among staff

4. Establishing and sticking to a weekly meeting time of at last 30 minutes to discuss school expectations and events, topical issues, and questions the new teacher may have

5. Sharing information and problem solving, when requested by the new teacher

Instructional Support and Development

6. Discussing state teaching standards and curriculum frameworks as they apply to the teaching assignments of the new teacher and mentor

7. Initiating and participating in a minimum of four collaborative coaching cycles, each of which include a planning conversation, observation of practice, data collection as requested by the new teacher, and a reflecting conversation, to promote the new teacher's reflection on practice

8. Facilitating observations of other teachers' instruction, as well as the mentor's

9. Utilizing a tool for self-assessment of instruction, such as The Framework for Teaching by Charlotte Danielson, to discuss areas of growth identified by the new teacher

Professional Support and Development

10. Role playing events, like parent-teacher conferences or formal teacher evaluation, to help the new teacher feel prepared to participate in them as is appropriate in the district

11. Collaborating on a project together, such as lesson planning, action research, or an event at school

12. Modeling what it means to be a professional, both within the context the mentor and new teacher share as well as in the larger arenas of state and national professional organizations and conferences

13. Introducing the new teacher to colleagues, organizations, and professional development events beyond the school

As you can see from the levels of support that mentors can provide, setting up a comprehensive mentoring program is a complicated endeavor that requires planning and the commitment of key shareholders in the school community.

WAYS MENTORS SUPPORT NEW TEACHERS

Mentors promote cultural proficiency regarding students and their families

New teachers need assistance when they are unfamiliar with the cultural diversity of their students and its relationship to their learning. New teachers might misinterpret students' classroom behaviors and, in so doing, may not respond to their students in ways that promote their achievement in school. Unfortunately, teachers who are not culturally proficient may identify the actions and words of students from different cultures as signals of lack of ability rather than displays of cultural diversity. Therefore, mentors need to teach strategies to novice teachers that address these possible failures in communication and understanding. In addition, as school reformers and activists, mentors are in a strong position to help change school policies and practices that are unsatisfactory for student learning.

Mentors provide emotional support and encouragement

Many new teachers feel a significant degree of self-doubt as they encounter the challenges of teaching students with diverse learning and emotional needs. Many wonder if they have made the right career choice or if they are able to become the teacher they envision. Teachers who have had mentors say repeatedly that it was the support and encouragement of their mentors, sometimes on a daily basis at the beginning of the year, that made the difference in their ability to see the possibility of becoming competent and successful teachers. Mentors establish trust and rapport with new teachers in as many ways as there are new teachers, yet what is true for all is a positive presupposition of the new teacher's worth and good intentions. When mentors convey this mind-set, they are able to help new teachers believe they will be able to meet their teaching responsibilities and put their energies toward learning more about their practice.

This may be particularly important when teachers who have been specifically recruited and hired because of their diversity enter a school system in which there are not many teachers who share their cultural identity. New teachers of color, as well as teachers of different ethnicities or religions, often face unique challenges if they are recruited into predominantly white school communities. For example, teachers in the minority are often called on when students who share their cultural identity are having problems. Colleagues often turn to them as if they were representatives of their race, ethnicity, or religion, instead of as individuals who have their own experiences and perspectives. Teachers who are different from others in their schools are often scrutinized and as a result may feel significant pressure to "be perfect." In addition, if people move to live in the communities in which they have been recruited to work, they may feel even more isolated.

Doreen Ballard, a protégé in a study of mentoring, commented,

> In order for someone—a female or someone of color—to be successful, they have to have a good support system, a good mentor who is willing to take the time to mentor them, to listen to them and to guide them, give them advice and be there for them. (Gardiner, Enomoto, & Grogan, 2000, p. 176)

Mentors of new teachers whose cultural identity is in the minority need to understand and acknowledge these additional factors and the possible impact on their partner's ability to deal with all the other issues faced by new teachers.

Mentors are in a position to make even more of a difference in their partners' adjustment and acceptance if they provide support based on greater awareness of these issues. Some consider it optimal for people to be mentored by teachers sharing their minority status because they have had common experiences. Cross-cultural mentoring also has benefits, as both teachers gain additional insight by hearing each other reflect on their experiences. Mentors may model how to initiate conversation with others about these kinds of issues or how to initiate further learning about cultural competence among staff members. Mentors may be strong advocates and in this way provide knowledge, skill, and emotional support.

Mentors provide information about the daily workings of the school and the cultural norms of the school community

Newcomers appreciate having guides and can benefit from their knowledge of the school and its culture. Experienced teachers know where the supplies are kept, are familiar with the way things are done, and are available to answer questions. Making the many routines and norms of interaction explicit is very useful to new teachers. This is an important and necessary component of any new teacher's entry.

Mentors can alert newcomers to things that they would not have found written anywhere and might only learn about after they had inadvertently gone against the norm. For example, suppose teachers in a school leave the school building within the same time frame that students are dismissed. There are many reasons why they might, including custodial hours, perceived safety of the neighborhood, stated preference of the administration, or unpublicized "work to rule" practices adopted by the teachers because of unresolved contractual issues. A new teacher who remained in that school after the other teachers had left could be treated with animosity, and she might not know why. In another school, teachers might remain in school for several hours after the students leave, collaborating and socializing with each other. A new teacher might prefer to leave school after student dismissal to go for a walk or care for an elderly relative before working long hours at home preparing for the next day. Yet in this situation, colleagues might think the new teacher isn't working hard because they don't see him working after school. New teachers need to know and understand more about the cultural norms before they can decide which ones they want to follow. Mentors can tell them "the way things are done here" in advance, or they can respond to new teachers' misperceptions when they arise, encouraging their mentees to make their own decisions, but based on a more complete understanding of their particular school context. Mentors may also help new teachers sort through the misunderstandings that may occur.

Mentors engage in collaborative coaching with their partners

When a mentor coaches a new teacher, significant growth is possible for both of them. Collaborative coaching, sometimes called peer coaching, is a powerful way for teachers at different stages in their careers to heighten each other's effectiveness through thoughtful reflection on practice. Collaborative coaching is a modified version of Cognitive Coaching, founded by Art Costa and Bob Garmston.

> Cognitive Coaching^{SM} is a supervisory/peer coaching model that capitalizes upon and enhances cognitive processes . . . a set of strategies, a way of thinking and a way of working that invites self and others to shape and reshape their thinking and problem solving capacities. (Center for Cognitive Coaching, n.d., para. 1)

Mentors can be very helpful to new teachers by using a coaching process that includes a pre-observation conference, called a planning conversation; nonjudgmental classroom observation; and a post-observation conference, called a reflecting conversation. They may prompt new teachers' self-reflection through collecting and sharing data from classroom observations and asking thoughtful questions that promote reflection. These are key strategies of successful collaborative coaching that benefit both mentee and mentor. In comprehensive mentoring programs that continue through the new teacher's second or third year in the system, collaborative coaching may provide an in-depth, continuous process for both teachers to examine their practices. Mentors who engage new teachers in collaborative coaching may, over time, establish peer coaching as a norm of behavior that will serve both new and experienced teachers well beyond their induction years. This collaborative coaching process is equally valuable for experienced colleagues, and that is why it is as relevant for experienced teachers who are new to a school or district to participate in a mentoring program as it is for beginning teachers.

The significant value of peer coaching has been documented by Bruce Joyce and Beverly Showers (2002) in a landmark study of training components. They looked at teachers' acquisition of knowledge, skill, and/or use of the skills in the classroom. They found that when peer coaching involving the study of theory, demonstration, and practice was added to training, teachers' use of the skills in the classroom rose significantly. Teachers achieved the following outcomes based on the cumulative benefit of each training component:

The Effects of Training and Coaching on Teachers' Implementation

TRAINING COMPONENTS	OUTCOMES*		
	Knowledge	Skill Demonstration	Use in the Classroom
Theory and Discussion	10%	5%	0%
Demonstration in Training	30%	20%	0%
Practice and Feedback in Training	60%	60%	5%
Coaching in Clinical Setting	95%	95%	95%

* Percentage of participants who demonstrated knowledge, demonstrated new skills in a training setting, and used new skills in the classroom.

These findings confirm the impact that on-the-job coaching has on gains in knowledge, skills, and use of skills in the classroom.

MENTOR PREPARATION

Mentors are most effective when they are explicitly taught about their role. Essential content for the professional development of mentors includes:

- Research on the needs of new teachers and implications for a mentor's role
- Roles and responsibilities of participants in the mentoring program (mentors, new teachers, administrators, colleagues who are not mentors)
- Communication and collaboration skills
- Cultural competence
- Collaborative coaching skills, including questioning and conferencing techniques
- Coaching observation approaches and data gathering strategies
- Frameworks for examining teaching, learning, and assessing (Dunne & Villani, 2007)

Mentors draw on different aspects of this knowledge base, depending on the level of knowledge, skills, and adult development of their new-teacher partners. Training and continuing support are key factors in the success of comprehensive mentoring programs as mentors attempt to respond appropriately to the changing needs of their mentees.

Alan Reiman and Lois Thies-Sprinthall (1998) have studied ways to promote mentors' skills. They have found that the combination of helping someone else learn, which they call role taking, and reflection yields the greatest learning for mentor trainees. Reflection can take the form of journaling, sequenced readings, or discussions of role-taking experiences. A balance between role taking and reflection is important, and they work best when there is guided reflection once a week (Reiman & Thies-Sprinthall).

An example of the way mentor development is done through a college course is SUCCEED, created by Reiman and his colleagues at North Carolina State University. SUCCEED is a professional development program that prepares veteran teachers to support new teachers. Applicable across grade levels, subject areas, and diverse school system populations, this program is based on a conceptual framework supported by 20 years of extensive research. The recommended schedule is a one-year intensive professional development course (90 hours) to train the mentors. The yearlong course has two components: a seminar and a practicum. The seminar includes courses in relationship building, modeling effective instruction, reflective coaching, and theories of adult development. During the practicum, participants apply new knowledge and skills as they mentor a new teacher. Experienced teachers are served by participating in the SUCCEED professional development curriculum, and new teachers are then served by them in their role as mentor.

STAGES OF MENTOR GROWTH

When teachers assume mentoring positions, they grow in their understanding of their role and of their own practice. Jean Casey and Ann Claunch (2005) have identified stages of mentor development that are useful for designing the training and ongoing support that mentors need.

Stages of Mentor Growth

Predisposition	• Seeks professional growth • Desires to assist and nurture others • Challenges self to improve • Practices effective interpersonal skills • Is open-minded and flexible
Disequilibrium	• Applies skills of time management and organization • Strengthens procedural knowledge • Shifts professional paradigm from teaching students to teaching adults • Has doubts, fears, and unclear expectations about mentoring roles • Has little self-confidence as a mentor • Experiences the "imposter phenomenon"
Transition	• Expands the understanding of mentoring roles • Expands knowledge base and vocabulary • Develops individualized mentoring strategies • Develops better questioning skills • Replaces personal agendas with the new teacher's agenda • Develops trusting relationships with colleagues • Reflects on and clarifies personal philosophy and beliefs
Confidence	• Understands job expectations • Continues the development of mentoring strategies • Refines listening and questioning • Begins to dissociate from the protégé's success • Finds a renewed sense of professionalism that includes collaboration, collegiality, and articulation • Trusts in his or her own beliefs • Begins to advocate for beginning teachers
Efficacy	• Develops a personal mentoring style • Continues to reflect on and adjust multiple strategies • Recognizes personal strengths as a mentor • Makes emotional shift to detachment and minimal response • Deepens the understanding of effective teaching • Moves from intuitive to intentional practice

SOURCE: From Casey, J., & Claunch, A. (2005). The stages of mentor development. In H. Portner (Ed.), *Teacher mentoring and induction: The state of the art and beyond.* Thousand Oaks, CA: Corwin.

If you already have a mentoring program, you may want to invite mentors to use the above stages as a way to self-assess their development. Their responses could inform their own plans for professional development. Additionally, this framework can help comprehensive mentoring program designers plan appropriate types of learning and support for mentors over time.

PROFESSIONAL DEVELOPMENT THAT ADDRESSES THE VARIED NEEDS OF NEW TEACHERS

Teachers new to the profession need more than orientation to the school system. They benefit from formally organized opportunities to learn skills related to the classroom, including classroom management, curriculum standards and assessment, and alternate ways to meet the needs of diverse student populations. They also may need professional development in, for example, promoting parent and community involvement, problem solving, conflict resolution, and time management.

Novice teachers also benefit from meeting with each other regularly. Their conversations together help them realize that they are not alone in their possible feelings of being overwhelmed, their uncertainty about their competence, and their confusion arising from their daily experiences in school. Meetings allow them to share coping strategies as well as things that have been successful in their classroom teaching.

New teachers who have changed careers, while having many of the same needs as those who have completed a teacher preparation program, often have additional needs. Some new teachers may find it easier to ask for help, at least initially, because they are just starting out. Career changers, on the other hand, are often accustomed to being highly competent and well respected in their former field. Beginning a new career, especially one for which they may not have had much training beyond their own experiences as a student, requires that they acknowledge that they are a novice. Being in such a different role is often difficult. Mentors, administrators, and other colleagues who are sensitive to the unique needs of career changers are in a much better position to support them.

Experienced teachers who are new to a school have somewhat different needs. They also need to be familiarized with the school's policies and practices, as well as the school's culture. Yet, they won't have the same needs for development as teachers new to the profession. Instead, professional development for experienced teachers may involve their participating in one or more school- or district-wide committees alongside teachers who have been in the district a number of years. In this way, they have a chance to get to know colleagues, their experience can be recognized, and they can contribute to work on curriculum and assessment, for example, with other experienced colleagues. Additionally, collaborative coaching may have great value to them as they choose to focus on broadening or deepening their teaching practice.

Sometimes, teachers who are not new to the school, but rather changing grade levels or subject areas, are included in mentoring programs. These teachers are familiar with school culture and norms as well as community history and priorities. They will most appreciate professional development and collegial support to familiarize them with the curriculum, and perhaps instructional strategies for a different age level or subject. Similarly, collaborative coaching may support their efforts to expand their teaching expertise. Differentiating the support of new teachers based on their preparation, background, and experience will make a big difference in the value they derive from the program.

A comprehensive mentoring program for new teachers that is part of a larger plan of professional development for all teachers in the school system has the potential for the greatest benefit. For example, if a school system uses backward mapping to plan curriculum and instruction, it will be ideal for new teachers to learn or review the backward mapping process during their induction. This will enable them to converse with other teachers in the system using a common language and knowledge base. When colleagues in different stages of their careers use the same language and focus on achieving the same student outcomes, the synergy in the school community can be transforming.

BENEFITS OF COMPREHENSIVE MENTORING PROGRAMS TO THE ENTIRE SCHOOL COMMUNITY

Comprehensive mentoring programs benefit school communities in many ways.

1. Enhanced and accelerated effectiveness of new teachers

We would not expect new teachers to be capable of achieving the same results in student learning that teachers with more experience achieve. Yet, Anthony Villar and Michael Strong (2007) found that

> classes taught by . . . new teachers in the comprehensive mentoring program realized reading gains that were equivalent to the gains of classes taught by more experienced teachers, despite being assigned to classrooms that had lower initial achievement and higher representation of ELLs. (p. 10)

Villar and Strong's findings are noteworthy because they make it clear that comprehensive mentoring programs have the potential to accelerate teacher performance.

2. Mentors' professional development and growth

Most experienced teachers who are motivated to become mentors for altruistic reasons find that they "get as much as they give." One experienced teacher, in describing the benefits of mentoring a novice colleague, wrote that she had gained "new ideas, viewpoints, rethinking my beliefs, fun, sense of being useful—sharing my own skills and knowledge—re-energizing" (personal communication, 1994). In fact, mentors are often energized when they teach other adults. Teachers find it rejuvenating to talk with colleagues who are interested in exploring with them the best practices in curriculum and instruction. Isolation, often one of the most difficult aspects of teaching, is usually reduced, if not eliminated, for teachers who participate in mentoring programs. Not only do they find that they learn more about their own teaching as they discuss what they know with new teachers, but they also find that collaborative coaching promotes their own reflection and improvement of their own practice.

Teaching, as a career, has a relatively flat structure. Especially at the elementary level, teachers teach or they leave the classroom to become administrators. For teachers who don't want to leave the classroom yet yearn for additional challenges, perhaps through working with adults, mentoring provides an excellent avenue to grow in different ways.

3. Financial savings to the district

Villar and Strong (2007) endeavored to calculate a benefit-cost analysis of a comprehensive mentoring program for beginning teachers in a medium-sized California school district. They concluded that, "assuming the costs of hiring a replacement represent 50% of a new teacher's salary, an investment in an intensive model of new teacher induction in a given district pays $1.66 for every $1 spent" (p. 16).

4. A positive school climate and the development of professional learning communities

An entire school culture may be positively affected by comprehensive mentoring programs for several reasons. Other teachers who are not directly participating in the program are often influenced by the enthusiasm and camaraderie of new teachers and their mentors. Since it takes more than one person to support a new teacher, experienced staff in the school may step up to share the responsibility. When this happens, many members of the school community are pursuing excellence through mutual support and growth. Many of the precepts of professional learning communities are made evident when districts have comprehensive mentoring programs.

5. Enhanced recruitment efforts

Aspiring teachers are becoming more aware of the benefits of mentoring programs. During interviews, they often ask what types of support are available for new teachers. A comprehensive mentoring program can offer districts a competitive advantage as they recruit and seek to retain new teachers.

Chapter 3 focuses on five factors that are important to consider while thinking about program development: goals, funding, the roles of shareholders, evaluation of new teachers and confidentiality, and the duration of the program.

3

Factors to Consider While Thinking About Program Development

A number of factors need to be considered prior to creation or revision of a comprehensive mentoring program. Some important ones are:

1. The goals of the program

2. Funding for the program

3. The roles of shareholders

4. Evaluation of new teachers and confidentiality

5. The duration of the program

Focusing on these factors will help you as you read and consider the different models in Part II.

1. GOALS

What are your goals for the program? Are they being driven primarily by state mandate, by recognized needs of the system, or by some combination of these? As you consider goals, keep in mind that a comprehensive mentoring program has potential benefits for a district that go well beyond initial orientation and support for new teachers. These include:

1. An integrated professional development program that blends the needs of new teachers with support for all staff in meeting the diverse learning needs of students and improving their achievement

2. Reinvigorated, experienced teachers who grow as a result of reflecting on their craft during their mentoring relationships

3. Higher retention rates among new teachers

4. A positive impact on school culture

You need to clarify your priorities as you consider options for inducting your new faculty. While satisfying mandated requirements must be addressed, that is only the beginning. You need to think about your system's new teachers and what is essential for their success. Promoting their personal and professional well-being and transmitting the culture of your system are basic ingredients in any comprehensive mentoring program. The biggest challenge you face in establishing or refining your program is how best to facilitate and enhance teacher performance, with the ultimate goal of heightening student achievement.

The programs described take various approaches to improving teachers' effectiveness. Your decisions will be shaped by your goals and the resources available to you. Focusing solely on new teachers yields a different program from one that addresses professional development for all faculty. If you decide on the latter approach, you need to be cognizant of the needs of teachers in different stages of their development as professional educators. Teachers certified after completing a degree in higher education will be prepared differently than new teachers who come to education from another career; experienced teachers who are new to your district will seek other supports from your comprehensive mentoring program. You must be mindful of all new teachers as you contemplate program design.

2. FUNDING

Funding is often the first consideration when envisioning a new program. You may be wondering if your district can afford a comprehensive mentoring program, especially one that encompasses your entire faculty. However, when you consider the cost of high teacher turnover at upward of $50,000 per new teacher hired (Villar & Strong, 2007) and the possibility of compromised student achievement, the question is rather, can you afford *not* to have a comprehensive mentoring program? We have a fiscal responsibility, as well as an educational and organizational duty, to keep as many as possible of the effective teachers we are hiring in the profession. Viewed this way, funding a program is a necessity, not a luxury.

Initially, please do not limit your thinking about establishing or enhancing a program because of cost considerations. Even if what you want seems beyond your district's or organization's budget, you should present its potential benefits to the decision makers. If cost is the only issue, there may be other ways to support your comprehensive mentoring program. These include the following:

- Federal funds, including monies for teacher quality, school improvement, and professional development
- Grants from local education funds and/or parent-teacher organizations
- Funding from your local teachers' association
- Other professional development monies in your budget
- Personnel sharing or reassignment

3. THE ROLES OF SHAREHOLDERS

While mentors are the primary supporters of new teachers, others are also positioned to ease their entry into teaching. Experienced faculty and staff need to know that their colleagueship is an important aspect of new teachers' success. In addition to the things teachers commonly do to welcome new staff, they can be encouraged to include new teachers in such things as lesson study and looking at student work. Administrators can make sure that new teachers aren't asked to face all the challenges of their first year alone. Parents and families should also be recruited to show their support of new teachers. When families know that there is a comprehensive mentoring program in place, they are reassured about their children's having a new teacher. They should be encouraged to value the strengths the new teachers bring to the school community and welcome them as potential assets.

Mentors: Who, How Often, and What Compensation?

When considering a comprehensive mentoring program, one of the first things you need to consider is who will mentor. Do you want to use experienced teachers in your district? If so, will they be expected to mentor in addition to their teaching responsibilities? Will you hire them as full-time mentors or as part-time mentors who will combine some teaching responsibilities with their mentoring work? Perhaps you want to invite recently retired teachers to be mentors. This idea is receiving increasing consideration, especially because the number of new teachers may actually exceed the number of experienced teachers in a particular grade level or department as so many teachers exit their roles each year.

The majority of mentoring programs throughout the country involve full-time classroom teachers mentoring new teachers on a one-to-one basis. There are benefits to having experienced teachers in a school mentor their new colleagues. Experienced teachers in the building are familiar with the issues classroom teachers address because they are facing them each day. Experienced classroom teachers have high credibility. They know the school culture and may be in the best position to introduce new teachers to the people and protocols in their school. Their knowledge of curriculum, especially if they are assigned to mentor a new teacher in their grade or subject area, is current and includes many instructional strategies for helping students achieve the desired learning outcomes.

On the other hand, classroom teachers have many responsibilities to their students and families. It may be difficult for them to make time to mentor new colleagues when they already have so many demands on them. Finding time to do collaborative coaching during the school day may be particularly difficult, especially if the school system cannot afford, or has a paucity of, substitute teachers to provide coverage. Using preparation periods for mentoring increases the amount of work mentors need to do after school hours. This is a lot to ask of people, especially when these teachers are often the ones who are also on many of the school system committees because of their capabilities and commitment. In addition, mentors who are full-time classroom teachers in that school have their own experiences, alliances, and opinions about school functioning that may be distracting to new teachers. Sometimes new teachers don't feel entirely trustful of a colleague who teaches next door to them.

Some programs have teachers divide their time between mentoring and teaching. For example, a teacher might teach specific classes and then mentor the rest of the time. Part-time teaching and part-time mentoring is often welcomed by experienced teachers who remain passionate about classroom teaching and want to support and promote adult development.

Full-time mentors are another possibility, and some districts are finding that the money they devote to salaries for full-time mentors is yielding improved student learning and achievement. Full-time mentors are able to devote themselves to new teachers and don't have the conflicting demands of a class of their own. They can be trained in many aspects of mentoring and have the time to provide support on instruction, curriculum, and assessment. Full-time mentors are much more flexible about when they do observations and conferencing because they aren't concerned about their own students. Nor is there the additional expense of substitutes. In addition, full-time mentors are not integrally involved in daily school issues and relationships, and new teachers are sometimes more comfortable with them as a result.

However, full-time mentors often coach new teachers in several schools and may not be available for spontaneous questions and unanticipated events. Such full-time mentors are not members of each specific school community, so their knowledge of school culture may be limited. Their credibility may be lower because they are not currently classroom teachers, depending on how many years it has been since they were teaching in the classroom. For this reason, some school systems with full-time mentors require that the mentors return to the classroom after a specified number of years, often two or three, so that they maintain their identity as classroom teachers. This has the added advantage of providing a number of experienced teachers with an opportunity for growth and reflection outside the classroom.

Increasingly, recently retired teachers are being asked to mentor new teachers in the schools at which they worked. They don't have the conflict of other teaching duties but still have close ties to the school community. If retired teachers are recruited as mentors, it is imperative that their remuneration be consistent with that of other mentors. Mentors need to be up-to-date on federal and state legislation, and therefore, it is crucial to include only recently retired teachers.

Mentors need to be acknowledged and valued for their time and efforts. In addition to monetary stipends, school systems may provide:

- Recognition in the school system for being a mentor: "status"
- Compensatory time, for professional or personal use
- Support to attend professional development opportunities outside the school system
- Released time from teaching to work with colleagues
- Common planning periods for mentors and new-teacher partners
- Reduction in duties such as supervision in study halls, in the cafeteria, or at recess

In all scenarios, it is likely that the skills of the support providers will be enhanced by their mentoring. Whether they remain in the classroom, return to the classroom after being a full-time mentor for a while, continue to be a support provider, or pursue other interests in their retirement, mentors consistently find the experience of mentoring beneficial.

Principals

Principals play a crucial role in the success of a comprehensive mentoring program. Keep in mind the importance of their understanding and support of the goals and components of the comprehensive mentoring program you are planning or revising. Hopefully, you will involve some building and district administrators in your planning committee.

Principals can support comprehensive mentoring programs in many ways. They may show their support of the comprehensive mentoring program by describing it during the interview process and mentioning it again when welcoming new teachers. Arranging common planning time for mentors and their new-teacher partners is a very visible way principals can demonstrate that new-teacher induction is a priority. Sometimes principals align specialist schedules so that mentors are able to meet with their new-teacher partners during common preparation times. In addition, principals help promote collaborative coaching as a value of the school, as well as of the mentor program, when they arrange classroom coverage so mentors may observe and coach new teachers. A principal's decisions about scheduling are a powerful way to support the program and promote collaboration among all teachers in the school.

The aspect of principal support that mentors mention most frequently is confidentiality. Mentors in most programs are working with new teachers confidentially, and in those programs, it is imperative that principals not discuss the new teacher with the mentor or ask the mentor how the new teacher is doing. Even when principals mean to support the mentors or show interest in the new teacher's progress, mentors may feel uncomfortable answering the principal or engaging in a conversation that does not include the new teacher. Principals may certainly speak with new teachers about their mentoring experience and even encourage or direct new teachers to work with their mentors on specific aspects of their practice. The key is that the principal is talking with the new teacher, not the mentor, about the new teacher's practice and professional development.

One of the conundrums of teaching is that new teachers are often assigned the most challenging situations: a high percentage of students with diverse learning and emotional needs, the least desirable schedules, inadequate classrooms and materials, and the largest number of class preparations. Administrators must be vigilant about safeguarding new teachers from these especially difficult assignments during their first three years. Administrators also need to consider the effect that coaching sports or being an advisor for extracurricular activities can have on new teachers. It may be tempting to think of new teachers' talents and enthusiasm for these additional roles when recruiting them. Furthermore, new teachers are often enthusiastic about such assignments because of a strong interest, the extra boost to what is usually a low salary, the sense of acceptance or connectedness they can provide, or the contact with students outside the classroom. However, new teachers may well have trouble balancing so many demands. Administrators need to be clear with teachers new to the profession that enhancing their teaching and growing professionally are their primary goals, and should not be compromised by activities outside the classroom during their first two years. (See Appendix A.)

School Staff

Teaching colleagues and other staff who are not mentors play important roles in the support and development of new teachers. Teachers who have similar jobs may encourage new teachers to visit their classrooms or offices while they work, and converse with them before and after the visits to process what they observed. Study groups, grade level or subject meetings, and sessions to look at student work and data are all ways that colleagues may involve new teachers in learning more about their practice and the endeavors of the school. It is important for teaching colleagues to speak to, and not about, new teachers. If colleagues want to support new teachers, they do so directly and don't try to involve the mentor by sharing things with the mentor that they think would benefit the new teacher.

As anyone who has worked in schools knows, the secretary and the custodian are two of the most important people in the building. There is a lot to be learned from people in these roles, as well as other support roles, because they deal directly with everyone in the school community and often have keen observations about school culture and key players. They also may be helpful to new teachers who are trying to figure out how to get things done, and can become, in addition to their mentors, their "go-to" people.

Coordinators/Steering Committee

Comprehensive mentoring programs need good coordination when being planned, implemented, or modified. When someone is designated as the program director or coordinator, things are more likely to operate smoothly. Mentors and new teachers know there is someone shepherding the program; parents, school committee members, and others know someone is in charge. Any unexpected difficulties, as well as the day-to-day issues of teaching and mentoring, may be addressed more expeditiously because someone takes that specific responsibility.

A building administrator is usually not the best choice for overseeing the comprehensive mentoring program because of issues of confidentiality. Principals are understandably interested in the induction of their new teachers, but their direct involvement in the comprehensive mentoring program may reduce new teachers' feeling of safety concerning evaluation.

Sometimes the assistant superintendent for curriculum and instruction coordinates the program, or the responsibility of coordination may be assigned to another person in the system who has experience in the program. When feasible, creating a position solely for the direction of the program is optimal.

Collaboration: Inside and Outside of School

School systems near a college or university have opportunities for coordinating preservice training and induction of new teachers with college faculty. Faculty in institutions of higher education may supplement and complement the induction and professional development of new teachers in a multitude of ways. Sometimes college faculty members support new teachers individually in their schools, and other times, they sponsor seminars or topical sessions for new teachers. Collaboratives and consortia are two popular ways that educational institutions are able to pool their talents and resources to assist in the induction of new teachers, as well as provide many other aspects of professional development.

Some school systems team up to train mentors and new teachers. Others hold jointly sponsored conferences or workshops that would not be individually affordable for any one of the districts. Telecommunication is another tool to be explored, especially in places where distance and low population density are factors that require special consideration.

Collaborations with the teachers' association, local institutions of higher education, and educational networks expand the ways that school systems can support their new teachers as well as their experienced teaching staff. Some bridges among these groups are already established in school systems, and others can be created with the common goal of inducting and retaining new teachers. The support of the teachers' association, the school committee, and the central office administration are invaluable to the success, if not the existence, of any program. When all members of the school community are united in their commitment to new teachers, all the energy is moving in the same direction. The new teachers and everyone else will then receive a clear message: "We are dedicated to supporting new teachers, and we're devoting resources to help them become the best teachers they can be."

4. EVALUATION OF NEW TEACHERS AND CONFIDENTIALITY

Evaluation is a key consideration in new-teacher induction. New teachers need to understand what is expected of them and how they are doing. In this context, the mentor's role needs to be very clear. Will mentors be nonevaluative supporters, or will they make recommendations about new teachers' continued employment? Mentoring is usually viewed as a separate function from supervision and evaluation. Traditionally, it has been considered a nonevaluative role, in which the new teacher presumably feels comfortable confiding in the mentor about his or her struggles and challenges. Many comprehensive mentoring programs have been predicated on the separation of mentoring and evaluation. However, as interest in mentoring and induction has grown, several states have formalized the induction of new teachers and linked it to licensure. Connecticut, for example, required that mentoring of new teachers be part of the certification process. When Connecticut's program was first developed, mentors were trained and assigned to support and evaluate new teachers; now the assessment function is done at the state level through a portfolio review process, and mentors support new teachers in portfolio development. In some comprehensive mentoring programs, peer evaluations are a significant factor in the continued employment of new teachers. The Peer Assistance and Review (PAR) program in Toledo, Ohio, developed in 1981, was the first such endeavor to gain nationwide attention, and others have been developed, including two described in this book: Rochester City, New York, and Columbus, Ohio. These programs are predicated on agreements between the teachers' union and the school administration regarding peer involvement in the induction and evaluation of new teachers. The PAR programs are noteworthy because they are contrary to the popular notion of mentoring. Advocates believe that experienced teachers are the most qualified to provide support for the profession as well as be its gatekeepers.

California's Beginning Teacher Support and Assessment (BTSA) program includes input from resource teachers in formative and summative assessment of new teachers. Advocates of mentors being part of new-teacher assessment make a strong case for teachers having a voice in performance standards. Sharon Feiman-Nemser has been very clear in articulating this viewpoint. This is an important and complex issue; thus, school systems need to give it careful consideration and be very clear about the mentor's role. Such clarity is essential to the success of a program because it establishes necessary boundaries.

We know that safety is a primary consideration in creating an environment conducive to learning. As new teachers decide how much to share with their mentors, they need to know whether their candidly shared concerns will be kept confidential. Trust is a key component in the relationship. Many programs assure new teachers that mentors will not share anything about them with administrators. In peer assistance and review programs negotiated by the union and the administration, new teachers know what aspects of their relationship with mentors are confidential, as well as the role the mentor will play in making recommendations regarding their rehiring. Adam Urbanski, president of the teachers' union in Rochester, New York, stated, "The relationship is confidential, though the outcome is public" (personal communication, 2001).

Other teachers and colleagues need to understand the nature of the mentoring relationship so that they may be supportive of new teachers and honor confidentiality. In a positive school climate, teachers form relationships with new colleagues and speak directly with them. Mentors should not discuss new teachers' performance and should not listen to comments about their partners from other teachers. When new teachers know that the members of their school community are interested in promoting their growth and success and are not talking behind their backs, they are more likely to thrive.

5. THE DURATION OF THE PROGRAM

An important goal of comprehensive mentoring programs is to get new teachers off to a good start. In that spirit, many mentoring programs have lasted only the first year of a new teacher's employment with the school system. New teachers were assumed to be ready to work on their own after that. However, school systems are extending mentoring for periods longer than one year because new teachers need more than a year to learn what they need to know.

Comprehensive mentoring programs span several years, bridge teachers' preservice and inservice education, establish collaborative relationships that provide opportunities for experienced teachers to share their craft wisdom, and have the potential to impact a school culture. For example, school cultures are positively affected when mentors who have been doing collaborative coaching with new teachers realize the benefits of this process for their own practice. They often tell others about it and do collaborative coaching with their more experienced colleagues, perhaps for the duration of their careers. In seeking to better train and retain new teachers, there is the potential to make teaching a more reflective and rewarding experience for all teachers.

As you read the program descriptions in Part II, think about the components of comprehensive mentoring programs mentioned in Chapter 1, the roles of mentors and the impact of comprehensive programs on the school community discussed in Chapter 2, and the factors that influence program development and implementation explored in Chapter 3. Most important, think about your goals and the goals of the different programs, considering how they address the needs of new teachers and experienced staff.

PART II

Charts of Program Highlights and Program Descriptions

Eighteen programs are described in this section. To help you decide which ones you want to read about first or focus on more completely, charts are included that summarize important aspects of these programs by answering 10 key questions. Some programs don't lend themselves to every chart, so some charts do not list every program. Complete program descriptions follow these charts.

1. HOW LARGE IS THE STUDENT POPULATION?

The programs range in size from Dover-Sherborn, Massachusetts, with a student population of 2,148 students, to Fairfax County, Virginia, with 138,000 students. The State of New Jersey has 1,393,791 students and provides mentoring guidelines and a toolkit to be used by every district.

District	Student Population
Dover-Sherborn, MA	2,148
Vicksburg, MI	2,630
North Haven, CT	3,962
Muscatine, IA	5,274
Oconee County, GA	6,424

(Continued)

(Continued)

District	Student Population
Cross-Career Learning Communities in Atlanta, GA	12,632
Glendale, AZ	15,197
Special School District of St. Louis County, MO	28,784
Stockton Unified, CA	38,617
St. Paul, MN	43,000
Rochester City, NY	44,000
Columbus, OH	55,235
Fairfax County, VA	138,000
State	
State of New Jersey	1,393,791

2. DOES THE PROGRAM SERVE AN URBAN, SUBURBAN, OR RURAL DISTRICT?

Five urban, five suburban, and two rural district programs are described. Six additional programs serve schools in urban, suburban, and rural areas.

Urban	Suburban	Rural
Stockton Unified, CA	Glendale, AZ	Muscatine, IA
Cross-Career Learning Communities in Atlanta, GA	Oconee County, GA	Vicksburg, MI
St. Paul, MN	Dover-Sherborn, MA	
Rochester City, NY	Special School District of St. Louis County, MO	
Columbus, OH	Fairfax County, VA	
North Haven, CT		
State of New Jersey		
e-Mentoring for Student Success (eMSS)		
Northern New England CoMentoring Network		
Middle School Science Mentoring Program		
Mentoring Unique Special Educators (MUSE)		

3. WHAT IS THE PER-PUPIL EXPENDITURE?

District per-pupil expenditures range from $6,290 to $14,617, and per-pupil expenditures in the State of New Jersey range from $7,000 to $18,000.

District or State	Per-Pupil Expenditure
Glendale, AZ	$6,290
St. Paul, MN	$7,000
Vicksburg, MI	$8,191
Muscatine, IA	$8,253
Oconee County, GA	$8,662
North Haven, CT	$9,902
Rochester City, NY	$11,000
Columbus, OH	$11,919
Special School District of St. Louis County, MO	$11,928
Dover-Sherborn, MA	$14,617
State of New Jersey	Varies from $7,000 to $18,000

4. IS THE PROGRAM MANDATED BY THE STATE?

Nine programs are mandated by their states and six are not. Some of the programs serve districts in more than more state, so they are not included in this chart. See Appendix B for information about state induction programs and mentoring for new and beginning teachers throughout the United States.

Mandated	Not Mandated
Stockton Unified, CA	Glendale, AZ
North Haven, CT	Cross-Career Learning Communities in Atlanta, GA
Muscatine, IA	Oconee County, GA
Dover-Sherborn, MA	St. Paul, MN
Vicksburg, MI	Fairfax County, VA
Special School District of St. Louis County, MO	Mentoring Unique Special Educators (MUSE)
State of New Jersey	
Rochester City, NY	
Columbus, OH	

5. HOW MUCH DOES THE PROGRAM COST?

Program costs vary dramatically even when size is taken into consideration. North Haven, Connecticut, has a program cost of $2,500, and Rochester City, New York, has a program cost of $3,500,000. Several multiyear programs have been funded by grants, including a three-year Wachovia grant of $750,000 for the Cross-Career Learning Communities piloted in Atlanta, Georgia, and a National Science Foundation grant of $2,300,000 for the Northern New England CoMentoring Network. As you read about these programs, it is important to notice whether they are continuing, and if so, in what capacity and through what funding.

District	Cost	Notes
North Haven, CT	$2,500	
Dover-Sherborn, MA	$24,400	
Oconee, GA	$30,000	Exclusive of director's salary
Muscatine, IA	$66,947	
Vicksburg, MI	$120,000	
Mentoring Unique Special Educators (MUSE)	$420,000	
Glendale, AZ	$718,453	
Cross-Career Learning Communities in Atlanta, GA	$750,000	This was a three-year grant.
Stockton Unified, CA	$806,000	Includes $450,000 from the state and $350,000 in kind from the district
Fairfax County, VA	$1,000,000	
Special School District of St. Louis County, MO	$1,061,500	This is the cost for the two years of mentoring.
Columbus, OH	$2,000,000	
Rochester City, NY	$3,500,000	
e-Mentoring for Student Success (eMSS)	$2,000 per beginning teacher	
Northern New England CoMentoring Network	$2,300,000	This was a three-year grant.

6. WHAT IS THE DURATION OF THE PROGRAM FOR NEW TEACHERS?

This book describes programs designed to last from one to three years for participants. Five last one year, five last two years, and four last three years. Several do not specify program length, and the number of years participants are involved varies.

One Year	Two Years	Three Years
Dover-Sherborn, MA	Stockton Unified, CA	Glendale, AZ
Rochester City, NY	North Haven, CT	Vicksburg, MI
Columbus, OH (may be longer)	Oconee County, GA	St. Paul, MN
State of New Jersey	Muscatine, IA	Special School District of St. Louis County, MO
Fairfax County, VA	Mentoring Unique Special Educators (MUSE)	
Middle School Science Mentoring Program (minimally two years)		
e-Mentoring for Student Success (eMSS)		
Northern New England CoMentoring Network		

7. ARE MENTORS FULL-TIME CLASSROOM TEACHERS, PART-TIME TEACHERS AND PART-TIME MENTORS, OR FULL-TIME MENTORS?

Most of the programs have mentors who are full-time teachers, although some of them have recruited retired teachers or consultants to be their mentors on some occasions. The mentors in the Glendale, Arizona, program have specific teaching assignments for part of each day and then devote the remainder of their time to mentoring. Three programs have full-time mentors, and another program has a full-time instructional specialist who also directs the program. The relative merits of these time allotments for mentoring have been discussed. You will need to consider your resources and contracts, as well as your goals, in deciding what mentoring job descriptions would be beneficial and plausible for your district.

Full-Time Teachers	Part-Time Mentors	Full-Time Mentors
Stockton Unified, CA	Glendale, AZ	Special School District of St. Louis County, MO (instructional facilitators)
North Haven, CT		Columbus, OH (consulting teachers)
Oconee County, GA		Mentoring Unique Special Educators (MUSE)
Muscatine, IA		
Dover-Sherborn, MA		
Vicksburg, MI	Vicksburg, MI (instructional specialist)	
Saint Paul, MN		

(Continued)

(Continued)

Full-Time Teachers	Part-Time Mentors	Full-Time Mentors
Special School District of St. Louis County, MO		
State of New Jersey		
Middle School Science Mentoring Program		
e-Mentoring for Student Success (eMSS)		
Northern New England CoMentoring Network		
Fairfax County, VA		
Cross-Career Learning Communities in Atlanta, GA		

8. HOW ARE MENTORS REMUNERATED?

Mentors receive a wide range of stipends and salaries, reflecting many variables, including job description and available resources. North Haven, Connecticut, pays mentors $100 per year, and Oconee County, Georgia, pays a "goodwill" stipend of $150 to $400, depending on whether the mentor is mentoring a first- or a second-year teacher. Some districts, such as Vicksburg, Michigan, make distinctions in remuneration for mentors depending on whether the mentee is in the first, second, or third year of employment; other programs, such as Stockton Unified, California, and e-Mentoring for Student Success, base compensation rates on whether the mentor is mentoring more than one new teacher. Stockton Unified pays mentors $2,250 for each teacher mentored, and this may reflect the fact that in California the legislature has allocated over $3,000 for each new teacher participating in the Beginning Teacher Support and Assessment (BTSA) program.

Glendale, Arizona, and Special School District in St. Louis, Missouri, pay mentors and instructional facilitators a teaching salary; Rochester City, New York, and Columbus, Ohio, pay mentors a teacher's salary plus a percentage of the base; and several programs pay the program director a separate salary.

District	Stipend	Teaching Salary	Teaching Salary +	Salary
Glendale, AZ		Mentors		
Stockton Unified, CA	$2,250 for each teacher mentored			
North Haven, CT	$100			
Oconee County, GA	$150 to $300			
Muscatine, IA	$1,000			
Dover-Sherborn, MA	Mentors: $950 Mentor teacher leaders: $1,300			

District	Stipend	Teaching Salary	Teaching Salary +	Salary
Vicksburg, MI	$1,500 for mentoring first-year teacher $600 for mentoring second-year teacher $300 for mentoring third-year teacher			Instructional specialist
St. Paul, MN	$700 for mentoring first-year teacher $300 for mentoring second-year teacher			
Special School District of St. Louis County, MO	$150 (mentors)	Instructional facilitators		
Rochester City, NY			Teacher's salary + 5% to 10% of the base	
Columbus, OH			Teacher's salary + 20% of the base	
e-Mentoring for Student Success (eMSS)	$1,800 for mentoring two teachers and another $400 for mentoring each additional teacher			
Northern New England CoMentoring Network	$1,000 per year for three years			
Mentoring Unique Special Educators (MUSE)			University salary	
Cross-Career Learning Communities in Atlanta, GA	$100 to $200 per day for five days for facilitators			

9. WHAT ARE SOME UNIQUE FEATURES OF THE PROGRAM?

The unique features of the programs are summarized in this chart; much more information is provided in the body of the program descriptions. To mention a few, Stockton Unified and North Haven are examples of their state's program for all new teachers: BTSA in California and Beginning Educator Support and Training (BEST) in Connecticut. Vicksburg, Michigan, has a creative way of affording a program director/instructional specialist position: they have hired a consultant to work for them and then release her 25 percent of the time to work for former clients, who then pay the district her consulting fees. These fees equal 60 percent of her salary in the district. E-Mentoring for Student Success is an entirely online support program for science and mathematics teachers. The Northern New England CoMentoring Network and Middle School Science Mentoring Program are two programs with a strong content component to support mathematics and science teachers. The Cross-Career Learning Communities were piloted in Atlanta, Georgia, and were a collaborative effort between Georgia State University and the National Council on Teaching and America's Future (NCTAF).

Program	Feature(s)
Glendale, AZ	Three-year program of support for new teachers in a high school regional district in which mentors are part-time classroom teachers and part-time mentors
Stockton Unified, CA	The way California teachers earn their clear credential
North Haven, CT	Part of the state's BEST program
Oconee, GA	A full week of induction activities prior to preplanning days when all teachers return to prepare for the opening of school
Muscatine, IA	Offers mentoring for experienced teachers who are new to the district even though this is not mandated by the state; lead mentors designed the program
Dover-Sherborn, MA	Mentor teacher leaders coordinate the program and do most of the training
Vicksburg, MI	Creative funding of instructional specialist and three-year program of coaching and coursework
St. Paul, MN	Joint effort of the district and union to improve the environment for new teachers with a two-tier approach of mentoring and coursework
Special School District of St. Louis County, MO	Instructional and professional development are linked and planned for teachers' first five years
State of New Jersey	All district local professional development committees develop a mentoring plan according to state guidelines
Rochester City, NY	Peer assistance and review program in which teachers and administrators support and evaluate new teachers
Columbus, OH	Peers mentor and evaluate entry-level teachers and experienced teachers in trouble
Middle School Science Mentoring Program	Uses inquiry as the basis for mentoring
e-Mentoring for Student Success (eMSS)	An entirely online program that is content specific, pairing mentors with beginning-teacher partners who teach the same grade level and content area
Northern New England CoMentoring Network	Focus on content and instruction in science and mathematics
Fairfax County, VA	Mentoring program for special education and new teachers
Mentoring Unique Special Educators (MUSE)	An IHE program of support for special education teachers, provided by full-time former special education teachers
Cross-Career Learning Communities in Atlanta, GA	Mentoring through learning communities that offer Critical Friends Group protocols, an online resource called the BRIDGE, and a professional growth plan

10. WHAT DATA ARE AVAILABLE ON TEACHER RETENTION?

Teacher retention data are one measure of program success. When this book was first published, retention data were difficult to obtain. With this edition, more information is available regarding the impact of the programs on teacher retention, and the results are promising. For example, Muscatine, Iowa, has had a three-year average retention rate of 89 percent, and Stockton Unified, California, has had a five-year average retention rate of 89 percent. Teacher retention in Special School District in St. Louis, Missouri, averaged 91 percent over three years, and Rochester City, New York, has averaged 88 percent in the past 22 years. These results are exciting, and we need even more collection of these data to inform program directors and committees.

Any correlation between comprehensive mentoring programs and student achievement is much more difficult to obtain. Usually, many variables affect student achievement, and it is very challenging to isolate these variables. Efforts to do so should be supported in any way possible because they will help us think even more fully about ways to enhance teacher effectiveness. That is why Anthony Villar and Michael Strong's preliminary findings (2007) are so exciting.

Program	Earlier Teacher Retention	Current Teacher Retention
Glendale, AZ	47% prior to the program	Retention of teachers hired between 2005 and 2008 averaged 79% in 2008
Stockton Unified, CA		88.9% rate from 2003 to 2008
Oconee, GA		Retention of teachers hired between 2005 and 2008 averaged 99% in 2008
Muscatine, IA		Retention of teachers hired between 2004 and 2007 averaged 89% in 2008
Special School District of St. Louis County, MO	74% from 1996 to 1997	Retention of teachers hired between 2005 and 2008 averaged 91% in 2008
Rochester City, NY	65% prior to the program	Over the past 22 years, the average retention rate has been 88%; retention of teachers hired between 2005 and 2008 averaged 91% in 2008
Mentoring Unique Special Educators (MUSE)		89% rate for 2007–2008

4

District Programs

The following descriptions have been written by the directors of the programs in conjunction with their colleagues and the author. Judgments about the programs are those of the program directors and their staff and not the opinion of the author. Unless stated otherwise, figures and information were true for the 2007–2008 school year.

GLENDALE UNION HIGH SCHOOL DISTRICT

GLENDALE, ARIZONA

John Croteau, Assistant Superintendent
7650 North 43rd Avenue
Glendale, AZ 85301
623–435–6000
Fax: 623–435–6078
JpCrotea@guhsdaz.org

The following information was obtained from telephone conversations and e-mail correspondence with John Croteau as well as program literature.

Demographics

Grade Levels	9–12
Student Population	15,197
Teacher Population	982
Urban/Suburban/Rural	Suburban
Ethnic Makeup*	
African American	8.4%
Asian American	3.1%

Caucasian	40.1%
Hispanic	45.5%
Native American	2.9%
% New Teachers	7% (69)
Per-Pupil Expenditure	$6,290

* The statistics available from the district delineated the ethnic makeup as shown. There was no information about students of more than one racial heritage.

Program Highlights

Unique Feature of Program	Three-year program of support for new teachers in this district	**Mentoring Is/ Is Not Mandated for Certification/Licensing**	Mentoring is not mandated
Coaching Is/Is Not a Component	Coaching is a component	**Mentors Do/Do Not Evaluate the New Teachers With Whom They Work**	Mentors do not evaluate
Cost of Program	$718,453 per year	**Funding**	District
Mentors Are Full-Time/ Part-Time Teachers	Mentors teach two classes per day and mentor the remainder of the time	**Mentor Remuneration**	Mentors are paid a teaching salary
How Long Program Has Been in Existence	15 years	**Duration of Program for New Teachers**	Three years
Higher Education Affiliation	Arizona State University–West	**Program Coordinator**	John Croteau

HISTORY

The Glendale Union High School District (GUHSD) had staff developers working with new teachers. When money got tight, those positions were eliminated. Since the district had a strong commitment to the professional development of teachers, a collaborative effort by the administration and union developed a system to promote teacher excellence.

It was decided that mentors would teach two classes a day and then be released from teaching the other three periods to support new teachers in their building. It was felt that having the mentors continue to teach would strengthen their identification with classroom teachers. Since the mentors were still classroom teachers, the union would support their positions.

STATE MANDATES

Is mentoring mandated for new teachers?

No, mentoring is not mandated for new teachers.

Is mentoring part of certification or licensure?

No, mentoring is not part of certification or licensure.

Is funding provided to support the mandate?

NA

GOALS

The goals of the program are to:

- Accelerate good teacher decision making in the classroom
- Retain quality first-, second-, and third-year teachers for a lifelong career in GUHSD
- Provide support and improvement in instructional skills
- Provide a solid grounding in the district learning system
- Assist teachers in developing a collegial network for support

PROGRAM DESIGN

What are the components and recommended schedule of the program?

New teachers are mentored for three years by experienced teachers in the district. There is one mentor per school, and there are nine high schools in the district. The mentors work with all new teachers in their building during their first three years of employment in GUHSD.

The new teachers come to work two weeks before the rest of the teachers, who return one week before the students. During the first two weeks, the new teachers work with their mentors to prepare their classrooms. Preparation includes instructional training based on Madeline Hunter's Essential Elements of Instruction (EEI), classroom management based on Harry Wong's ideas, and discipline instruction based on Fred Jones's guidelines. The new teachers confer with a building team colleague, who shares lessons for the first nine weeks of school. The teachers are paid to participate in these 10 days of training.

Are there any programs that complement the mentoring program?

District curriculum coordinators complement the mentoring program by providing content workshops.

Who designed the mentoring program?

Vernon Jacobs, retired associate superintendent of curriculum and instruction and superintendent of GUHSD, and Norman Smalley, retired and former district staff developer and district principal, developed the mentoring program in collaboration with the union.

PROGRAM ADMINISTRATION

Who coordinates the mentoring program?

John Croteau, the assistant superintendent, coordinates the program.

How is information communicated to shareholders?

John Croteau communicates with members of the school communities.

Who coordinates integration of the mentoring program with other professional development opportunities and requirements in the schools and district?

John Croteau coordinates this program with other professional development opportunities as part of his role as assistant superintendent. He works closely and meets frequently with the lead mentor and lead curriculum coordinator.

PARTICIPANTS

Who is served?

All teachers who are new to GUHSD participate in the program their first three years.

Is participation of new teachers voluntary or mandatory?

Participation is mandatory. Much of the professional conversation in GUHSD schools regards the Essential Elements of Instruction and the district learning system. Experienced teachers as well as teachers new to the profession need to be familiar with the work of Madeline Hunter and the structure and expectations of the learning system.

Who provides the mentoring/induction?

The mentoring team inducts new teachers.

What are the criteria for being a mentor?

Mentors must:

- Have experience in GUHSD schools
- Be master teachers and very familiar with the Essential Elements of Instruction
- Offer workshops on curriculum and induction in the school and for the district

MENTOR RESPONSIBILITIES AND REMUNERATION

What are the job responsibilities of mentors?

Mentors work with teachers for their first three years of employment in GUHSD. Mentors observe teachers and do coaching with them.

Are mentors required to do peer observation and coaching?

Yes, mentors are required to do observation and coaching.

Do mentors have full-time classroom teaching responsibilities?

Mentors teach two classes a day and are released from teaching the other three periods to mentor new teachers.

How are mentors available to participate in the program?

Mentors are released from teaching three periods a day. Their schedule is created accordingly.

Do mentors evaluate new teachers?

No, mentors never evaluate new teachers.

Is the mentor–new teacher relationship confidential?

Mentors never speak with administrators about the performance of new teachers. An administrator may tell a mentor that she or he told the new teacher to work with the mentor on a specific skill or issue and may ask the mentor if the teacher followed up. The mentor can answer that kind of question as long as there isn't any discussion of the teacher's performance.

Are mentors paid?

Mentors are paid a teacher's salary.

MENTOR SELECTION, MATCHING, TRAINING, AND SUPERVISION

How are mentors selected?

Experienced teachers are invited to apply to be in a pool of trained mentors. They go through a screening process that includes observing a lesson taught by another teacher, scripting it, and then analyzing it. They are also interviewed. If they are accepted into the pool of mentors, they are then able to apply if a position becomes available at one of the schools.

If an opening occurs, the principal interviews mentors from the pool who applied, then selects one for the position. All things being equal, preference is given to a master teacher who works in the school that has the opening. It has been found that familiarity with school culture is important knowledge for a mentor to have.

How are mentors and new teachers matched?

Mentors work with all new teachers in their building, regardless of content area.

Are mentors trained?

Mentors are trained by experienced mentors. All mentors are provided with ongoing staff development through the National Staff Development Council, district curriculum coordinators, and district administrators. Several mentors have also received training from the New Teacher Center at the University of California, Santa Cruz.

Who supervises the mentors?

John Croteau supervises the mentors.

SUPPORTS FOR MENTORS

Is professional development available for mentors?

Mentors train each other, by sharing different areas of expertise. They meet at the district office every Friday to support each other, plan together, and train each other.

Who provides this professional development?

In addition to the mentors, consultants are sometimes hired to do specific training with mentors.

What resources are available for mentors?

Mentors have each other, consultants, and the district administrators as resources.

PROGRAM COSTS AND FUNDING

What resources are required for the program?

The cost of the program is $718,453.

Mentor salaries (including benefits): $472,025

Regular workshop for first-, second-, and third-year teachers: $110,660

Summer workshops for first-, second-, and third-year teachers: $134,152

Books, pamphlets, publications, and supplies: $1,658

What are the funding sources?

The district budget funds the program.

Who requests the funding?

John Croteau requests funding for the program.

PROGRAM EVALUATION

How is the program evaluated?

First-, second-, and third-year teachers are surveyed regarding the program. The mentor team and John Croteau carefully consider the teachers' feedback and their experiences in being mentored, then make an effort to improve the program based on what is said in the survey.

Who sees the results of the evaluation?

The results are shared at meetings with the school board and are therefore available to the public.

RECRUITMENT, HIRING, AND RETENTION OF NEW STAFF

How many new teachers are recruited and hired?

Fifty to 100 new teachers are hired each year.

Are there any data that correlate the mentoring program with the retention of new teachers?

Teacher retention in GUHSD has improved substantially since the implementation of the mentoring program. Before the program began in 1991, 47 percent of teachers remained within the district for 10 years. Recent statistics show the following retention rates:

Year of Hire	Teachers Remaining in the District as of August 2008
2005	82%
2006	70%
2007	85%

INDICATORS OF PROGRAM SUCCESS

What are the indicators of program success?

Personnel at GUHSD believe they are successfully retaining quality teachers, and the data support that belief. It appears that teachers who need to be counseled out of teaching are identified earlier in their teaching careers.

OCONEE COUNTY SCHOOL SYSTEM TEACHER INDUCTION PROGRAM

OCONEE, GEORGIA

Jean Anne Marra, Induction Specialist
Oconee County School System
P.O. Box 146
34 School Street
Watkinsville, GA 30677
706–769–5130
jmarra@oconee.k12.ga.us

The following information was obtained from telephone conversations and e-mail correspondence with Jean Anne Marra.

Demographics

Grade levels	K–12	Urban/Suburban/Rural	Suburban
Student Population	6,424	**Ethnic Makeup***	African American 5% Asian 3% Caucasian 85% Hispanic 4% Native American 0.01% Multiracial 2.3%
Teacher Population	550	**% New Teachers**	5%; varies each year
		Per-Pupil Expenditure	$8,662

* The statistics available from the district delineated the ethnic makeup as shown.

Program Highlights

Unique Feature of Program	A full week of induction activities prior to preplanning days	**Mentoring Is/Is Not Mandated for Certification/Licensing**	Mentoring is not mandated
Coaching Is/Is Not a Component	Coaching is a component	**Mentors Do/Do Not Evaluate the New Teachers With Whom They Work**	Mentors do not evaluate
Cost of Program	$30,000 not including director's salary	**Funding**	Local and Title IIA
Mentors are Full-Time/Part-Time Teachers	Mentors are full-time teachers	**Mentor Remuneration**	$150 to $350 per year
How Long Program Has Been in Existence	Eight years	**Duration of Program for New Teachers**	Two years
Higher Education Affiliation	None now; University of Georgia assisted in program development and evaluation	**Program Coordinator**	Jean Anne Marra

HISTORY

The Oconee County School System's Teacher Induction Program (TIP) was started in 2001 when direct assistance was provided for first- and second-year teachers working in the district. There was one induction specialist who worked with the new teachers, their mentors, and the principals. A needs assessment was done to determine the system's needs, and national research was studied to see what established, successful programs were doing to support their novice professionals. Over the years, the program has grown into what it is today, providing support services to beginning teachers and their mentors through many activities such as TIP Week, model classrooms, demonstration classrooms, seminars, collaborative planning, and peer observations. In 2007, when the program had existed for seven years, the Magna Award was presented by the National School Boards Association.

STATE MANDATES

Is mentoring mandated for new teachers?

No, mentoring is not mandated for new teachers.

Is mentoring part of certification or licensure?
No, mentoring is not part of certification or licensure.

Is funding provided to support the mandate?
NA

GOALS

The goals of the program are to:

- Develop quality teachers to increase student achievement
- Increase the retention of promising beginning teachers
- Transmit the culture of the school system to newly hired teachers
- Provide support for inductees, their mentors, and the principals

PROGRAM DESIGN

*What are the components and
recommended schedule of the program?*

- Jean Anne Marra, the induction specialist, is the director of the program, and she works with two other retired principals, also called induction specialists, who assist as necessary. The induction specialists work with new teachers and their mentors.
- Each new teacher is assigned a mentor.
- A five-day program for new teachers begins the week before all teachers return to school. Components of these five days include:
  - Model classrooms for K–5, 6–8, and 9–12
  - Information on legal mandates regarding instructional modifications for students
  - "The Pyramid of Intervention": identifying modifications and tracking which ones are successful
  - Training on differentiated instruction
  - Two days of training on Max Thompson's learning-focused schools instructional model
  - One day of training on classroom management by Dr. Jordan Walker with Resources for Professionals, in which mentors also participate and work with their protégé teachers.
  - Time in the buildings for setting up the classroom

- With each new teacher, the induction specialists (who are also referred to as coaches) do a dress rehearsal for teacher evaluation using the instruments and forms that principals will use during formal evaluations. The induction specialists then debrief the new teachers on the experience.

- Monthly seminars on critical issues are provided after school, usually for 90 minutes. Usually, the topics are chosen in preparation of professional development that all teachers will do, or in preparation of such things as parent-teacher conferences or state-mandated testing.

- In October, a follow-up day on classroom management is provided by Resources for Professionals.

- Mentors have a plan of action that they follow.
- Coaches do regular classroom visits and e-mail periodically.

Are there any programs that complement the mentoring program?

No, there are no programs that complement TIP.

Who designed the mentoring program?

Jean Anne Marra, the induction specialist, designed the program with a TIP planning team, composed of mentor teachers, beginning teachers, an Oconee teacher of the year, and a building administrator, after conducting a needs assessment throughout the system. The planning team became what is now called the oversight team.

PROGRAM ADMINISTRATION

Who coordinates the mentoring program?

Jean Anne Marra coordinates the program.

How is information communicated to shareholders?

- Once a month, Jean Anne Marra attends a leadership meeting with the superintendent, leadership cabinet, principals, and most directors to share information about the program.
- E-mail is widely used as an informal means of communication.
- Low-cost and no-cost strategies to support beginning teachers are distributed to principals. Some of the strategies that have been implemented include the following:
  - ○ Teachers should not be assigned to teach in trailers (rented, portable structures located separate from the school building as a temporary solution to a need for more space).
  - ○ In a four-period day at the high school level, it is recommended that a TIP teacher not have more than two preparations during the first semester. (The high school uses a block schedule, which is a four-period day. Each of the two semesters represents a full year of instruction.)
  - ○ At the elementary level, principals refrain from putting new enrollees into classes once the year has started. They discourage placing students with the most complicated IEPs in a TIP teacher's classroom.

Who coordinates integration of the mentoring program with other professional development opportunities or requirements in the schools and district?

Jean Anne Marra coordinates the program with the human resources department and the curriculum office, where her office is located.

PARTICIPANTS

Who is served?

Participants in the TIP program are teachers who have just graduated from college and have less than two years of teaching experience. Teachers who have taught one year in another program are also eligible for TIP; if they are included, they participate for two years. If a teacher has been out of the profession for a number of years, it is likely that the principal will enroll him or her in the TIP program. This program is not for experienced teachers who are new to the district.

Is participation of new teachers voluntary or mandatory?

Participation in TIP is mandatory based on the principal's recommendation.

Who provides the mentoring/induction?

Mentors and coaches provide mentoring and induction of new teachers.

What are the criteria for being a mentor?

Principals select mentors in collaboration with the coaches. Mentors are teachers who:

- Have great interpersonal skills
- Want to be mentors
- Are excellent teachers
- Are willing to put in the time that it takes

The State of Georgia once had a teacher support training course, and some teachers sought and received that endorsement on their state certificate. Now that there is no longer state funding for mentoring, these endorsements are not sought and the teachers who carried the endorsement are retired or retiring. TIP is planning to craft its own training course. Some of the new mentors are former TIP participants who have been hired within the last eight years.

MENTOR RESPONSIBILITIES AND REMUNERATION

What are the job responsibilities of mentors?
Mentors are required to follow the plan of action as specified by the planning team.

Are mentors required to do peer observation and coaching?
Yes, mentors are required to do peer observation and coaching.

Do mentors have full-time classroom teaching responsibilities?
Yes, mentors are full-time classroom teachers.

How are mentors available to participate in the program?
Mentors are contracted to perform their responsibilities as specified in the plan of action.

Do mentors evaluate new teachers?
No, neither mentors nor coaches evaluate new teachers.

Is the mentor–new teacher relationship confidential?
Yes, the relationship between mentor and new teacher is confidential.

Are mentors paid?
Mentors are paid $150 to $300, depending on whether they are mentoring a second- or first-year teacher.

MENTOR SELECTION, MATCHING, TRAINING, AND SUPERVISION

How are mentors selected?

Principals select mentors and notify the induction specialist of their decisions.

How are mentors and new teachers matched?

Principals match mentors and beginning teachers.

Are mentors trained?

Now that the state is not providing training for mentors, the district will roll out local training in 2009. This training will have a cognitive coaching component, including giving appropriate feedback. It will be based on a clinical supervision model, with pre and post conferences around an observation.

Who supervises the mentors?

Principals provide building-level oversight of mentors. Mentors might talk with the coaches about situations they would not discuss with the principals because of the confidentiality of the mentoring relationship. The coaches support the mentors but don't evaluate them. Regarding issues of safety or ethics, a mentor or coach would speak with the principal.

SUPPORTS FOR MENTORS

Is professional development available for mentors?

Professional development for mentors is being planned since there is no longer state training. It will be at least 20 hours in the beginning. The person who did the state training will consult with Oconee County to develop training for mentors.

Who provides this professional development?

Coaches, through the curriculum department, will offer professional development to mentors.

What resources are available for mentors?

Mentors are given the classroom management resource manual. As members of the staff, they are trained in learning-focused schools.

PROGRAM COSTS AND FUNDING

What resources are required for the program?

The cost of the program is $30,000, not including the project director's salary. These costs include:

- Materials. The classroom management manual and other materials are provided for all new teachers.
- Stipends. The stipend for mentors is $150 to $300 per year, depending on whether the mentee is a second- or a first-year teacher.
- Substitutes to cover mentors' released time for observation of their protégés if they are not able to use their planning time or get coverage from another mentor.

- Office furnishings and equipment.
- Professional development for the project director when she assumed leadership of the program.

Mentor training is done by the coaches, with needed support from area professional organizations including the Georgia School Superintendents Association, the Regional Educational Services Agency (RESA), and the University of Georgia. The district takes responsibility for new-teacher orientation. Business partners called Partners in Education underwrite the cost of food for meetings.

What are the funding sources?

The program is funded locally, supplemented by Title IIA funds.

Who requests the funding?

Each year, Jean Anne Marra submits a budget for the program to the assistant superintendent for curriculum and instruction.

PROGRAM EVALUATION

How is the program evaluated?

During the first few years, the University of Georgia did external evaluations of the program. Now, TIP evaluates itself. There are separate evaluations for TIP Week before school begins, as well as evaluations after the first and second semesters. Mentors also do an evaluation at the end of the year. All these evaluations are combined into a final report.

Who sees the results of the evaluation?

The results of evaluations are public; they are shared with TIP teachers, mentors, and administrators and included in the board report each fall.

RECRUITMENT, HIRING, AND RETENTION OF NEW STAFF

How many new teachers are recruited and hired?

From 2001 to 2008, the number of new teachers varied from 12 to 30.

Are there any data that correlate the mentoring program with the retention of new teachers?

Retention Data for TIP Teachers, 2001 to 2008

Year	Number of Teachers Hired	Number Remaining in Oconee as of 2007	Percentage Remaining in Oconee as of 2007	Percentage Serving in Education Elsewhere as of 2007	Percentage Remaining in Education as of 2007
2001–2002	16	9	56	4	81
2002–2003	12	9	75	3	100

Year	Number of Teachers Hired	Number Remaining in Oconee as of 2007	Percentage Remaining in Oconee as of 2007	Percentage Serving in Education Elsewhere as of 2007	Percentage Remaining in Education as of 2007
2003–2004	9	8	89	1	100
2004–2005	16	12	75	4	100
2005–2006	25	22	88	2	96
2006–2007	25	25	100	0	100
2007–2008	15	14	93	1	100

Although the TIP program can't take full credit, there are links between beginning teachers and student achievement. For instance, in reading and math at the elementary level, teachers with five years of experience or less have more students meeting and exceeding standards on their criterion-referenced tests than teachers with more than 15 years of experience.

The data are currently reported by a team at the middle school level, and they are planning to change their reporting so that they can see the results for each teacher. While some might say that because classroom assignments were carefully planned, test outcomes were affected accordingly, many think the results are indicative of the strength of TIP.

INDICATORS OF PROGRAM SUCCESS

What are the indicators of program success?

Of the nine schools in the Oconee district, four of the schools have selected former TIP teachers as their teacher of the year. Teachers have to work in the district at least three years to qualify for teacher of the year. Since the fourth year of TIP's existence, 50 percent of teachers of the year have been former TIP teachers. Teachers of the year are featured in demonstration classrooms, and TIP teachers observe instructional and managerial strategies in the demonstration classrooms. Principals are using TIP as a recruiting tool, and Oconee County has a huge pool of applicants. Principals hire young teachers by design to keep a diversity of age in their faculty. The Oconee County school board was awarded the 2007 Magna Award by the National School Boards Association, and they were chosen because of TIP. TIP has been adopted and adapted by other systems in Georgia.

MUSCATINE COMMUNITY SCHOOL DISTRICT

MUSCATINE, IOWA

Sue Johannsen, Mentoring Program Director
2900 Cedar Street
Muscatine, IA 52761
563–263–0411
skjohann@muscatine.k12.ia.us

The following information was obtained from telephone conversations and e-mail correspondence with Sue Johannsen.

Demographics

Grade levels	PreK–12	Urban/Suburban/Rural	Rural
Student Population	5,274	**Ethnic Makeup***	African American 3% Asian 1% Hispanic 22% Native American 1% White 74%
Teacher Population	416	**% New Teachers**	12.7%
		Per-Pupil Expenditure	$8,253

* The statistics available from the district delineated the ethnic makeup as shown.

Program Highlights

Unique Feature of Program	Offers mentoring for experienced teachers who are new to the district, even though it is not mandated by the state; lead mentors designed the program	**Mentoring Is/Is Not Mandated for Certification/Licensing**	Mentoring is mandated
Coaching Is/Is Not a Component	Coaching is a component	**Mentors Do/Do Not Evaluate the New Teachers With Whom They Work**	Mentors do not evaluate
Cost of Program	$66,947	**Funding**	State and district
Mentors are Full-Time/Part-Time Teachers	Mentors are full-time teachers	**Mentor Remuneration**	$1,000 per year
How Long Program Has Been in Existence	Since 2000	**Duration of Program for New Teachers**	Two years
Higher Education Affiliation	Eastern Iowa Community College	**Program Coordinator**	Sue Johannsen

HISTORY

The mentoring program was initiated as a pilot program in 2000. The program gained national recognition in 2002 when it received the NEA-Saturn/UAW Partnership Award. The number of participants has grown each year.

The originators of the program started out using Pathwise, but then they began creating their own local materials. They are about to adopt a new statewide model, Journey to Excellence. For the first time, they will offer training to surrounding school districts.

STATE MANDATES

Is mentoring mandated for new teachers?

Yes, mentoring is mandated for new teachers.

Is mentoring part of certification or licensure?

Yes, mentoring is part of certification and licensure.

Is funding provided to support the mandate?

Yes, funding is provided by the State of Iowa: $1,300 per year per beginning educator.

GOALS

The goals of the program are to:

- Provide a structure for the training and ongoing support of new teachers
- Create a process to support the retention of new teachers in the profession so that after a three-year period promising teachers remain committed, lifelong learners
- Build a supportive, collaborative environment between existing staff and beginning teachers
- Create a structure for the professional development of mentors, beginning teachers, and all staff using "plan, teach, reflect, apply" as an ongoing growth experience in the profession

PROGRAM DESIGN

What are the components and recommended schedule of the program?

The program focuses on the Iowa Teaching Standards; the Iowa Professional Development Model of "plan, teach, reflect, apply"; Charlotte Danielson's book *Enhancing Professional Practice: A Framework for Teaching*; and *Mentoring Matters: A Practical Guide to Learning-Focused Relationships* by Laura Lipton and Bruce Wellman with Carrlette Humbard.

Year One

- Focus on supporting beginning teachers as they learn the culture of Muscatine Community School District (MCSD)
- Creating a classroom environment to enhance student learning
- Coaching
- Classroom management
- Creating relationships among staff

Year Two

- Focus on student work
- Classroom management
- Building a support system to retain beginning teachers through collaborative relationships between existing staff and beginning teachers

Are there any programs that complement the mentoring program?

All professional development at MCSD is data driven and aligned to the district, building, individual, and comprehensive school improvement plans. The Iowa Professional Development Model provides the structure of planning, teaching, reflecting, and applying. These components plus the Iowa Teaching Standards form the basis of the program's evaluation system.

Who designed the mentoring program?

The lead mentors developed the program using their knowledge of Danielson's *Enhancing Professional Practice*, Lipton and Wellman's *Mentoring Matters*, the Iowa Teaching Standards, and the needs of the district.

PROGRAM ADMINISTRATION

Who coordinates the mentoring program?

Sue Johannsen coordinates the program along with lead mentors who are full-time teachers, all of whom she describes as experienced and excellent.

How is information communicated to shareholders?

An annual report about the program is provided to the board of education and the public. Faculty and administrative meetings include updates on or discussion of the mentoring program.

Who coordinates integration of the mentoring program with other professional development opportunities and requirements in the schools and district?

Sue Johannsen, coordinator; Becky Furlong, assistant superintendent; and six lead mentors coordinate integration of the mentoring program with other professional development opportunities in the schools and district.

PARTICIPANTS

Who is served?

The coordinator and five lead mentors provide training for the building mentors. Building mentors provide support for beginning teachers. Supporting and promoting retention of beginning teachers serves the whole community.

Is participation of new teachers voluntary or mandatory?

Participation of new teachers is mandatory.

Who provides the mentoring/induction?

Lead mentors, building mentors, and administration provide the mentoring.

What are the criteria for being a mentor?

Selected mentors meet the following criteria:

- Valid practitioner's license under Iowa Code Chapter 272
- Teaching contract with a local school district or area education agency in the State of Iowa
- Four years of successful teaching practice
- Employment as a classroom teacher on a nonprobationary basis

In determining the type of teacher who would perform well as a mentor, the administration selects candidates who are:

- Outstanding, experienced teachers whose teaching reflects excellent content, knowledge, and adherence to curriculum frameworks
- Aware of the merits of different teaching styles
- Knowledgeable about the resources of the school and staff
- Willing and able to invest time to develop mentoring skills and participate in the program for the duration of the two-year process
- Able to maintain a confidential relationship

Successful candidates possess knowledge of district and site policies, procedures, routine, curriculum, courses of study, and competencies. Candidates also demonstrate a professional commitment to the improvement of teaching and learning and the development of beginning teachers. Mentors present substantial evidence of dedication to the profession through their ability to model effective teaching strategies, relate effectively to adult learners, work collaboratively with colleagues, and reflectively articulate the art and science of teaching. Mentors are committed to serving as advocates for beginning teachers within the district and sharing knowledge with other mentors and educators. Mentors are trustworthy and are respected by their colleagues. Mentors also possess personal qualities such as strong interpersonal communication skills and time management skills.

MENTOR RESPONSIBILITIES AND REMUNERATION

What are the job responsibilities of mentors?

Mentors attend training and meet regularly with their new-teacher partner to meet her or his needs.

Are mentors required to do peer observation and coaching ?

Yes, peer observation and coaching are required for mentors.

Do mentors have full-time classroom teaching responsibilities?

Yes, mentors are full-time classroom teachers.

How are mentors available to participate in the program?

Training is held before school starts in the summer and after contract hours during the school year. Mentors find time to meet with their beginning teacher before school, during planning time, at lunch, or after school.

Do mentors evaluate new teachers?

No, mentors do not evaluate new teachers.

Is the mentor–new teacher relationship confidential?

Yes, the relationship between mentor and new teacher is confidential.

Are mentors paid?

Yes, mentors are paid $1,000 to mentor probationary teachers in their first and second years. Mentors of teachers who are new to the district but have experience are paid $500 out of local funds.

MENTOR SELECTION, MATCHING, TRAINING, AND SUPERVISION

How are mentors selected?

All mentors apply and some are recruited. Building principals and the assistant superintendent make recommendations to the coordinator, and reference calls are made.

How are mentors and new teachers matched?

Mentors are matched to new teachers by building, subject area, and/or grade level as closely as possible.

Are mentors trained?

Yes, 30 hours of training are provided to mentors.

Who supervises the mentors?

The six lead mentors supervise the mentors.

SUPPORTS FOR MENTORS

Is professional development available for mentors?

Yes, mentors are given 30 hours of training.

Who provides this professional development?

Lead mentors provide mentor training.

What resources are available for mentors?

Mentors receive three training days before school starts, four meetings during the school year, resource books such as *Mentoring Matters* and *A Framework for Understanding the Iowa Teaching Standards and Criteria*, and forms. Six lead mentors are available to support them.

PROGRAM COSTS AND FUNDING

What resources are required for the program?

The cost of the program is $66,947. Costs include:

- Mentor training: 30 hours of training for 60 mentors/full-time teachers
- New-teacher orientation, including half a day with mentors prior to the start of school

- Snacks and beverages
- Materials: paper, copying, books
- Stipends for mentors: $1,000 per mentor working with beginning teachers in the first or second year of teaching and $500 per mentor working with experienced teachers new to the district
- Substitutes for released time, when needed
- Portion of project director's salary related to mentoring: $3,000

What are the funding sources?

The State of Iowa and MCSD fund the program.

Who requests the funding?

MCSD requests funds from the State of Iowa.

PROGRAM EVALUATION

How is the program evaluated?

Mentors complete written evaluations after each training meeting. An end-of-year evaluation is given to mentors and beginning teachers. Data are compiled and tracked over time.

Who sees the results of the evaluation?

Lead mentors, the assistant superintendent, the school board, and the public see the results of the evaluation.

RECRUITMENT, HIRING, AND RETENTION OF NEW STAFF

How many new teachers are recruited and hired?

Each year the number seems to increase. In 2007–2008, there were 50 new hires and 25 second-year teachers.

Are there any data that correlate the mentoring program with the retention of new teachers?

Yes, as follows:

Year of Hire	Percentage of New Professionals Who Have Been Recommended for Licensure	Percentage of New Professionals Who Continue Working for MCSD
2006–2007	100%	93%
2005–2006	93% (one teacher decided not to apply for a teaching license)	86%
2004–2005	100%	81%

INDICATORS OF PROGRAM SUCCESS

What are the indicators of program success?

The indicators of success of the program are:

- Continued participation of building mentors year after year
- Training for other school districts beginning in the fall of 2008. In Iowa, small districts may not have people trained to be trainers, so the program provides training to teachers from two other districts. They travel to Muscatine, receive training, and return to their districts to mentor beginning educators
- Continual program change and improvement
- Academic achievement of students
- High retention rate of beginning teachers
- Positive formative and summative evaluations. Each training meeting includes an evaluation from participants, and an end-of-year program evaluation is completed by mentors and beginning educators. The results of these evaluations have indicated understanding of materials presented at the training meetings and satisfaction with the total program

The success of the program motivates teachers to accept the role of mentor. Many mentors have returned to serve other beginning educators year after year. Teachers who have not mentored in the past show interest in becoming mentors.

DOVER-SHERBORN PUBLIC SCHOOLS MENTOR TEACHER LEADER PROGRAM

DOVER, MASSACHUSETTS

Jim Baroody, High School Mentor Teacher Leader
9 Junction Street
Dover, MA 02030
baroodyj@doversherborn.org

Dara Johnson, Middle School Mentor Teacher Leader
155 Farm Street
Dover, MA 02030
djohnson@doversherborn.org

The following information was obtained from telephone conversations and e-mail correspondence with Martin Moran, one of the original mentor teacher leaders, who is now an administrator in the district.

Demographics

Grade Levels	K–12	Urban/Suburban/Rural	Suburban
Student Population	2,148	**Ethnic Makeup***	African American 2% Asian American 3% Caucasian 95%

Teacher Population	213	% New Teachers	16.5%
		Per-Pupil Expenditure	$14,617

* The statistics available from the district delineated the ethnic makeup as shown. There was no information about students of more than one racial heritage.

Program Highlights

Unique Feature of Program	Mentor teacher leaders coordinate the program and do most of the training	Mentoring 1s/ Is Not Mandated for Certification/ Licensing	Mentoring is mandated
Coaching Is/ Is Not a Component	Coaching is a component	Mentors Do/Do Not Evaluate the New Teachers With Whom They Work	Mentor do not evaluate
Cost of Program	$24,400	Funding	Local budget
Mentors Are Full-Time/ Part-Time Teachers	Mentors and mentor teacher leaders are full-time teachers	Mentor Remuneration	Mentors: $950; mentor teacher leaders: $1,300
How Long Program Has Been in Existence	10 years	Duration of Program for New Teachers	One year
Higher Education Affiliation	None	Program Coordinators	Jim Baroody, Dara Johnson

HISTORY

John Moore, the former middle school principal, had been matching new teachers with veteran staff in an informal way to promote the integration of new staff into the school community. He wanted to formalize this matching process by creating a mentoring program for new staff to facilitate their success and to promote their development as teachers. After a presentation to the administrative council, a program was started and eventually evolved into a program coordinated by mentor teacher leaders in all four schools.

STATE MANDATES

Is mentoring mandated for new teachers?

Yes, mentoring is mandated by the State of Massachusetts.

Is mentoring part of certification or licensure?

Yes, mentoring is a requirement for certification and licensure.

Is funding provided to support the mandate?

No, the state does not support mentoring at the district level.

GOALS

The school district is faced with the challenge of replacing experienced staff members with those who are less experienced. The quality and excellence of the school system must be maintained during the transition. To facilitate this goal, the school system aims to utilize the expertise of the experienced veteran staff.

The two major goals of the program are to attract and retain quality professionals and to improve the quality of instruction. The establishment of the program has the potential to raise regard for the profession in the community and provide improved collegiality and morale. It also affords the opportunity for renewal of the veteran staff.

PROGRAM DESIGN

The design of the program is one-to-one mentoring, a new teacher with an experienced teacher, coupled with professional development opportunities.

What are the components and recommended schedule of the program?

The components of the program are:

- Mentor training at the end of August
- Meetings of mentor-mentee pairs, at least weekly but in many cases daily, throughout the school year
- Afterschool and/or inservice workshops
- Peer observations and collaborative coaching three times a year (optimally)

The program officially begins when mentors are chosen in the spring and trained at the end of August. Just before school starts, the new teachers are told who their mentors will be for the school year.

The program technically ends at the close of school in June. However, some mentors are chosen again for the following year, so their participation is cyclical. Some of the mentors, also referred to as mentor teacher leaders, work on the design and plans for implementation of the program for the next year.

Are there any programs that complement the mentoring program?

In addition to the mentors, a support team is developed in each school to assist all the new teachers. The support team might include the principal or headmaster, the assistant headmaster, a teacher leader, a department head, or other appropriate staff members.

Faculty who are not mentors support their new colleagues by welcoming them into their classrooms for observations and assisting them when appropriate. Sometimes mentor teacher leaders videotape colleagues (with their permission) whose teaching demonstrates different ways to approach some of the issues and questions raised by new teachers. The mentor teacher leaders use the tapes at afterschool or inservice meetings with the new teachers. Two subjects that have been videotaped in recent years include Transitions and How to Begin a Lesson.

Who designed the mentoring program?

Kathy Dunne, an educational consultant with Learning Innovations at WestEd, was hired by John Moore to help him design and implement the initial mentor training. The first few years, she worked with a select group of mentor teacher leaders to:

- Enhance their capacity to facilitate mentor training
- Prepare them to serve as classroom coaches to support mentors in deepening their coaching skills in working with new teachers
- Design and facilitate afterschool workshops for new faculty

Since that time, Kathy has returned periodically to work with the mentor teacher leaders, but for the most part the mentor teacher leaders plan the program, design and present the training, run the workshops, and meet together throughout the year to coordinate and oversee the program.

PROGRAM ADMINISTRATION

Who coordinates the mentoring program?

The mentor teacher leaders are the linchpin in the operation of the mentoring program. They are responsible for meeting with the other mentors to coordinate the mentoring program for the entire system, and they also work in conjunction with their building administrator(s) in coordinating the mentoring program for their building. The mentor teacher leaders are responsible for overseeing the day-to-day operation of the program, providing the initial training of mentors, holding afternoon workshops, and organizing observation days by hiring substitutes and arranging the schedules of mentors and new teachers. If there are extra slots in a substitute's schedule, other teachers are welcome to use the time for peer coaching. Mentor teacher leaders typically do not mentor new teachers: they coach the mentors. On rare occasions when it is needed, a teacher leader may mentor a new teacher.

How is information communicated to shareholders?

All members of the school community have been familiarized with the program. When it was first created, it was introduced to all adult shareholders.

Efforts are made by the mentor teacher leaders and administrators to ensure that everyone is aware of the mentoring program and familiar with its workings and the benefits it accrues. The mentor teacher leaders, mentors, and new teachers are the most directly involved in such communication, and the administrators also discuss the program with faculty, school board members, and parents.

In addition, the mentor teacher leaders have presented their program at different workshops and conferences, including the annual conferences of the National Staff Development Council (NSDC) in Atlanta and Boston. They have familiarized other educators with the mentor teacher leader program they have created and implemented and have assisted them with what they might want to do in their own districts.

Who coordinates integration of the mentoring program with other professional development opportunities and requirements in the schools and district?

The mentor teacher leaders speak with the administrative liaison throughout the year. The superintendent has said that this program is the cornerstone of professional development in the district. A new professional development committee has been formed and discussions are underway to coordinate its efforts with those of the mentoring program.

PARTICIPANTS

Who is served?

The program is designed for teachers who are new to the school system, either as novices or as veteran educators from another school system.

Is participation of new teachers voluntary or mandatory?

The mentoring program is discussed during the interviewing and hiring process, and it is seen as a benefit of employment. Participation in the program is mandatory for all new staff.

Who provides the mentoring/induction?

Mentors, who are also teachers, are in a strong position to offer support and to promote reflection without the presence of concerns about evaluation and continued employment. The premise is that teachers are best able to support their colleagues in a nonjudgmental and nonthreatening way.

What are the criteria for being a mentor?

The criteria for being a mentor are:

- Previous teaching experience, with at least three years in the district
- Demonstrated excellence in teaching
- Demonstrated leadership in the school community
- Strong communication skills

Mentor Responsibilities and Remuneration

What are the job responsibilities of mentors?

Mentors are selected in the spring and trained in the summer. Each new teacher is assigned a mentor, with whom he or she meets frequently at the beginning of the school year and approximately weekly thereafter. Optimally, the mentors do collaborative coaching with their new-teacher partners two to three times during the year. Substitutes are provided so that new teachers and mentors can observe each other teaching as they participate in the collaborative coaching cycle. The mentor teacher leaders, who coordinate the program, arrange the schedule for the substitutes. Mentor teacher leaders also plan the afterschool and inservice meetings for the new teachers and their mentors. These meetings last approximately one hour.

Are mentors required to do peer observation and coaching?

Yes. Ideally, peer observation and coaching are done at least three times during the school year.

Do mentors have full-time classroom teaching responsibilities?

Yes, mentors have full-time teaching responsibilities.

How are mentors available to participate in the program?

Training for mentors is offered at the end of August, before school begins. Substitutes are hired and scheduled by the mentor teacher leaders to provide new teachers and their mentors the opportunity to do peer observations and collaborative coaching. Workshops are scheduled monthly after school or during inservice days.

Do mentors evaluate new teachers?

No, mentors are involved in a nonjudgmental relationship with the new teacher and do not evaluate.

Is the mentor–new teacher relationship confidential?

Yes, the mentor–new teacher relationship is completely confidential.

Are mentors paid?

Yes, mentors are paid $900 a year, and mentor teacher leaders are paid $1,300 a year.

MENTOR SELECTION, MATCHING, TRAINING, AND SUPERVISION

How are mentors selected?

Teachers volunteer to be mentors, sometimes at the request of building administrators. They are chosen by the building principal, often in consultation with mentor teacher leaders, in accordance with the set of established criteria. These leaders are deemed effective teachers by the principals and have knowledge of cognitive coaching. It is presumed that other teachers will assume these roles in the future so that the program will be self-sustaining.

How are mentors and new teachers matched?

Building administrators match new teachers with their mentors, often speaking first with the mentor teacher leaders about their ideas for matches. The grade level or subject area of new teachers influences the choice of optimal partnerships.

Are mentors trained?

Yes, mentors are trained for one day in the summer, before school begins.

Who supervises the mentors?

The teacher leaders supervise the mentors.

SUPPORTS FOR MENTORS

Is professional development available for mentors?

Afterschool and inservice meetings are provided for new teachers and their mentors. The mentor teacher leaders plan and implement these meetings. The involvement of other teachers has greatly affected the school culture. Sometimes experienced teachers who are not part of the mentoring program are videotaped, and these video clips are used during afterschool meetings to exemplify topics being discussed.

The mentor teacher leaders meet three times a year. They discuss the program and ways to make it even stronger. Some have worked with other school systems during the summer and occasionally during the school year to consult about mentor teacher leadership and mentoring.

Who provides the professional development?

Mentor teacher leaders provide professional development for the mentors and coach them throughout the school year.

What resources are available for mentors?

Mentors and mentor teacher leaders have access to professional libraries and the audiovisual equipment they need for the program.

PROGRAM COSTS AND FUNDING

What resources are required for the program?

The cost of the program is $24,400. Resources for the program include:

- Mentor's handbooks, new teacher's handbooks, and supplies for afterschool and inservice workshops
- Stipends for mentors at $900 per person
- Stipends for mentor teacher leaders at $1,300 per person
- Substitutes for observations and teacher leader meetings

What are the funding sources?

Initially the Dover-Sherborn Education Fund provided the money to develop this mentoring program, but now the funding is a regular part of the school budget.

Who requests the funding?

NA

PROGRAM EVALUATION

How is the program evaluated?

Mentor teacher leaders gather feedback from the new teachers and their mentors in informal focus groups at the end of the school year. Based on some of this feedback, the mentor teacher leaders determine what the new teachers are most interested in learning during the workshops. They use this feedback to inform and influence their design of the program for the following year.

Who sees the results of the evaluation?

See above.

RECRUITMENT, HIRING, AND RETENTION OF NEW STAFF

How many new teachers are recruited and hired?

Each year is different. The number of new teachers has ranged from 15 to 27 in the past 10 years.

Are there any data that correlate the mentoring program with the retention of new teachers?

No, retention data have not been collected.

Indicators of Program Success

What are the indicators of program success?

The culture of the school system has dramatically changed. Teachers are in and out of each other's classrooms. Experienced teachers welcome new teachers and encourage them to sit in on their classes. The camaraderie among the mentors has benefited the entire faculty of the school.

When the mentor teacher leaders arrange the schedules of substitutes to cover new teachers and their mentors for observations and collaborative coaching, sometimes there are extra time slots. Classroom teachers have requested substitutes so that they can do peer observations with other staff. This has been a significant change in school culture. Exact data have not been documented, but in the last few years, many teachers in the district have completed three years of service to the district and are or soon will have earned professional status. Each building is finding that its new-teacher numbers are down from previous years. John Moore's primary vision when he initiated this mentoring program approximately 10 years ago was to improve teacher retention throughout the district. He would be proud of the program's success in the last 10 years, particularly the district's ability to retain excellent teachers.

VICKSBURG COMMUNITY SCHOOLS LEADERSHIP TRAINING FOR MENTOR TEACHERS AND NEW TEACHER INDUCTION PROGRAM

VICKSBURG, MICHIGAN

Pat Wilson O'Leary, Instructional Specialist
301 South Kalamazoo Avenue
Vicksburg, MI 49097
269–321–1038
Fax: 616–321–1055
patwo@vicksburg.k12.mi.us

Patricia Reeves, Ed.D.
Western Michigan University
Kalamazoo, Michigan
269–720–3285
patricia.reeves@wmich.edu

The following information was obtained from telephone conversations and e-mail correspondence with Pat Wilson O'Leary.

Demographics

Grade Levels	K–12	Urban/Suburban/Rural	Rural
Student Population	2,630	**Ethnic Makeup***	African American 0.8% Asian 0.5% Caucasian 97.5% Hispanic 0.8% Native American 0.4%
Teacher Population	165	**% New Teachers**	11% (includes all teachers in their first, second, or third year)
		Per-Pupil Expenditure	$8,191

* The statistics available from the district delineated the ethnic makeup as shown. There was no information about students of more than one racial heritage.

Program Highlights

Unique Feature of Program	Creative funding of an instructional specialist; three-year program of coaching and coursework	Mentoring Is/Is Not Mandated for Certification/Licensing	Mentoring is mandated, but not for licensure
Coaching Is/Is Not a Component	Coaching is a component	**Mentors Do/Do Not Evaluate the New Teachers With Whom They Work**	Mentors do not evaluate
Cost of Program	$120,000	**Funding**	District, creatively
Mentors are Full-Time/Part-Time Teachers	Mentors are full-time teachers; the instructional specialist is a part-time mentor director	**Mentor Remuneration**	$1,500 for a first-year teacher, $600 for a second-year teacher, and $300 for a third-year teacher
How Long Program Has Been in Existence	Nine years	**Duration of Program for New Teachers**	Three years
Higher Education Affiliation	Central Michigan University, Western Michigan University	**Program Coordinator**	Pat Wilson O'Leary

HISTORY

The program began when the school district became interested in providing more support for new teachers. The superintendent devised a creative way to be able to offer those professional development opportunities.

New-teacher induction classes were begun in 1997. In 1999, the district developed a "buddy" system with a coordinator, who called six meetings during the year to provide mentor support and information. In 2000, the program was expanded and became more comprehensive.

STATE MANDATES

Is mentoring mandated for new teachers?

Yes. As of 1993, Section 1526 of the Michigan State Code states that for the first three years of employment in classroom teaching, a teacher will be assigned by the school to one or more master teachers, college professors, or retired master teachers who will act as mentors. Schools will also provide 15 days of intensive staff development, above and beyond regular teacher inservice.

Is mentoring part of certification or licensure?

No, mentoring is not part of certification or licensure. It is a district responsibility.

Is funding provided to support the mandate?

No, the state does not provide funding for mentoring.

GOALS

The following is a statement of the program's goals, and the five beliefs of the mentoring model are the assumptions on which the program was created.

Mentoring Model

1. Maintain and improve student learning
   a. to regularly gather and evaluate data to make change
   b. to keep our focus on student-centered learning as we make program decisions
   c. Set high standards for teaching excellence

2. Create a community of learners
   a. welcome and integrate new teachers into system, culture, and professional expectations
   b. provide resources and skills to support, encourage and renew all teachers
   c. provide consistent opportunities for new and veteran educators to reflect and grow in their practice as they network across grade levels and content areas

---

(Continued)

(Continued)

Five Beliefs of the Mentoring Model

Our mentoring program does not exist in isolation. It is part of the whole district's culture. At the basis of our culture and program are five major beliefs:

1. Every teacher is a lifelong learner, and strives for excellence

2. Reflection is part of the job

3. All educators are part of a community of learners

4. We are responsible for student achievement

5. Using best practice makes a difference, regardless of demographics

Smitley, Wilson O'Leary
Vicksburg Community Schools, 2006

SOURCE: Provided by Pat Wilson O'Leary.

Another program goal is to recognize capable veterans and enable them to consider new professional perspectives.

The goal of professional development offered in Vicksburg is to support teachers in meeting the state requirements in ways that address the district's goals and the teachers' individual development plans (IDPs).

PROGRAM DESIGN

What are the components and recommended schedule of the program?

This program is for teachers in their first three years in the district.

Year One

- New teachers are assigned a building mentor. Mentors orient their new-teacher partners to the building and procedures, help them prepare their room, and begin building a supportive relationship with them.
- Each first-year teacher meets with the principal, curriculum coordinator, and human resources director before school begins.
- First-year teachers who are new to teaching and veteran teachers new to Vicksburg Community Schools (VCS) are required to attend six sessions (approximately 36 hours) of professional development. This course, called Instructional Skills, focuses on starting school, classroom management, and instructional skills. Graduate credit is available. The course runs from August to May. Teachers who are new to the

district but have taught elsewhere take a course called Instructional Skills Refresher. When this course was first offered, 40 percent of all veteran staff participated.

- All new teachers receive the following materials:
  - *The First Days of School: How to Be an Effective Teacher* by Harry and Rosemary Wong (2004)
  - *Transforming Classroom Grading* by Robert Marzano (2000)
  - The journal *Reflections on Teaching* (VCS Press, 2000)
- Course packets of approximately 250 pages of text, containing samples of previous participants' and veteran teachers' lists of procedures, discipline plans, communications to and from parents, grading rubrics, lessons plans, and so forth, are offered to new teachers as springboards for their preparation for instruction in and management of their own classrooms.
- All new teachers, K–12, are observed by and conference with Pat Wilson O'Leary one time each semester. Mentors observe their partners six times a year. Pat also provides demonstration lessons for any teacher who requests them. Observations by mentors and instructional specialists are nonevaluative.
- During the new teacher's first year, her or his mentor is expected to:
  - Meet with the new teacher prior to the onset of the school year to discuss curriculum, classroom setup, and procedures
  - Meet with the new teacher 20 to 30 minutes weekly to discuss planning, classroom management, and instructional and assessment strategies
  - Observe the new teacher a minimum of six times per year; two observations (one per semester) should be at least 30 minutes in length
  - Hold pre- and post-observation conferences with the new teacher
  - Maintain logs of each meeting with the new teacher
  - Attend mentor training four times per year (one of these training sessions, for first-time mentors only, is in the summer)
  - Attend bimonthly mentor meetings (five per school year, one hour each)

Year Two

- Second-year teachers are required to attend five sessions of professional development (approximately 24 hours) that focus on the use of cooperative learning. Graduate credit is available. The course runs from August to April.
- Second-year teachers are observed by their mentors and the instructional specialist or the instructional consultant.
- Second-year teachers receive *A Guidebook for Cooperative Learning: A Technique for Creating More Effective Schools* by Dee Dishon and Pat Wilson O'Leary (Learning Publications, 1998).
- During the new teacher's second year, his or his mentor is expected to:
  - Meet with the new teacher for 20 to 30 minutes every other week to discuss planning, classroom management, and instructional and assessment strategies
  - Observe the new teacher a minimum of six times per year; two observations (one per semester) should be at least 30 minutes in length
  - Hold pre- and post-observation conferences with the new teacher
  - Maintain logs of each meeting with the new teacher
  - Arrange for the new teacher to observe the mentor or another teacher and then conference with the new teacher about the observation
  - Attend bimonthly mentor meetings (five per school year, one hour each)

Year Three

The professional development plan for the third year is designed in consultation with the principal. An individual development plan is tailored to each teaching assignment and each teacher's own strengths and areas of needed growth. Observations by Pat Wilson O'Leary and mentors continue as described above.

During the new teacher's third year, her or his mentor is expected to:

- Meet with the new teacher for 20 to 30 minutes on a monthly basis to discuss planning, classroom management, and instructional and assessment strategies
- Observe the new teacher a minimum of six times per year; two observations (one per semester) should be at least 30 minutes in length
- Hold pre- and post-observation conferences with the new teacher
- Maintain logs of each meeting with the new teacher
- Arrange for the teacher to observe the mentor or another teacher and then conference with the new teacher about the observation
- Attend bimonthly mentor meetings (five per school year, one hour each)

Are there any programs that complement the mentoring program?

All staff development programs are organized around district goals and complement each other.

All K–12 staff, administrators, and secretaries are provided the journal *Reflections on Teaching* (VCS Press, 2000). This student- and staff-designed journal is used at staff meetings and professional development sessions for personal reflections and conversation starters.

Who designed the mentoring program?

In 1999, Pat Wilson O'Leary, Annette Smitley, and Patricia Reeves, the superintendent, created the program after looking at the literature on mentoring programs, considering personal and district experiences, and networking with other program directors and mentors. Presently, Pat and the new superintendent, Charles Glaes, continue to support and adapt the program to meet changing needs.

PROGRAM ADMINISTRATION

Who coordinates the mentoring program?

Pat coordinates the program. She is part of the PIT (principals and instructional team) Crew. This team supports the mentoring program and makes recommendations that align with the district's professional development needs and initiatives.

How is information communicated to shareholders?

Pat shares information with the superintendent, mentor trainees, Total Learning Council, and PIT Crew, who communicate with the shareholders in the district.

All mentors, new and veteran, attend six 1-hour meetings per school year for communication, updates on the mentoring literature, and training in new skills.

Who coordinates integration of the mentoring program with other professional development opportunities and requirements in the schools and district?

The instructional team coordinates integration of this program with other professional development opportunities and requirements in the district, examples of which include Journaling, Shared Leadership, Courage to Teach, Differentiated Instruction, Software/Hardware Applications, Professional Learning Communities, and Using Assessment to Guide Instruction.

PARTICIPANTS

Who is served?

This program serves teachers in their first, second, and third years in VCS, regardless of past experience or tenure elsewhere.

Is participation of new teachers voluntary or mandatory?

Participation of first-, second-, and third-year teachers new to the district is required.

Who provides the mentoring/induction?

Pat Wilson O'Leary mentors the new teachers as well as the district mentors at all school sites. Pat also teaches the courses offered in the first and second years.

What are the criteria for being a mentor?

A mentor must:

- Be tenured
- Have four or more years of experience in the district
- Express an interest in being a mentor
- Be viewed as a master teacher by colleagues
- Be a lifelong learner
- Have a recommendation from the principal
- Be ready to attend training and carry out the mentor's role
- Be invited by Pat or the principal

MENTOR RESPONSIBILITIES AND REMUNERATION

What are the job responsibilities of mentors?

Job responsibilities are outlined in detail in the Program Design section above (pages 68–70).

Are mentors required to do peer observation and coaching?

Yes, mentors of first-year teachers are asked to observe their mentees, leave notes, and discuss the lesson with them three times per semester (six times per year). Art Costa's model of cognitive coaching is the basis for the coaching mentors perform.

Do mentors have full-time classroom teaching responsibilities?

Mentors have full-time teaching responsibilities. Pat is an instructional specialist whose responsibilities relate to professional development.

How are mentors available to participate in the program?

Mentors are released from their teaching duties for training. They are required to observe new teachers, and the principals have offered to provide substitutes so that mentors can observe. The extra-duty contract pay covers some of the activities and time mentors give to their mentees.

Do mentors evaluate new teachers?

No, mentors do not evaluate new teachers. They support and coach them.

Is the mentor–new teacher relationship confidential?

Yes, the relationship is confidential. Some issues are discussed in mentor training as a means of supporting, instructing, and encouraging the new teacher–mentor relationship and the growth of professionalism.

Are mentors paid?

Mentors of a first-year teacher are paid $1,500. For mentoring a second-year teacher, a mentor is paid $600, and for mentoring a third-year teacher, a mentor is paid $300.

MENTOR SELECTION, MATCHING, TRAINING, AND SUPERVISION

How are mentors selected?

An invitation to be a mentor may come from either a principal or Pat, often after a teacher expresses interest and/or a colleague suggests that a teacher be a mentor.

How are mentors and new teachers matched?

Grade level, subject matter, location, and willingness to support new teachers are all considered in matching mentors with new teachers.

Are mentors trained?

Yes, new mentors are trained at four leadership sessions (approximately 30 hours total); one of these is scheduled before the school year, and the other three are held throughout the school year. Released time is provided. All mentors also attend six 1-hour afterschool meetings spaced out from September through May. (See Appendix C.)

Who supervises the mentors?

Pat Wilson O'Leary and the principals supervise the mentors.

SUPPORTS FOR MENTORS

Is professional development available for mentors?

Yes. The following are three professional development options for mentors:

- Coach-to-coach support from Pat
- College credit for the courses taken
- State board continuing education units

Who provides the professional development?

Pat trains the mentors.

What resources are available for mentors?

Mentors have access to the following resources:

- Substitutes are provided for three training days and time to observe.
- The district has purchased journals, books, and videotapes for the professional library and made them available for training sessions and to all mentors.
- Mentors receive packets of materials from training sessions.
- Mentors collaborate with other mentors.

PROGRAM COSTS AND FUNDING

What resources are required for the program?

The approximate cost of the program is $120,000 for remuneration of mentors, the director's salary, and training materials. Additional costs include a day of pay for each new teacher who attends summer orientation, hardware and software, and payment for substitute teachers.

What are the funding sources?

Pat Wilson O'Leary's position as an instructional specialist is funded in an unusual way. She is hired by VCS to work 210 days a year. She works approximately 75 days a year for other school systems (former clients of Pat's when she was an independent consultant), who pay her fee to VCS. These fees offset 60 percent of Pat's salary and part-time secretarial costs.

The remainder of Pat's salary and other costs of the program are paid through graduate credit tuition reimbursement, sale of VCS Press journals, tuition from outside participants, and the school district's budget.

Who requests the funding?

VCS approves this process upon request of the superintendent.

PROGRAM EVALUATION

How is the program evaluated?

Perceptual surveys are given to new teachers and mentors. Discussion occurs among administration and staff. These surveys provide specific data that indicate whether the program is supporting teachers and providing mentors with rewarding experiences.

Who sees the results of the evaluation?

The PIT Crew, Pat, mentor teachers, mentees, and the superintendent see the results. All results are public information.

RECRUITMENT, HIRING, AND RETENTION OF NEW STAFF

How many new teachers are recruited and hired?

Due to Michigan's economy, the number of new teachers is 5 to 10 per year on average. Forty-three percent of the staff was hired between 1995 and 2000, and 32 percent was hired between 1997 and 2000.

In 2005–2006, VCS hired six teachers. At the end of the year, one teacher moved and one was laid off. The latter has been recalled for the 2008–2009 school year.

In 2006–2007, VCS hired 14 new teachers. Four left at the end of that year, three on a voluntary basis; one had a semester-only position.

In 2007–2008, VCS hired four teachers and none have left.

Pat believes that the school board of VCS is to be commended for maintaining high standards for this program in tough economic times. Their creative funding allows this to happen.

Are there any data that correlate the mentoring program with the retention of new teachers?

In recent years, teachers have left mainly to retire. According to exit interviews, the second biggest reason has been family relocation (spouse employment or desire to be near parents). Only three teachers have left the district for higher salaries in larger schools.

INDICATORS OF PROGRAM SUCCESS

What are the indicators of program success?

Principals report that teachers new to VCS (first-year or veteran) who have been through Instructional Skills and Cooperative Learning are better prepared for the high expectations for classroom performance than beginning teachers have been in the past. They are said to be performing with more skill and confidence by the time they have been in the district three or four years than their predecessors did without the assistance.

Due to the hiring of good people and the provision of support, new teachers are moving quickly into professional committee and voluntary support positions. During the last two years (2006–2007 and 2007–2008), four second- and third-year teachers have been appointed as literacy coaches—teachers seen by their colleagues as masters at teaching students to read and write well. Ten teachers who have been teaching less than four years have volunteered or have been asked to present a variety of professional development classes. These Choice PD programs enable all VCS teachers to meet their state-required training days.

Five regional districts send their teachers to Vicksburg mentor training or hire Pat to replicate the VCS mentor model in their district.

The model has been featured twice in the Michigan Department of Education publication *Leading Change*, once in the Fall 2005 issue and again in the Spring 2007 issue (Volume 5, Issue 2; http://www.cenmi.org/Documents/LeadingChange.aspx). VCS is proud of this coverage and enjoys sharing its program with others.

One goal of the Vicksburg program was to recognize capable veterans and enable them to consider new professional perspectives. These quotations from mentors' reflections are another indicator of success:

> After I called my mentee in the summer, I found myself getting excited about the start of the school year. In talking with her, I realized how routine the start of school had become for me, and the conversation helped me understand just how far I had come in the field of education. . . . Our conferencing after an observation reminded me how important it is for new teachers (along with veterans) to get feedback not only from students, but from colleagues as well.
>
> —Jeff Briggs, seventh-grade math teacher

> It was interesting for me to mentor someone who is older and more experienced than me. Since my mentee came from another school district, I found it very interesting to talk to him about the differences between the two districts. I really came to appreciate the student. . . . I believe that I am a better teacher for this experience.
>
> —Kim Roberts, computer education teacher

> Being a veteran teacher can be like acting in a well-rehearsed play. When I mentor, I relive what it is like to begin again. I am energized every year by this feeling of starting over again.
>
> —Annette Smitley, high school English teacher

ST. PAUL PUBLIC SCHOOLS CAREER IN EDUCATION PROGRAM

ST. PAUL, MINNESOTA

Kate Wilcox-Harris, Director
Career in Education Program
St. Paul Public Schools
1001 Johnson Parkway
St. Paul, MN 55106
651–793–5400
kate.wilcox-harris@spps.org

The following information was obtained from telephone conversations and e-mail correspondence with Kate Wilcox-Harris and Marilyn Baeker as well as from program literature. Additional information may be found on the district's Web site: www.spps.org

Demographics

Grade Levels	K–12	Urban/Suburban/Rural	Urban
Student Population	43,000	Ethnic Makeup*	African American 30% Asian 30% Caucasian 25% Hispanic 13% Native American 2%
Teacher Population	3,277	% New Teachers	18%
		Per-Pupil Expenditure	Approximately $7,000

* The statistics available from the district delineated the ethnic makeup as shown. There was no information about students of more than one racial heritage.

Program Highlights

Unique Feature of Program	Joint effort of district and union to improve the environment for new teachers with a two-tier approach of mentoring and coursework	Mentoring Is/Is Not Mandated for Certification/Licensing	Mentoring is not mandated; administrator observations are required
Coaching Is/Is Not a Component	Coaching is a component	Mentors Do/Do Not Evaluate the New Teachers With Whom They Work	Mentors do not evaluate
Cost of Program	$230,000	Funding	District funds for staff development; Saint Paul Federation of Teachers
Mentors are Full-Time/Part-Time Teachers	Mentors are full-time teachers	Mentor Remuneration	$700 for mentoring a first-year teacher, $300 for mentoring a second-year teacher
How Long Program Has Been in Existence	This version has been in operation since 2004–2005; some version of this program has been in operation for more than 10 years	Duration of Program for New Teachers	Three years
Higher Education Affiliation	Hamline University provides credit options for some of the coursework	Program Coordinator	Hamline University, Kate Wilcox-Harris

HISTORY

The mentoring program is part of the St. Paul Public Schools (SPPS) Career in Education Program, a joint union-district program that began in the 2000–2001 school year. That program asked participants to pair up and collect a stipend for their work. The current version added training, accountability, and feedback from mentors and mentees.

STATE MANDATES

Is mentoring mandated for new teachers?

No, mentoring is not mandated for new teachers.

Is mentoring part of certification or licensure?

No, mentoring is not part of certification or licensure.

Is funding provided to support the mandate?

NA

GOALS

The program goals are to:

1. Provide support and assistance for new teachers.
2. Provide "at the elbow" professional development that allows new teachers to learn and implement district curricula.
3. Match new teachers with a coach if the mentor is unable to take this role. (Mentors are often content coaches. All schools in SPPS have at least a half-time coach.)
4. Guide the new teacher into district and union professional development courses. For example, a new elementary teacher is expected to implement Reader's Workshop. Mentors help mentees get the direct instruction (district workshop) and coaching they need to do that. SPPS provides specific classes that teachers are expected to take to achieve tenure.
5. Help new teachers navigate the system—everything from how to use a whiteboard to where school supplies are located.

PROGRAM DESIGN

What are the components and recommended schedule of the program?

It is the responsibility of every nontenured teacher to work with his or her mentor and principal to ensure that all required workshops are completed by the end of the third year of teaching. Completion of required workshops is recorded by each staff member. Continued employment in SPPS depends on achieving tenure.

Probationary teachers are required to receive mentoring assistance; they select a qualified mentor and participate in the program requirements. Stipends, released time, or in-service credits are provided to mentors, with their principal's approval, for all training days as specified by the Career in Education Program. Mentors provide peer coaching support to eligible probationary teachers.

Site staff development coordinators are responsible for training staff in their building on the Career in Education Program, maintaining records, coaching professional development teachers, reviewing professional development plans, and other duties outlined in the job posting. They may also serve as coaches. The site staff development committee selects coordinators at their site. Site staff development coordinators receive a stipend.

Are there any programs that complement the mentoring program?

Yes, the Achievement of Tenure Program complements the mentoring program. Please go to http://hr.spps.org/sites/796838e5-b16a-499a-8c29–8e37dabb6712/uploads/TenureChart.pdf for a graphic representation of this program.

Who designed the mentoring program?

The mentoring program arose from teacher requests. The St. Paul Federation of Teachers responded, and district implementation of the program began in 1999. It has gone through a variety of metamorphoses over the years in response to teacher feedback.

PROGRAM ADMINISTRATION

Who coordinates the mentoring program?

Marilyn Baeker oversees the program, while the principals and building site staff development coordinators help facilitate it within each building.

How is information communicated to shareholders?

Because the program is a collaboration between the union and the district, teachers receive information from a variety of sources: human resources, St. Paul Federation of Teachers, their principal, and the staff development coordinator.

Who coordinates integration of the mentoring program with other professional development opportunities and requirements in the schools and district?

The Office of Professional Development and building principals help coordinate multiple professional development opportunities.

PARTICIPANTS

Who is served?

First-year teachers are served. Teachers without teaching experience may opt for a second year.

Is participation of new teachers voluntary or mandatory?

Participation is strongly encouraged, but not mandatory.

Who provides the mentoring/induction?

Experienced master teachers, preferably in the same building, provide the mentoring.

What are the criteria for being a mentor?

Master teachers with experience in the district's reform models are eligible to be mentors.

MENTOR RESPONSIBILITIES AND REMUNERATION

What are the job responsibilities of mentors?

Mentors are asked to meet the mentee during opening week to plan for the first day or first week of school, or meet within two weeks of the new teacher's start date if the mentee is beginning or transferring to the school or site during the school year. Mentors must complete and submit all required online documentation by the deadline to receive compensation.

For first-year mentees who teach a full year at SPPS, the mentor's responsibilities are to:

- Meet or confer with the mentee at least weekly to discuss problems, share information, and get updates on how the mentee is doing
- At least six times during the school year, observe and/or model lessons in the mentee's classroom or have the mentee observe the mentor. Meet after each observation to discuss the lesson
- Complete six mentor classroom observation records and submit them using the online mentor report form
- Help the mentee claim two released days during the year for mentoring activities

For first-year mentees who join SPPS later in the school year, the mentor's responsibilities are to:

- At least three times during the school year, observe and/or model lessons in the mentee's classroom or have the mentee observe the mentor. Meet after each observation to discuss the lesson
- Complete three mentor classroom observation records and submit them using the online mentor report form
- Help the mentee claim one released day for mentoring activities

For second-year mentees, the mentor's responsibilities are to meet monthly with the mentee and report those meetings using the online second-year mentor report form.

Are mentors required to do peer observation and coaching?

Yes, peer observation and coaching are required for first-year teachers.

Do mentors have full-time classroom teaching responsibilities?

Yes, mentors are full-time classroom teachers.

How are mentors available to participate in the program?

Mentors are given two full days of substitute coverage per year for mentoring work.

Do mentors evaluate new teachers?

No, mentors do not evaluate new teachers.

Is the mentor–new teacher relationship confidential?

Yes, the mentor–new teacher relationship is confidential.

Are mentors paid?

Yes, mentors are paid $700 to mentor a first-year teacher.

Mentor Selection, Matching, Training, and Supervision

How are mentors selected?

Mentors volunteer and are selected by the principal, coordinator, and teacher.

How are mentors and new teachers matched?

Mentors and new teachers are matched through a collaboration among the building principal, site staff development coordinator, and new teacher.

Are mentors trained?

Yes, mentors are trained. Marilyn Baeker does one training session for mentors each year and is available for questions. Since the same teachers often serve as mentors year to year, the training needs are not as great as they are in some districts. In 2008–2009, a two-hour training session was provided, focusing on coaching, mentoring, and how to report mentoring activities to receive stipends.

Who supervises the mentors?

Building site staff development coordinators, principals, and district support (Marilyn Baeker) supervise the mentors.

SUPPORTS FOR MENTORS

Is professional development available for mentors?

Yes, professional development is available for mentors.

Who provides the professional development?

District personnel, under Marilyn Baeker, provide professional development for the mentors.

What resources are available for mentors?

Principals, coaches, and other district support are available for mentors.

PROGRAM COSTS AND FUNDING

What resources are required for the program?

The cost of the program is $230,000. Resources required for the program include:

- Mentor training
- New-teacher orientation
- Materials
- Stipends for mentors
- Substitutes for released time

What are the funding sources?

District and building staff development funds pay for the program.

Who requests the funding?

The program is funded through the district's building staff development budget.

PROGRAM EVALUATION

How is the program evaluated?

The program is evaluated through constant dialogue among all parties and oversight by a joint committee, the Career in Education Committee.

Who sees the results?

All parties involved see the results of the evaluation.

RECRUITMENT, HIRING, AND RETENTION OF NEW STAFF

How many new teachers are recruited and hired?

Seventy-four new teachers were hired in 2007–2008.

Are there any data that correlate the mentoring program with the retention of new teachers?

This is difficult to establish because of fluctuating educational funding, declining enrollment, and more stringent licensing requirements.

INDICATORS OF PROGRAM SUCCESS

What are the indicators of program success?

A survey is carried out at the end of each year to assess the effectiveness of the program. There are no data linking the mentoring program to longer tenure in the district. However, survey results from both mentors and mentees have consistently indicated high rates of satisfaction with the program. Mentees regularly report that their mentors have helped them navigate the systems in their schools, have been great people to listen to concerning any problems they have encountered as new teachers, and have provided a lot of practical ideas for improving instruction.

New teachers, mentor teachers, and principals have provided many anecdotal testimonials. Even during tight fiscal times, this program remains a priority for administrators throughout the district. Academic gains continue to be recognized, and the district recently received an award from the Council of the Great City Schools for ELL achievement. Students are learning.

ROCHESTER CITY SCHOOL DISTRICT CAREER IN TEACHING PLAN

ROCHESTER, NEW YORK

Marie Costanza, Mentoring Program Coordinator
131 West Broad Street
Rochester, NY 14614
585–262–8541
Fax: 585–262–8795
marie.costanza@rcsdk12.org

The following information was obtained from telephone conversations and e-mail correspondence with Adam Urbanski, Carl O'Connell, and Marie Costanza.

Demographics

Grade Levels	PreK through adult ed	Urban/Suburban/Rural	Urban
Student Population	44,000	**Ethnic Makeup***	African American 65% Hispanic 21% Caucasian 12% Other 2%
Teacher Population	3,600	**% New Teachers**	12%
		Per-Pupil Expenditure	$11,000

* The statistics available from the district delineated the ethnic makeup as shown. There was no information about students of more than one racial heritage.

Program Highlights

Unique Feature of Program	Peer assistance and review	Mentoring Is/Is Not Mandated for Certification/Licensing	Mentoring is mandated
Coaching Is/Is Not a Component	Coaching is a component	**Mentors Do/Do Not Evaluate the New Teachers With Whom They Work**	Mentors do evaluate
Cost of Program	$2.7 million	**Funding**	District, state, and grants

Mentors Are Full-Time/Part-Time Teachers	Mentors teach 50% and mentor 50% if they work with four new teachers; otherwise, they are full-time teachers	**Mentor Remuneration**	Mentors receive a teacher's salary plus 5% to 10% of base
How Long Program Has Been in Existence	22 years	**Duration of Program for New Teachers**	One year, or longer if requested by teacher or panel
Higher Education Affiliation	None	**Program Coordinator**	Marie Costanza

HISTORY

Adam Urbanski is president of the Rochester Federation of Teachers and vice president of the American Federation of Teachers. Through his association with Dal Lawrence, president of the American Federation, Adam became familiar with the Peer Assistance and Review (PAR) program in Toledo, Ohio, which started in 1981. Adam proposed a variation of that program for Rochester in 1986. After multiple meetings, consensus was reached within the Rochester Federation and PAR was proposed in negotiations. It was included in the 1987 contract.

STATE MANDATES

Is mentoring mandated for new teachers?

Yes, mentoring is mandated for new teachers.

Is mentoring part of certification or licensure?

Yes, mentoring is part of certification and licensure.

Is funding provided to support the mandate?

Yes, the state provides some of the funding for mentoring.

GOALS

The goals of the program are to:

- Cultivate good teaching
- Create the best possible teaching staff among new teachers
- Retain teachers

PROGRAM DESIGN

What are the components and recommended schedule of the program?

- Each new teacher is assigned a mentor, who works closely with her or him throughout the school year. New teachers are "interns" on the career level in the Rochester City School District.

- The mentor coaches and evaluates the intern and, at the end of the school year, makes a recommendation to the Career in Teaching (CIT) panel regarding the teacher's continued employment in the school system.
- Mentors are trained before school starts. They also participate in monthly meetings and receive training throughout the school year.
- Throughout the year, over 60 percent of the mentors voluntarily meet in collegial circles to discuss conferencing techniques and provide peer review of their peer coaching skills.
- A four-day new-teacher orientation is scheduled the week before school starts. Ongoing professional development is available for all new teachers throughout the year.
- The CIT panel, composed of teachers and administrators, reviews the performance of interns and mentors. The CIT panel also arranges training.

Are there any programs that complement the mentoring program?

The school district recognizes several career levels as follows:

- Intern: Newly employed teachers are considered intern teachers. Newly employed teachers who have had previous experience may be excluded from internship and assigned resident status.
- Resident: Teachers who successfully complete the intern teacher level move to the resident teacher level.
- Professional: Tenured teachers.
- Lead: Teachers who are master teachers and have additional responsibilities.

A professional development group within the union collaborates with the CIT department. This group makes recommendations about professional development, which are often funded by the union and the district. Typically there are over 50 professional development opportunities during the school year. The Rochester Teacher Center collaborates with the CIT department to provide professional development opportunities.

Tenured teachers may voluntarily request support—peer assistance—which is confidential. In these cases, mentors are assigned to teachers, and they work together throughout the school year. No written reports are filed.

Who designed the mentoring program?

Initially, Adam Urbanski designed the program, and then he collaborated with the superintendent, Peter McWalters, and the chair of the CIT panel, Tom Gillett. In 1991, Carl O'Connell joined the group, and he and school-based mentors also collaborated on design revisions.

PROGRAM ADMINISTRATION

Who coordinates the mentoring program?

Marie Costanza is the mentoring program coordinator.

How is information communicated to shareholders?

Information is shared through bulletins, e-mails, the union Web site, and articles and publications about the program. It is also shared at orientation meetings and trainings throughout the school year.

Who coordinates integration of the mentoring program with other professional development opportunities and requirements in the schools and district?

The CIT panel works to coordinate the program with other professional development opportunities, and works closely with curriculum directors as well.

PARTICIPANTS

Who is served?

The following are served by the program:

- First-year teachers, newly graduated from college
- Teachers from out of state
- Alternatively certified teachers (through partnerships with Roberts Wesleyan College and Empire State College)
- Teachers changing tenure areas

Is participation of new teachers voluntary or mandatory?

Teachers listed above must participate in the mentoring program. Resident-level and professional-level tenured teachers have the option of requesting support.

Who provides the mentoring/induction?

Mentors are classroom teachers. This is a practitioner-based model.

What are the criteria for being a mentor?

The criteria for being a mentor are:

- Seven years' teaching experience, five in the district
- Tenure
- References from six colleagues, including the supervisor and union representative
- An interview with and recommendation by a team from the CIT Panel
- Successful participation in a mandatory mentor training

MENTOR RESPONSIBILITIES AND REMUNERATION

What are the job responsibilities of mentors?

The job responsibilities of a mentor are those of gatekeeper and evaluator as well as advocate.

Mentors must:

- Participate in the training, before school and during the school year
- Attend monthly meetings
- Observe and conference with intern(s)
- Do demonstration lessons and peer coaching
- Write reports about intern performance
- Recommend whether intern(s) should be rehired

Are mentors required to do peer observation and coaching?

Yes, peer observation and coaching are required of mentors. Typically mentors observe their interns 30 to 40 times and conference with them 50 to 60 times per year.

Do mentors have full-time classroom teaching responsibilities?

All mentors are at the "lead teacher" career level. Mentors of one intern have full-time classroom teaching responsibilities and are released on a per-diem basis for their mentoring. Mentors who have four interns are released from 50 percent of their teaching.

How are mentors available to participate in the program?

Mentors who have one intern are released on a per-diem basis, and mentors who are released 50 percent of the time to mentor four interns job-share a position. The reaction to this arrangement has been favorable, and parents often request that their children be placed in the classrooms of mentors who are job-sharing.

Do mentors evaluate new teachers?

Yes, mentors evaluate their peers. Mentors submit two status reports during the school year, as well as a final report, to the CIT panel. The CIT panel then writes its recommendation about future employment to the superintendent and the board of education. In addition, the principal evaluates new teachers.

Is the mentor–new teacher relationship confidential?

Yes, the relationship is confidential. All notes taken by the mentor during observations and conferences with the intern are confidential. The CIT panel is given two status reports and a final evaluation, and the only thing that goes into the new teacher's personnel file is the letter from the CIT panel regarding recommendation for future employment.

Are mentors paid?

Mentors are lead teachers, and they are paid an additional 5 to 10 percent of their base salary, depending on their responsibilities.

MENTOR SELECTION, MATCHING, TRAINING, AND SUPERVISION

How are mentors selected?

The CIT panel selects mentors. Selection is based on:

- Application and statement
- References
- Interview

How are matches made between mentors and new teachers?

Marie Costanza carefully matches interns and mentors. She gives priority to proximity and certification area. It is preferable for interns to be mentored by teachers in their buildings, yet if those teachers have not taught in their certification area, other mentors are assigned.

Are mentors trained?

Yes, mentors are trained before school starts and then throughout the school year.

Who supervises the mentors?

Marie supervises the mentors. In addition, twice a year, the interns write evaluations of the mentors, which are reviewed by the CIT panel. Members of the panel share responsibility for observing each mentor.

SUPPORTS FOR MENTORS

District personnel support the mentors. They are given materials, including books about beginning teaching, that are also given to interns.

Is professional development available for mentors?

Yes, professional development is available for mentors.

Who provides the professional development?

Professional development is provided by people from within and outside of the system, as the need requires.

What resources are available for mentors?

The monthly meetings are an opportunity for mentors to receive support and discuss issues.

PROGRAM COSTS AND FUNDING

What resources are required for the program?

The cost of the program is $2.7 million per year. It costs approximately $5,000 per intern. The resources required are:

- Mentor training: $15,000
- New-teacher orientation: $60,000
- Books for mentors and interns: $30,000
- Stipends for mentors $2,300,000
- Coverage for mentors to be released: $100,000
- Coordinator's and secretary's salaries: $150,000
- Additional costs: $45,000
- Conferences for interns to attend
- Conferences for mentors to attend
- Supplies and materials

What are the funding sources?

The funding sources are local, state, and federal grants.

Who requests the funding?

Marie Costanza requests the funding.

PROGRAM EVALUATION

How is the program evaluated?

The program is evaluated throughout the school year in many ways, including:

* Mentors' evaluations: Mentors write a self-reflection, which is reviewed by the CIT panel. Additionally, mentors write an assessment of the program and the program coordinator.
* Interns' evaluations: Two times per year, interns write assessments of their mentors. At the end of the year, interns complete a survey in which they evaluate the program.
* Administrators' evaluations: At the end of the year, administrators write an evaluation of the mentor(s) who worked with their interns. The administrators also evaluate the effectiveness of the program.
* Teachers who leave the district complete an exit interview survey in which they evaluate the program.
* CIT panel observations and review of mentors' records: Throughout the year, CIT panel members are assigned to approximately 15 mentors. The panel member observes the mentor and intern's interaction and provides feedback to the mentors. Additionally, two times a year, the panel member reviews the status reports written by the mentor about the intern. At the end of the year, the panel member meets with each mentor to assess the mentor's records.

Who sees the results of the evaluation?

The results of the evaluations are seen by Marie, the union president, the superintendent, and the CIT panel.

RECRUITMENT, HIRING, AND RETENTION OF NEW STAFF

How many new teachers are recruited and hired?

An average of 400 new teachers are hired each year.

Are there any data that correlate the mentoring program with the retention of new teachers?

Yes, there are data that correlate the mentoring program with the retention of new teachers. In 1986, before the program was started, 65 percent of new teachers remained in the district. The first year of the program, 1987, the retention rate grew to 91 percent. Over the last 22 years, the average retention rate has been 88 percent.

INDICATORS OF PROGRAM SUCCESS

What are the indicators of program success?

In addition to the retention rate are several other indicators of program success. An independent evaluation, "RCSD and the English Language Arts State Examination," was conducted in 1999–2000 by Guillermo Montes of Children's Institute. Guillermo studied the forces underlying the English language arts (ELA) scores of young students in the district. It was a retrospective study, following current fourth-graders back to first grade, and was quite robust: 2,900 students for four years, from first grade through fourth. Nineteen variables per child per year were taken into account—or around 360,000 variables in all. Guillermo, one of the area's top economists, used structural equation modeling, simultaneous equations, and multivariate regression. His study is a prototype of many of the current growth models now out there. After studying the information regarding the fourth-grade ELA results of students whose teachers were interns with mentors, the Education Testing and Research Department in the Rochester City School District concluded that "In short, the ELA longitudinal study offered tantalizing evidence that the mentoring program is an effective intervention in improving student performance."

Each year, surveys of administrators and interns are conducted. The data collected indicate a high correlation between teacher retention and mentoring services received.

Intern surveys consistently show that Rochester City School District interns attribute their successful performance and the performance of their students to the assistance they receive from their mentors. The following quotes are taken from the 2008 Career in Teaching program evaluation questionnaire:

> My mentor was an excellent resource and support. She encouraged, challenged, and motivated me to improve my practice. She fostered my love for teaching and was enthusiastic about it in her own practice. My students and I grew immensely due to her support and guidance.

> This program has immediate and long-term benefits. The mentorship provides guidance, confidence and direction, which is needed for new teachers. Due to the confidence instilled in me by my mentor, my students were able to gain a great deal. When I study the results obtained by my students at the end of the year in comparison to the preliminary assessments in the beginning of the year, I know their success is due in part to the strategies modeled for me by my mentor.

COLUMBUS PUBLIC SCHOOLS PEER ASSISTANCE AND REVIEW PROGRAM

COLUMBUS, OHIO

Rhonda Johnson, President
Columbus Education Association
929 East Broad Street
Columbus, OH 43205
614–253–4731
rjohnson@ceaohio.org

The following information was obtained from telephone conversations and e-mail correspondence with John Grossman, former president of the Columbus Education Association (CEA), and current CEA president Rhonda Johnson, as well as materials distributed by the CEA.

Demographics

Grade Levels	K–12 plus	Urban/Suburban/Rural	Urban
Student Population	55,235	Ethnic Makeup*	African American 61.6% Asian 1.9% Caucasian 27.7% Hispanic 5.6% Multiracial 3.0% Native American .2%
Teacher Population	4,100	% New Teachers	5%
		Per-Pupil Expenditure	$11,919

* The statistics available from the district delineated the ethnic makeup as shown.

Program Highlights

Unique Feature of Program	Peers mentor and evaluate entry level teachers and experienced teachers in trouble	Mentoring Is/ Is Not Mandated for Certification/Licensing	Mentoring is mandated
Collaborative Coaching Is/Is Not a Component	Coaching is a component	Mentors Do/Do Not Evaluate the New Teachers With Whom They Work	Mentors do evaluate
Cost of Program	$2,000,000	Funding	District and state grants
Mentors Are Full-Time/Part-Time Teachers	Consulting teachers are full-time in that role	Mentor Remuneration	Teacher's salary plus 20% of the base
How Long Program Has Been in Existence	23 years	Duration of Program for New Teachers	One year; may be longer
Higher Education Affiliation	Ohio State University	Program Coordinator	Seven-member panel (four union, three administrative)

HISTORY

In the mid-1980s, a group of administrators and teachers in the Columbus schools researched a number of program designs to assist new teachers. Their hope was to improve retention rates for teachers in urban districts, since it was not uncommon for over half of new teachers to leave within their first year or two, and Columbus was no exception.

Teachers often began in Columbus because of competitive salaries and access to graduate programs at local colleges, including Ohio State University (OSU). However, these were not enough to keep them in a challenging urban teaching environment that offered little support in coping with the daily problems they faced as new teachers.

The team of administrators and teachers did a number of site visits to look at induction models. After much deliberation they decided to fashion their program on a model being used in Toledo. It was a similar district, also in Ohio, and it included mentoring and review functions. New teachers would be supported by successful, experienced faculty members, who after a year of observation and reflection would serve as their primary evaluators. They decided to call the program Peer Assistance and Review (PAR).

STATE MANDATES

Is mentoring mandated for new teachers?

Yes, mentoring is mandated for new teachers.

Is mentoring part of certification or licensure?

Yes, mentoring is part of certification and licensure.

Is funding provided to support the mandate?

No. There is some grant money, but it is available to districts only every other year.

GOALS

The goals of the Columbus Peer Assistance and Review Program are to:

- Retain new teachers
- Put experienced teachers on career ladders, which might offer incentives to them as well as take advantage of the expertise gained by their years of experience

PROGRAM DESIGN

What are the components and recommended schedule of the program?

The program includes a variety of professional development experiences for new teachers.

The intern phase is for beginning teachers and involves having mentor teachers visit their classrooms and coach them.

The other part of the program is the intervention phase; this is for experienced teachers having extreme difficulty. This part of the program does many of the same things as the intern phrase, yet there is not the limit of one year to make a decision about rehiring.

New-teacher orientation lasts one week, the mentoring component being on Thursday and Friday.

Consulting teachers work with new teachers, called interns.

Are there any programs that complement the mentoring program?

Yes. Teachers have the option of taking any of three graduate courses offered, including an action research course and a common issues course. District staff and university faculty jointly teach these courses. They are part of the Outreach and Engagement partnership with Ohio State University's College of Education and Human Ecology.

Who designed the mentoring program?

The program was jointly designed by the school board and the union in 1986.

PROGRAM ADMINISTRATION

Who coordinates the mentoring program?

The union and the school administration jointly coordinate the program.

Responsibility for the entire management of PAR rests on a seven-member governing panel, referred to as the PAR panel. Members include the union president, three teachers, the executive director of human resources, the director of human resources administration, and a building principal. The chair of the panel rotates between administration and union on a yearly basis. All governing decisions are made by this body, including selection of consulting teachers, monitoring of consulting teachers' duties and reports, establishing program policy, and ensuring that the philosophical base for PAR is maintained and refined as necessary.

How is information communicated to shareholders?

Information is communicated through a weekly union newspaper.

Administrative members are responsible for maintaining open lines of communication with the school board and administrative personnel. The union members of the PAR panel seek to keep their faculty representatives and members informed of the purpose and activities of the PAR program as well as advise all members that their legal and contractual rights will be protected whether they are intern teachers in the PAR program or not.

Who coordinates integration of the mentoring program with other professional development opportunities and requirements in the schools and district?

The PAR panel coordinates integration of the program with other professional development opportunities.

Participants

Who is served?

Entry-level teachers are served by the PAR program, as well as experienced teachers who are having significant difficulties with their practice.

Is participation of new teachers voluntary or mandatory?

Participation of new teachers is mandatory.

Who provides the mentoring/induction?

Consulting teachers provide mentoring and support of new teachers.

What are the criteria for being a mentor?

The criteria for selection of consulting teachers include:

- Five years' classroom experience in Columbus
- Outstanding classroom teaching ability
- Talent in written and oral communications
- Ability to work cooperatively and effectively with staff members
- Extensive knowledge of a variety of management and instructional techniques

In addition, each applicant must submit the following documents directly to the manager of personnel:

- A reference from his or her building principal or immediate supervisor
- A reference from his or her union senior faculty representative
- References from two other teachers with whom the applicant is currently working

Each applicant selected for an interview is given a set of questions requiring written responses. These are reviewed for what they reveal about the applicant's attitudes and knowledge as well as written communication skills. The applicant then has an extensive oral interview with the panel as the final step in assessing her or his qualifications to be a PAR consulting teacher.

Consulting teachers are expected to be among those most respected by their peers. Because of the importance of their role, in addition to their being outstanding teachers, their integrity must be above question. Teachers may serve as consulting teachers for no more than three years before returning to the classroom. Thus, no one in the PAR program has been far from the classroom for long. Rather, these teachers have sought change and challenge as a way to improve themselves while serving in a vital role for new teachers.

Once selected, potential consulting teachers join a pool of teachers who may be called on to join the PAR program as the need arises. Selections are made as necessary, determined by the number of intern teachers within a particular grade level or content area.

MENTOR RESPONSIBILITIES AND REMUNERATION

What are the job responsibilities of mentors?

Consulting teachers are required to:

- Meet with each intern teacher 25 times a year for peer observation and coaching
- Mentor, support, and provide continuous feedback
- Make an assessment of how each teacher is doing and make a recommendation of whether the person should be hired the next year (reviewed by the PAR panel)

Are mentors required to do peer observation and coaching?

Yes, peer observation and coaching are required of consulting teachers.

Do mentors have full-time classroom teaching responsibilities?

No, consulting teachers are full time in their role.

How are mentors available to participate in the program?

Consulting teachers are released from classroom teaching and are full-time supporters of new teachers. They work with 16 to 18 new teachers.

Do mentors evaluate new teachers?

Yes, consulting teachers evaluate new teachers. This is a central tenet of the Columbus program, and it is contrary to the belief that mentoring and evaluation are conflicting roles. The PAR program assumes that the two functions can be successfully performed by one person. Theoretically, the final evaluation of a beginning teacher would reflect the dialogue that began in September. It wouldn't contain anything new; there would be no surprises.

Therefore, a lot of attention is given to the need for honesty and candor, as well as support, to be the hallmarks of the relationship between the two teachers. This is a demanding role for consulting teachers, and they are carefully chosen for their ability to balance these factors. They are colleagues, not professional evaluators, and their final recommendations stem from their relationships as supportive consulting teachers.

Is the mentor–new teacher relationship confidential?

Yes, the relationship between consulting teacher and new teacher is confidential.

Are mentors paid?

Consulting teachers are paid an additional 20 percent of their base salary.

MENTOR SELECTION, MATCHING, TRAINING, AND SUPERVISION

How are mentors selected?

The PAR panel selects consulting teachers.

How are mentors and new teachers matched?

Mentors and new teachers are matched, as closely as possible, according to teaching level and area of certification or licensure.

Are mentors trained?

Consulting teachers are offered a variety of graduate courses, depending on their professional needs and prior education. The PAR panel determines what courses they are required to take. Consulting teachers also participate in professional development activities every other Friday for the three years they are in the program.

Who supervises the mentors?

The PAR panel supervises the consulting teachers.

SUPPORTS FOR MENTORS

Is professional development available for mentors?

Consulting teachers receive ongoing staff development. When the program first started, OSU faculty planned a series of graduate courses for consulting teachers. These courses were intended to ensure that participants understood the dynamics of observation and conferencing. They were also aimed at underscoring the importance of a supportive relationship between intern and consulting teacher.

Over the years, collaboration with OSU increased to the point where, in 1998, a part-time position was established for consultation with PAR staff. A professor who had been very involved with the PAR staff development program was given the appointment.

Central to the university's program is the notion that consulting teachers need to look back on their experiences and reflect on how they have evolved from beginners to competent professionals. As part of this process, they are expected to look at the educational research on the needs and growth of teachers.

Consulting teachers consider that entry-level teachers progress through a series of stages in their professional development and that part of the mentoring role is to understand these stages and to help beginners move from one stage to the next.

Preservice training is provided by active PAR consulting teachers.

Who provides this professional development?

See above.

What resources are available for mentors?

Consulting teachers are supported by the CEA, Columbus City Schools (CCS), and OSU.

PROGRAM COSTS AND FUNDING

What resources are required for the program?

The cost of the program is approximately $2,000,000.

- Salaries for consulting teachers: $1,500,000
- New-teacher orientation: $50,000
- Salaries for one full-time and one part-time secretary: Varies
- Furniture and supplies: Varies
- Materials: Varies

What are the funding sources?

In 1986, the school board agreed to fund the million-dollar program. There is sometimes state funding through a grant.

Who requests the funding?

The school board funds the program as a line item in the school budget.

Administrative members of the seven-member panel are responsible for securing necessary financial support of the program.

PROGRAM EVALUATION

How is the program evaluated?

Consulting teachers and new teachers are surveyed.

Who sees the results of the evaluation?

The PAR panel sees the results.

RECRUITMENT, HIRING, AND RETENTION OF NEW STAFF

How many new teachers are recruited and hired?

The number of new teachers hired varies. In 2007–2008, approximately 200 teachers were hired, and about as many were anticipated for 2008–2009.

Are there any data that correlate the mentoring program with the retention of new teachers?

Yes. Three surveys of staff have assessed the retention rate of teachers after five years in the district. Compared to the 50 percent retention rate that is often the case in urban districts, the results in Columbus have been much higher:

- In the first five years, 80 percent of the teachers remained, and of the 20 percent who left, 4 to 6 percent of them were terminated in their first year.
- In the second five-year cycle, 4 to 6 percent were terminated and 81 percent remained.
- In the third five-year cycle, the retention rate dropped to 67 percent.

The union and the district started a research project to determine the reasons for the decline. Preliminary results say that the program has become so accepted in the region that suburban districts are trying to lure teachers away. Of the teachers who have left, the majority of them have remained in the profession.

INDICATORS OF PROGRAM SUCCESS

What are the indicators of success?

In addition to the retention of new teachers, there are several indicators of success.

The Columbus Public Schools have worked with Sandra Stroot at OSU. She has studied when teachers gain competence, and this information helps consulting teachers know how best to help their intern teachers.

Research has been done on the 6,000 to 7,000 teachers who have participated in the PAR program. Data have been collected about the colleges the teachers attended, and feedback has been given to the universities about what is working and what needs improvement.

Praxis III is teacher testing mandated by the State of Ohio. All PAR consultants have been trained to administer and access the Praxis III test. PAR consultants have deep knowledge of what is required and are incorporating this knowledge into their practice with their intern teachers.

The district has made it clear that the PAR program is the last program that will ever be cut. The explicit due process in the program, along with all of the data that are collected, addresses issues of job performance long before any disagreement about tenure can occur. It has put an end to questions of job performance and disputes between the union and the school system.

State Programs

The following descriptions have been written by the directors of the programs in conjunction with their colleagues and the author. Judgments about the programs are those of the program directors and their staff and not the opinion of the author. Unless stated otherwise, figures and information were true for the 2007–2008 school year.

STOCKTON UNIFIED SCHOOL DISTRICT BEGINNING TEACHER SUPPORT AND ASSESSMENT INDUCTION PROGRAM

STOCKTON UNIFIED, CALIFORNIA

Lori Walker, BTSA Director
Stockton Unified School District
1503 St. Marks Plaza
Stockton, CA 95207
209–933–7030, Ext. 2324
lwalker@stockton.k12.ca.us

The following information was obtained from telephone conversations and e-mail correspondence with Lori Walker. This is an urban, single-district program.

Demographics

Grade Levels	K–12 and alternative	Urban/Suburban/Rural	Urban
Student Population	38,617	**Ethnic Makeup***	African American 12.9%
			Asian 12.4%
			Filipino 5.2%
			Hispanic 55.7%

(Continued)

(Continued)

			Native American 3.4% Pacific Islander 0.6% White 9.7% Multiple/No Response 0.1%
Teacher Population	1,778	**% New Teachers**	+/– 10%
		Per-Pupil Expenditure	$7,977

* The statistics available from the district delineated the ethnic makeup as shown.

Program Highlights

Unique Feature of Program	As per Senate Bill 2042, BTSA induction is the means by which California teachers receive their clear credential	**Mentoring Is/Is Not Mandated for Certification/Licensing**	Mentoring is mandated
Coaching Is/ Is Not a Component	Coaching is a component	**Mentors Do/Do Not Evaluate the New Teachers With Whom They Work**	Support providers do not evaluate
Cost of Program	$3,084 per participating teacher; for 2008–2009, total cost was $456,000 plus district in kind of $350,000	**Funding**	State and district
Mentors are Full-Time/Part-time Teachers	90% of support providers are full-time classroom teachers; 10% are specialists, retired teachers, etc.	**Mentor Remuneration**	Support providers receive $2,250 for each participating teacher they serve
How Long Program Has Been in Existence	The program has been in existence three years; it began as a Pathwise mentoring program in 1995	**Duration of Program for New Teachers**	Two years
Higher Education Affiliation	Chapman University	**Program Coordinator**	Lori Walker, BTSA Director; Cate Rockstad, Program Specialist

HISTORY

California has been a leader in legislating support for new teachers and supporting that mandate with funds for new-teacher induction.

The California Beginning Teacher Support and Assessment (BTSA) Induction Program provides formative assessment, individualized support and advanced content for newly-credentialed, beginning teachers, and is the preferred pathway to a California Professional (Clear) Teaching Credential. The BTSA Induction program is co-administered by the California Department of Education (CDE) and the California Commission on Teacher Credentialing (CCTC). The BTSA Task Force and State Leadership Team provide support and technical assistance to local BTSA Induction Program leaders. There are currently over 164 SB 2042–approved BTSA Induction Programs across California. (California BTSA, n.d., para. 1)

California's Beginning Teacher Support and Assessment (BTSA) program was based on research from the California New Teacher Project (CNTP). A central finding of this research identified the need to provide beginning teachers with focused induction support. To be useful, this support must be provided at a sufficient level of intensity to make a difference in the performance, retention, and satisfaction of beginning teachers. The 1997 Mazzoni legislation that established BTSA encouraged collaboration among local school districts, county offices of education, colleges, and universities to organize and deliver professional development for beginning teachers.

The *Induction Program Standards* (Commission on Teacher Credentialing, 2008) as well as the objectives stated in Section 44279.2(b) of the California Education Code guide the design and implementation of support and professional development services for teachers participating in BTSA induction programs.

STATE MANDATES

Is mentoring mandated for new teachers?

Yes, mentoring is mandated for new teachers to clear their California preliminary credential.

Is mentoring part of certification or licensure?

Yes, mentoring is part of certification and licensure.

Is funding provided to support the mandate?

Yes, funding is provided. The state gives $3,085 per participating teacher, and the district gives $2,000 in kind.

GOALS

The purposes of California's BTSA program as set out in Education Code Section 44279.2(b) are as follows:

1. To provide an effective transition into the teaching career for first-year and second-year teachers in California

2. To improve the educational performance of students through improved training, information, and assistance for new teachers

3. To enable beginning teachers to be effective in teaching students who are culturally, linguistically, and academically diverse

4. To ensure the professional success and retention of new teachers

5. To ensure that a support provider provides intensive individualized support and assistance to each beginning teacher

6. To improve the rigor and consistency of individual teacher performance assessments and the usefulness of assessment results to teachers and decision makers

7. To establish an effective, coherent system of performance assessments based on the California Standards for the Teaching Profession (CSTP)

8. To examine alternative ways in which the general public and the educational profession may be assured that new teachers who remain in teaching have attained acceptable levels of professional competence

9. To ensure that an individual induction plan for each beginning teacher is based on an ongoing assessment of the beginning teacher's development

10. To ensure continuous program improvement through ongoing research, development, and evaluation

PROGRAM DESIGN

What are the components and recommended schedule of the program?

The Stockton Unified School District (SUSD) BTSA Induction Program provides comprehensive, extended preparation and professional development for participating teachers that focus on CSTP in relation to state-adopted academic content standards and performance levels for students and state-adopted curriculum frameworks. Professional growth is guided by the development and implementation of an annual individual induction plan (IIP) and documented in the participant's portable file. Completion of all program requirements leads to a recommendation for the California professional credential.

Enrollment Procedures

- Meet with a credentials analyst
- Attend a SUSD BTSA Induction Program orientation meeting
- Complete and submit a participating teacher application form
- Complete and submit a state consent form (online registration)
- Submit a Teaching Performance Assessment (TPA) when available
- Work with an assigned support provider who will advise the participating teacher about his or her involvement in the induction program, provide formative feedback about his or her participation in and progress toward completion of the program, and support the participating teacher in accumulating evidence of professional growth

Program Completion Requirements

- Accumulate evidence of reflective practice, document all professional credential requirements, and, at the end of the program, organize this evidence in support of one's application for a California professional credential
- Attend a BTSA/California Formative Assessment and Support System for Teachers (CFASST) induction orientation meeting

- Attend a CFASST overview meeting
- Attend all BTSA quarterly meetings
- Meet with the support provider before school begins to discuss school procedures and classroom arrangement (if possible)
- Meet with the support provider at least once a week to discuss the support and assessment process
- Attend one full-day workshop on lesson planning, content standards, or classroom management
- Each semester, attend one workshop on Induction Standards program and/or content with the support provider
- Attend an appropriate Toward Equity workshop
- Complete one CFASST cycle each semester and develop an IIP at the end of each cycle (an IIP must be turned in to the program director for each cycle)
- Submit an activity log at the end of each month to the program director in the curriculum office
- Attend an end-of-year colloquium
- Complete professional development activities for Induction Standards 5 (Pedagogy: Equity and Diversity) and 6 (Universal Access: Teaching English Learners and Special Populations)
- Complete the SUSD BTSA Induction Program

Upon completion of all program requirements, the SUSD BTSA Induction Program, in collaboration with school district personnel, recommends eligible participating teachers to the California Commission on Teacher Credentialing for their California professional credential.

Are there any programs that complement the mentoring program?

Yes, most professional development activities and programs support the formative assessment process as experienced by BTSA participating teachers.

Who designed the mentoring program?

The program was designed by the BTSA induction director in conjunction with curriculum department staff. The program was designed in response to the California standards for professional teacher induction programs and has been approved by the California Commission on Teacher Credentialing.

PROGRAM ADMINISTRATION

Who coordinates the mentoring program?

Lori Walker, the BTSA induction program director and new-teacher support program specialist, coordinates the program.

How is information communicated to shareholders?

Shareholders receive information through informational meetings, professional development (training and seminars), a monthly bulletin, and one-on-one consultations.

Who coordinates integration of the mentoring program with other professional development opportunities and requirements in the schools and district?

The BTSA induction director works in conjunction with curriculum department staff and the human resources department.

PARTICIPANTS

Who is served?

The program serves:

- First- and second-year teachers with a preliminary credential
- Out-of-state teachers with less than five years' experience
- Out-of-country teachers

Is participation of new teachers voluntary or mandatory?

Participation is mandatory by contract and as per California state requirements to clear the preliminary credential.

Who provides the mentoring/induction?

Mentoring and induction are provided by BTSA induction support providers.

What are the criteria for being a mentor?

A support provider must be a caring, supportive teacher willing to assist a teacher participating in the BTSA induction program.

Selection criteria are consistent with the support provider's specified roles and responsibilities, including but not limited to the following:

- Knowledge of beginning teacher development
- Knowledge of state-adopted academic content standards and performance levels for students, state-adopted curriculum frameworks, and CSTP
- Willingness to participate in professional training to acquire the knowledge and skills needed to be an effective support provider
- Willingness to engage in formative assessment processes, including nonevaluative, reflective conversations about formative assessment evidence with participating teachers
- Willingness to share instructional ideas and materials with participating teachers
- Willingness to deepen understanding of cultural, ethnic, cognitive, linguistic, and gender diversity
- Effective interpersonal and communication skills
- Willingness to work with participating teachers
- Demonstrated commitment to personal professional growth and learning
- Willingness and ability to be an excellent professional role model

The support provider position is a commitment of at least two years, the length of time a participating teacher spends in the BTSA induction program. After four consecutive years of service, support providers are asked to submit a current letter of recommendation from their site administrator. Support providers are assigned on an as-needed basis. The honorarium is subject to prorating according to time and length of assignment (participating teachers may be hired late or leave the district during the year) as determined by the BTSA leadership team. The availability, site, grade level, and content areas of participating teachers are considered in determining support provider assignments.

MENTOR RESPONSIBILITIES AND REMUNERATION

What are the job responsibilities of mentors?

Support providers are responsible to:

1. Participate in Formative Assessment for California Teachers (FACT) training during the school year; training may be up to five full days, or whatever is appropriate for the assigned participating teacher

2. Attend the BTSA induction orientation meeting in August

3. Attend one FACT overview meeting (choices are available)

4. Attend all BTSA quarterly meetings (should an unavoidable conflict arise for the second-, third-, or fourth-quarter meeting, contact the program director in advance to complete a makeup assignment)

5. Meet with the participating teacher within one week of assignment to discuss their role as the BTSA support provider and assist with classroom startup

6. Meet with a site administrator once a year to discuss the BTSA induction program

7. Meet with the participating teacher at least once a week to discuss the support and assessment process

8. Attend training (one day at minimum) focused on coaching skills and/or participating teacher needs

9. Attend an appropriate Toward Equity training

10. Attend at least one Induction Standards focus meeting each semester with the participating teacher

11. Complete one formative assessment cycle each semester and develop an IIP at the end of each cycle; an IIP and descriptions of practice (DOP) must be turned in to BTSA office for each cycle

12. Submit an activity log to the BTSA office at the end of each month

13. Attend the end-of-year colloquium; if unable to attend, prepare a portfolio or write a paper describing their experience in BTSA

14. Maintain satisfactory or better teacher evaluation during service as a support provider

Are mentors required to do peer observation and coaching?

Yes, peer observation and coaching are required.

Do mentors have full-time classroom teaching responsibilities?

No, support providers do not have full-time classroom teaching responsibilities.

How are mentors available to participate in the program?

Support providers are released from teaching to provide formative assessment, perform coaching and training, and complete observations.

Do mentors evaluate new teachers?

No, induction program support providers do not evaluate participating teachers.

Is the mentor–new teacher relationship confidential?

Yes, the relationship is confidential.

Are mentors paid?

Induction program support providers are paid $2,250 per participating teacher.

MENTOR SELECTION, MATCHING, TRAINING, AND SUPERVISION

How are mentors selected?

The following are required of applicants:

- A letter of recommendation from a current site administrator (an application with a "not recommended" will not be considered)
- A letter of recommendation from a fellow teacher (an application with a "not recommended" will not be considered)
- A letter of intent to the curriculum department explaining why the applicant wants to become a BTSA induction program support provider, along with the applicant's résumé and qualifications
- A valid California clear teaching credential; permanent status and a minimum of three years of successful teacher experiences in SUSD
- A score of satisfactory or better on the most recent teacher evaluation
- A minimum of four of the following experiences:
  - Successful completion of an intern support teacher, professional development teacher, consulting teacher, or BTSA support provider appointment
  - Participation in any California subject matter project
  - Authorization to teach English language learners; language development specialization (LDS), or current cross-cultural language and academic development (CLAD), bilingual cross-cultural language and academic development (BCLAD), or bilingual cross-cultural (BCC) certification.
  - Experience as a successful staff development presenter within the district and/or site
  - Prior training in peer coaching
  - A record of continuing professional growth

   ○ Membership in the site leadership team or school site council or another leadership role (department chair, etc.)
   ○ Membership in the site curriculum team, district curriculum council, or another district curriculum committee or cadre

How are mentors and new teachers matched?

The intent of the program is to match a participating teacher with a supportive member from the teacher's grade level or content area. Pedagogical needs and local context are considered in the match.

Are mentors trained?

Yes, induction program support providers are trained in the formative assessment system used by the program and in cognitive coaching.

Who supervises the mentors?

The program director supervises induction program support providers.

SUPPORTS FOR MENTORS

Is professional development available for mentors?

Yes, training is provided on FACT system components, cognitive coaching, and equity and diversity.

Who provides this professional development?

Program specialists, trainers, and professional development staff provide support for support providers.

What resources are available for mentors?

Mentors receive training as described as well as support from the program director.

PROGRAM COSTS AND FUNDING

What resources are required for the program?

Total funding for 2008–2009: $456,000 plus district in-kind funding of $350,000. The costs are:

- Two positions (program specialist and support staff)
- Support provider stipends
- Professional development
- State conferences and training for program leadership
- Substitutes to cover released time for training and observations
- Consultants
- Books and instructional materials for participating teachers

The BTSA director is paid by the BTSA program and the general fund. The new-teacher support program specialist is paid by Title II funds. The support staff are paid by BTSA funds.

What are the funding sources?

The state grants $3,085 per participating teacher, and the district provides $2,000 in kind.

Who requests the funding?

The program director requests the state grant award.

PROGRAM EVALUATION

How is the program evaluated?

External and state-level evaluation is a required part of the program. An annual review process is required.

Who sees the results of the evaluation?

All stakeholders see the results of the evaluations.

RECRUITMENT, HIRING, AND RETENTION OF NEW STAFF

How many new teachers are recruited and hired?

On average, 150 new teachers are hired each year.

Are there any data that correlate the mentoring program with the retention of new teachers?

Yes, SUSD has had an 88.9% retention rate over five years for BTSA induction program participants.

INDICATORS OF PROGRAM SUCCESS

What are the indicators of program success?

The indicators of success are the number of teachers completing the program successfully and receiving their California clear credential, the retention data, and participant program evaluations. When asked what is most valuable, participating teachers generally comment on the support and availability of support providers, opportunities for professional development and reflective practice, examination of student work, and program monitoring for credential requirement completion. Support providers, when asked what is the most valuable, generally comment on their coaching training and experience and mutual professional growth (they learn as much from their participating teachers as the participating teachers learn from them). Principals see value in the formative assessment process, observation by support providers, and general support as a good match for formal evaluation. They appreciate knowing that the strong structure and support help new teachers through their first two years of teaching.

NORTH HAVEN PUBLIC SCHOOLS BEGINNING EDUCATOR SUPPORT AND TRAINING PROGRAM

NORTH HAVEN, CONNECTICUT

Ann Cappetta, BEST Facilitator
Sue Bass, BEST Facilitator
North Haven High School
21 Elm Street
North Haven, CT 06473
203–239–2614, Ext. 1914
cappetta.ann@north-haven.k12.ct.us

Excerpts from *A Guide to the BEST Program for Beginning Teachers*, published by the Connecticut Department of Education's Bureau of Program and Teacher Evaluation, are included in the following description of the North Haven Public Schools program, along with information obtained from Marie Diamond, past coordinator of the program, and Sue Bass, BEST facilitator, in telephone conversations and e-mail correspondence.

Demographics

Grade Levels	PreK–12	Urban/Suburban/Rural	Urban, suburban, and rural
Student Population	3,962	Ethnic Makeup*	African American 4.5%
			Asian 6.8%
			Hispanic 4.1%
			Native American 0.2%
			White 84.4%
Teacher Population	269	% New Teachers	11%
		Per-Pupil Expenditure	$9,902

* The statistics available from the district delineated the ethnic makeup as shown. There was no information about students of more than one racial heritage.

Program Highlights

Unique Feature of Program	This program is part of the state's BEST program	Mentoring Is/Is Not Mandated for Certification/Licensing	Mentoring is mandated
Collaborative Coaching Is/Is Not a Component	Coaching is a component	Mentors Do/Do Not Evaluate the New Teachers With Whom They Work	Mentors do not evaluate

(Continued)

(Continued)

Cost of Program	$2,500	Funding	The districts fund their programs
Mentors Are Full-Time/Part-Time Teachers	Mentors are full-time teachers	Mentor Remuneration	$100 per year
How Long Program Has Been in Existence	18 years	Duration of Program for New Teachers	Two years, three if needed
Higher Education Affiliation	None	Program Coordinator	Ann Cappetta

HISTORY

The Education Enhancement Act of 1986 was highly significant in raising standards for teacher education and licensing as well as increasing teacher salaries to the highest in the nation. Born in the 1980s, the Beginning Educator and Support Training (BEST) program provided all new teachers with foundational competencies and a set of professional standards that uniformly raised the level of performance of all beginning teachers. The BEST program ensures all new teachers a full year of mentoring. Most districts provide two full years of mentoring, especially in the second year when new teachers must complete detailed portfolios documenting the teaching, learning, and assessment of an 8 to 10-hour unit of instruction. (More information can be obtained by accessing the following link: www.sde.ct.gov/sde/cwp/view.asp?a=2607&Q=319186&sdePNavCtr=|#45440.) This "balanced equation" of higher teacher salaries matched by increased professional standards has been found extremely successful in attracting more academically qualified individuals into Connecticut's schools.

Connecticut's Common Core of Teaching (CCT) defines the knowledge, skills, and competencies teachers need to attain to ensure that students learn and perform at high levels. The CCT is used across the career continuum of teachers. The CCT includes foundational skills and competencies that are common to all teachers and discipline-specific professional standards that represent the knowledge, skills, and competencies that are unique to teachers of elementary education, English language arts, history/social studies, art, special education, math, music, science, world languages, physical education, and health.

STATE MANDATES

Is mentoring mandated for new teachers?

Yes, mentoring is mandated for new teachers by the State of Connecticut.

Is mentoring part of certification or licensure?

No, initial certification is granted for three years. After successful completion of the portfolio and a successful third year, the state grants provisional certification for five years and then a professional certification thereafter.

Is funding provided to support the mandate?

No, funding is no longer provided by the state, although the state recommends a first-year mentoring stipend of $2,500 followed by another $500 for the second year. Most districts are not able to pay this to mentors. In North Haven, due to serious budget constraints, mentors have not been paid in several years. Mentors view what they do as their professional duty, which North Haven appreciates and views as quite admirable.

GOALS

North Haven and the State of Connecticut share the same goals with regard to new-teacher induction: that every student be taught by a qualified and skilled teacher; hence, through contact with an involved and well-trained mentor, new teachers are expected to demonstrate competence in both the foundational skills and competencies and discipline-based professional standards through the completion of the BEST program. These foundational skills and competencies include all of the following (from Connecticut's Common Core of Teaching document on foundational skills and competencies):

I. Teachers have KNOWLEDGE of

STUDENTS

- Teachers understand how students learn and develop
- Teachers understand how students differ in their approaches to learning

CONTENT

- Teachers are proficient in reading, writing, and mathematics
- Teachers understand the central skills, concepts, tools of inquiry, and structures of the discipline they teach

PEDAGOGY

- Teachers know how to design and deliver instruction
- Teachers recognize the need to vary their instructional methods

II. Teachers APPLY this knowledge by

PLANNING

- Teachers plan instruction based upon knowledge of subject matter, students, the curriculum, and the community
- Teachers select and/or create learning tasks that make subject matter meaningful to students

INSTRUCTING

- Teachers establish and maintain appropriate standards of behavior and create a positive learning environment
- Teachers create instructional opportunities that support students' academic, social, and personal development
- Teachers use effective communication techniques which foster individual and collaborative inquiry
- Teachers employ a variety of instructional strategies that enable students to think critically, solve problems, and demonstrate skills

ASSESSING AND ADJUSTING

- Teachers use various assessment techniques to evaluate students' learning and modify instruction as appropriate

III. Teachers DEMONSTRATE PROFESSIONAL RESPONSIBILITY through

PROFESSIONAL AND ETHICAL PRACTICE

- Teachers conduct themselves as professionals in accordance with The Code of Professional Responsibility for Teachers (Section 10-145d-400a of the Connecticut Certification Regulations)
- Teachers share responsibility for student achievement and well-being

REFLECTION AND CONTINUOUS LEARNING

- Teachers continuously engage in self-evaluation of the effects of their choices and actions on students and the school community
- Teachers seek out opportunities to grow professionally

LEADERSHIP AND COLLABORATION

- Teachers serve as leaders in the school community
- Teachers demonstrate a commitment to their students and a passion for improving their profession

PROGRAM DESIGN

What are the components and recommended schedule of the program?

According to state mandate, each new teacher is assigned a certified mentor (hopefully in the same subject area, grade, and school) for his or her first year of teaching. The mentor is responsible to meet with the teacher for at least one hour once per week and must be given released time to observe and/or meet with the new teacher on at least eight occasions during the first year. Mentors are expected to assist the new teacher in any way—whether it be in planning lessons, dealing with parents, planning open house activities, or getting involved in the school community by moderating a club or coaching a sport. During the second year, the state does not mandate mentoring, but most districts maintain the mentoring relationship during the crucial second year when new teachers must create a lengthy portfolio documenting 8 to 10 hours of instruction and assessment.

Are there any programs that complement the mentoring program?

State-based support sessions in the second year include:

- Portfolio overview sessions
- Portfolio videotape sessions
- Discipline-specific seminars

Submission of a teaching portfolio is required by May 1 of the teacher's second year.

Who designed the mentoring program?

The BEST program was designed by the Connecticut Department of Education. Every school superintendent must appoint a district BEST facilitator, who coordinates and oversees the program. The district facilitator goes to three or four meetings a year and is brought up to date on the BEST program by the state. The state sets BEST guidelines and requirements, and the BEST district facilitators find ways to address them and support new teachers in their system. Ann Cappetta is the North Haven Public Schools BEST facilitator.

PROGRAM ADMINISTRATION

Who coordinates the mentoring program?

Ann Cappetta coordinates the program in North Haven.

How is information communicated to shareholders?

The Bureau of Program and Teacher Evaluation publishes many documents that are distributed to all beginning teachers as well as other school personnel. In addition, the district BEST facilitator disseminates relevant materials about district and state programs.

Who coordinates integration of the mentoring program
with other professional development opportunities and
requirements in the schools and district?

Ann Cappetta is the BEST facilitator for the North Haven school system. Often, similar programs are coordinated by assistant superintendents or directors of curriculum. Ann is North Haven's K–12 art coordinator, which is an unusual position. However, Ann has worked for the past 20 years at the state level and is well positioned to coordinate integration of the BEST program and the district's induction program with other professional development.

PARTICIPANTS

Who is served?

Teachers who must participate in the BEST program are beginning teachers who:

- Are employed as teachers in Connecticut's public schools or an approved private special education facility
- Hold one of the following certificates:
  - ○ Initial educator certificate
  - ○ Interim initial educator certificate
  - ○ Temporary 90-day certificate
  - ○ Durational shortage area permit
- Are full time or part time
- Are hired under long-term substitute status (provided they are teaching under a valid certificate as noted above and in the corresponding endorsement area of that certificate)

The BEST program does not stipulate any support for teachers who change grade levels or subjects; districts may provide assistance. In some cases, teachers are permitted to submit their required portfolio in their third year because of changing subjects.

Is participation of new teachers voluntary or mandatory?

Participation is mandatory. BEST is a two-year program, with a third year available if necessary. However, the third year is the last opportunity to complete the BEST program requirements. Individuals who fail to complete participation in three years will not be eligible for reissuance of the initial educator certificate.

Who provides the mentoring/induction?

Experienced North Haven Public Schools teachers who are trained by the state as BEST support teachers provide the induction support as mentors.

In addition, there are support teams led by a school staff member who has completed BEST support team training. A support team may support one or more beginning teachers at the district or building level. Other members of the team may include teachers in the same content areas or grade level as the beginning teacher, a previously trained Common Core of Teaching (CCT) assessor or BEST portfolio scorer, master mentor, the principal, a department chair, a curriculum specialist, and past "graduates" of the BEST program.

What are the criteria for being a mentor?

The guidelines for district selection of support teachers (mentors and cooperating teachers) define eligible educators as teachers holding a professional or provisional education certificate and who have attained tenure. Further, they are teachers who:

- Demonstrate success as an educator
- Possess a variety of educational experiences and training
- Are able to impart knowledge and understanding about effective teaching practices to others
- Demonstrate knowledge of effective teaching practices as defined by the CCT or its equivalent
- Are committed to improving the induction of student and beginning teachers into the profession
- Are able to relate to adult learners and work cooperatively as part of a team
- Demonstrate effective communication skills

MENTOR RESPONSIBILITIES AND REMUNERATION

What are the job responsibilities of mentors?

Regardless of whether support is provided by a mentor or a support team, the mentor or support team is responsible for assisting the beginning teacher in:

- Exploring a variety of teaching strategies that address diversity in students and their learning styles
- Identifying effective teaching strategies that conform to the foundational skills and competencies as well as discipline-specific standards of the CCT
- Reflecting on the effectiveness of teaching and how well students are learning
- Documenting the types and frequency of support provided to the beginning teacher

The professional responsibilities of mentors and support teams are to:

- Meet regularly (at a minimum, once every two weeks) with beginning teachers
- Provide instructional support through such activities as observing the beginning teacher's teaching (either in person or through videotaping), discussing lesson planning, analyzing student work, and assisting with videotaping
- Assist the beginning teacher in demonstrating effective teaching as defined by the CCT and in preparing for the BEST portfolio assessment
- Help secure the resources (e.g., equipment, video camera operation) beginning teachers need to videotape their classrooms for the portfolio assessment as well as for general professional development
- Identify and engage other instructional staff (as needed) in providing the beginning teacher with instructional support in her or his content area and/or grade level.
- Participate in professional development activities related to supporting beginning teachers and enhancing one's own professional practices
- Seek information from the BEST program district facilitator regarding district policies for using professional development funds (funds provided to school districts by the state to support beginning teachers and their mentors)

Are mentors required to do peer observation and coaching?

Yes, mentors and other support team members may either observe a beginning teacher or view a videotape of teaching to provide feedback about the following critical questions:

- How well were the lesson elements tied together so that students could see a connection between lesson elements, as well as with past and future learning?
- How well were lessons developed to move students toward achieving objectives?
- What were the teacher's and the students' roles in classroom discourse?
- How effectively did the teacher monitor understanding and make adjustments as appropriate?

When the BEST program was first implemented, assessors were trained by the state to observe and evaluate beginning teachers. That component of the program has been replaced by the requirement of a portfolio, which is submitted in the teacher's second year. Now the state trains people to assess the portfolios over the summer.

Do mentors have full-time classroom teaching responsibilities?

Yes, mentors are full-time classroom teachers.

How are mentors available to participate in the program?

The BEST program requires that districts provide new teachers with at least eight half days to observe or be observed by their mentors or support teams or for activities related to professional development. Districts face difficulty in finding substitute teachers to fulfill their requirement. Sometimes the district finds other ways to cover classrooms for the observations to occur.

Do mentors evaluate new teachers?

Mentors do not evaluate beginning teachers. They provide support to new teachers.

Is the mentor–new teacher relationship confidential?

Mentors, as coaches, are in nonevaluative positions and should not communicate any concerns to anyone, except if there has been a breach of the code of ethics or there are concerns about the safety of students.

Are mentors paid?

Mentors receive a stipend of $100 per year.

MENTOR SELECTION, MATCHING, TRAINING, AND SUPERVISION

How are mentors selected?

There is an application and informal interview process for prospective support teachers. In addition to inviting applications, Ann asks administrators and especially program coordinators to recommend teachers to her. Then Ann forwards applications and urges them to consider applying.

How are mentors and new teachers matched?

Principals, along with the director of instruction and personnel, Patricia K. Brozek, review the need for mentors and the requirements of mentors who are to be trained. Periodic training of new mentors and updates for existing mentors are provided by the district through the Area Cooperative Educational Service (ACES). Whenever possible, beginning teachers are matched with mentors who have taught at the same grade or subject level. If teaching experience is not directly matched, BEST facilitators, principals, and the director of instruction and personnel work to ensure that teachers have a mentor in their building.

Are mentors trained?

Support teachers, who may also mentor teachers who work with student teachers, are trained by the state through ACES. They participate in professional development that includes mentor update training, master mentor training, portfolio scoring, and a host of other workshops.

Who supervises the mentors?

As district facilitator, Ann oversees the program with the assistance of the administrative team. She speaks with mentors to get their assurances that they have met the requirements of the program.

SUPPORTS FOR MENTORS

Is professional development available for mentors?

There are periodic mentor update workshops offered by the state and district.

Who provides this professional development?

The Department of Education, through the Regional Education Centers, offers training for the mentors.

What resources are available for mentors?

Ann is available to work with mentors and support teams as well as their beginning teacher partners. Mentors have resource materials and workshops available to them from ACES and Ann.

PROGRAM COSTS AND FUNDING

What resources are required for the program?

The cost of the program is $2,500.

- First-day orientation expenses
- Materials for new teachers
- Stipends for mentors
- A video camera and food for meetings

What are the funding sources?

The state does not provide the district with any funding for the BEST program.

Further support of the program in North Haven comes from the professional development budget of the district.

Who requests the funding?

NA

PROGRAM EVALUATION

How is the program evaluated?

The state does extensive evaluation of the BEST program through feedback from teachers and analysis of data regarding student achievement and teacher performance. Some people think that the portfolio is very difficult to do and that there is not enough support from the state. Mentors are spending a lot of time with the new teachers, and the state is no longer compensating the mentors for their time.

In the spring of 2008, the state legislature of Connecticut voted to restructure the BEST program to a Mentor Assistance Program (MAP). The details of this new program will be forthcoming. The 2008–2009 school year was the last year for new teachers to complete the portfolio as originally devised, although they were not required to complete the video segment.

Who sees the results of the evaluation?

Ann periodically speaks with district administrators. State officials see the results of the evaluations.

RECRUITMENT, HIRING, AND RETENTION OF NEW STAFF

How many new teachers are recruited and hired?

Fifteen new teachers were hired in North Haven for the 2007–2008 school year.

Are there any data that correlate the mentoring program with the retention of new teachers?

No retention data are available.

INDICATORS OF PROGRAM SUCCESS

What are the indicators of program success?

In 2007–2008, 75% of new teachers in North Haven passed the BEST portfolio requirement for certification.

Evidence of BEST success includes rising Connecticut mastery test scores and anecdotally the rise in teachers with advanced degrees in their content areas. There has been an increase in teachers who come with a bachelor's or master's in a content area and then do further mastery work in education. The state has mandated that universities that offer certification programs do so consistently, so it is seeing better-qualified and better-prepared candidates. A few key universities are actually asking education students to intern in schools for an entire year before they student-teach.

Anecdotally, because of better preparation and mentoring, new teachers appear to be more successful in the profession. New teachers who have mentors in their building and subject area routinely report great satisfaction with the program overall. They appreciate the nonjudgmental assistance the mentors provide. They are more confident going into the portfolio year.

MENTORING FOR QUALITY INDUCTION

STATE OF NEW JERSEY

Victoria Duff, Mentoring Program Coordinator
New Jersey Department of Education
Office of Professional Standards, Licensing, and Higher Education Collaboration
P.O. Box 500
Trenton, NJ 08725–9500
609–292–0189
Victoria.duff@doe.state.nj.us

Cathy Pine, Director
Office of Professional Standards, Licensing, and Higher Education Collaboration

Eileen Aviss-Spedding, Manager
Office of Professional Standards

Judy Cifone, Manager
Provisional Teacher Program (Licensing)

The following information was obtained from telephone conversations and e-mail correspondence with Victoria Duff. Figures and information were true for the 2006–2007 school year.

Demographics

Grade Levels	PreK–12, 2,430 schools in 6,161 districts	Urban/Suburban/Rural	Urban, suburban, and rural
Student Population	1,393,791	Ethnic Makeup	African American 17% Asian American 8% Caucasian 55% Hispanic 19% Other 1%
Teacher Population	110,964	% New Teachers	8%
		Per-Pupil Expenditure	Varies from district to district: $7,000–$18.000

* The statistics available from the district delineated the ethnic makeup as shown. There was no information about students of more than one racial heritage.

Program Highlights

Unique Feature of Program	All district local professional development committees (four teachers, two administrators) develop a mentoring plan according to state guidelines; mentoring plan development is guided by *The Mentoring for Quality Induction Toolkit*	Mentoring Is/Is Not Mandated for Certification/ Licensing	Mentoring is mandated for all novice teachers who hold a certificate of eligibility (CE—alternate route) or a certificate of eligibility with advanced standing (CEAS—traditional route); the Provisional Teacher Program oversees new-teacher licensing requirements
Coaching Is/Is Not a Component	Coaching is a recommended part of mentor training	Mentors Do/Do Not Evaluate the New Teachers With Whom They Work	Mentors do not evaluate

(Continued)

(Continued)

Cost of Program	Dependent on the district's program and mentoring plan	**Funding**	2004–2008: Partial state funding ($2,500,000) for mentor stipend reimbursement; no district program funding 2009: No funding
Mentors are Full-Time/Part-Time Teachers	Dependent on the district's mentoring plan; the majority of mentors in New Jersey are full-time teachers	**Mentor Remuneration**	$550 for mentoring traditionally prepared teachers (30 weeks) $1,000 for mentoring alternate route teachers: $450 for first 20 days, $550 for remaining 30 weeks
How Long Program Has Been in Existence	Since 1985; the program began as a result of New Jersey's alternate route program	**Duration of Program for New Teachers**	30 weeks for traditionally prepared teachers or alternate route teachers undergoing a state-approved clinical experience 34 weeks for all other alternate route teachers
Higher Education Affiliation	Two colleges are in the process of developing online mentor training components	**Program Coordinator**	Victoria Duff, Judy Cifone

HISTORY

In 1985, an alternate route program was created to open the doors of the teaching profession to a pool of potential candidates with content-specific expertise to support teaching and learning within the schools of New Jersey. Commissioners Saul Cooperman and Leo Klagholz took the lead in developing a comprehensive system for teachers entering through the alternate route. These teachers were enrolled in the newly created Provisional Teacher Program (PTP), which oversaw 200 hours of regional training in pedagogy, summative and formative evaluations by principals, and mentoring within the schools. In 1993, the PTP grew to include those teachers entering the profession through traditional preparation programs. They were required to undergo the formative and summative evaluations and receive a full year of mentoring. In 2000, Governor Christie Whitman identified the need for a more structured mentoring experience for novice teachers. Pilot districts spent two years identifying key components of mentoring and providing guidance to the state on effective mentoring programs. In 2004, the state department provided all district professional development committees with a framework for mentoring programs and guidance on the development of mentoring plans through the *Mentoring for Quality Induction* toolkit. Districts submitted their first mentoring plan in 2005 and completed a second plan to be implemented in September 2008.

STATE MANDATES

Is mentoring mandated for new teachers?

Yes, mentoring is mandated for all first-year teachers holding an instructional certificate.

Is mentoring part of certification or licensure?

Mentoring is part of the certification requirement for traditionally prepared and alternate route teachers in their first year of teaching. The state requires that all novice teachers be enrolled in the PTP. During the provisional teaching year, all those enrolled in the PTP must be mentored by a certified teacher and undergo a satisfactory formal state evaluation (two formative and one summative) administered by the school principal and submitted to the Department of Education for issuance of the standard certificate.

Is funding provided to support the mandate?

Since 2004, the state has funded partial mentor stipend reimbursements to novice teachers. Because of an enormous state budget deficit, those funds were cut for the 2009 fiscal year.

The state does not fund the district mentoring programs but rather expects districts to develop and fund mentoring plans aligned to the professional standards for teachers, the Quality Single Accountability Continuum (QSAC), which is the state monitoring system, and state regulations.

GOALS

The goals of the mentoring program are to:

- Enhance teacher knowledge and strategies related to the New Jersey Core Curriculum Content Standards to facilitate student achievement
- Support the novice in identifying and implementing exemplary teaching skills and educational practices necessary to acquire and maintain excellence in teaching
- Assist novice teachers in the performance of their duties and adjustment to the challenges of teaching

PROGRAM DESIGN

What are the components and recommended schedule of the program?

The Mentoring for Quality Induction toolkit, developed by the Department of Education, National Staff Development Council (NSDC), and New Jersey Mentoring Task Force, provides the local professional development committee in each district with the necessary components of the mentoring plan and tools to implement it. The mentoring toolkit can be accessed online at www.nj.gov/education/njpep/pd/mentor_toolkit/index.html. Districts are required to develop a mentoring plan every three years with annual revisions based on evaluation of the plan. The following are the major components required for the mentoring plan:

- Vision statement
- Needs assessment
- Criteria for mentor selection
- Roles and responsibilities of mentors, novice teachers, and principals
- Professional learning components for mentors
- Professional learning components for novice teachers
- Action plan for implementation
- Overview of mentoring for alternate route teachers in their first 20 days of teaching
- Resource options

- Funding resources
- Program evaluation

Novice teachers entering through the alternate route must undergo intensive mentoring in their first 20 days of teaching, ideally with a certified teacher in the classroom for the entire time. Districts may develop a plan for the 20 days that includes other means of intensive mentoring. In addition, all alternate route teachers receive 200 hours of training at regionally accredited training centers.

Are there any programs that complement the mentoring program?

District professional development (a state requirement for all districts) should complement the mentoring program in the district.

Who designed the mentoring program?

The mentoring program was designed by the New Jersey Department of Education, NSDC, and the New Jersey Mentoring Task Force (a group of stakeholders from all areas of the educational community).

PROGRAM ADMINISTRATION

Who coordinates the mentoring program?

The program is coordinated at the state level by a teacher quality coordinator in the Office of Professional Standards and at the district level by a designated individual (assistant superintendent or director of curriculum and instruction, staff development coordinator, principal or superintendent in a one-school district, mentor coordinator, or teacher leader). Additionally, the PTP in the Office of Licensure oversees the enrollment of novice teachers in the program and the collection and analysis of the evaluations for the standard certificate.

How is information communicated to shareholders?

Districts share their mentoring program with all stakeholders within the district.

Who coordinates integration of the mentoring program with other professional development opportunities and requirements in the schools and district?

The local professional development committee, which develops and implements the professional development plan and the mentoring plan, helps to integrate professional learning opportunities for novice teachers and mentor teachers. Additionally, many districts assign the responsibility for oversight to the office of curriculum and instruction or the human resources department. The licensing code also places responsibility for implementation and support of mentoring on the principal in each school.

PARTICIPANTS

Who is served?

All novice teachers holding instructional certificates are required to be mentored according to the district mentoring plan in their first year of teaching. Districts have the option of mentoring other novice professionals or veterans who are new to the district.

Is participation of new teachers voluntary or mandatory?

Participation of novice teachers who hold instructional certificates is mandatory.

Who provides the mentoring/induction?

The mentor, with the principal as the lead, provides direct mentoring. In addition, districts may supplement the mentoring with content and instructional coaching. Mentors are required to ensure that mentoring activities and discussions are confidential.

What are the criteria for being a mentor?

The mentoring criteria are set minimally by state regulations and further developed by the district's mentoring plan. Mentors should have:

- Three years of teaching experience
- Certification and experience in the subject area of the novice, where possible
- Strong interpersonal skills
- Leadership skills
- Credibility with peers and administrators
- Curiosity and eagerness to learn
- Respect for multiple perspectives
- A commitment to spending time to develop the mentor–novice relationship and to supporting the novice in developing competency in instruction and content

Mentors should:

- Be trained in the basic foundations of effective mentoring
- Be knowledgeable about and supportive of building an understanding of school and district culture and policies
- Be committed to the goals of the local mentoring plan
- Maintain confidentiality in the mentor–novice relationship
- Demonstrate an exemplary command of content and instructional knowledge
- Have knowledge of basic resources and opportunities within the district

MENTOR RESPONSIBILITIES AND REMUNERATION

What are the job responsibilities of mentors?

The responsibilities of the mentor are set minimally by state regulations and further developed by the district's mentoring plan. It is expected that all mentors will engage in professional learning for their position, professional learning opportunities with the novice, and at least biweekly meetings with the novice that are documented by topic. Those mentoring alternate route teachers must provide intensive daily mentoring for the first 20 days that the teacher is in the classroom.

Are mentors required to do peer observation and coaching?

Peer observation and coaching are recommended in the training of mentors but not mandated.

Do mentors have full-time classroom teaching responsibilities?

The majority of mentors in the state have full-time teaching responsibilities.

How are mentors available to participate in the program?

Mentors participate in the mentoring program in accordance with the district's mentoring plan.

Do mentors evaluate new teachers?

Mentors may not evaluate new teachers in any capacity.

Is the mentor–new teacher relationship confidential?

The mentor–novice relationship is strictly confidential.

Are mentors paid?

All mentors of novice teachers receive a state-mandated stipend. In lieu of state funding, novice teachers are responsible to pay the mentoring stipend. Mentors of traditionally prepared teachers and alternate route teachers who have undergone a preservice clinical experience are paid $550 for 30 weeks of mentoring. Mentors of those in the alternate route program are paid $450 for the first 20 days of intensive mentoring and $550 for the additional 30 weeks of mentoring.

MENTOR SELECTION, MATCHING, TRAINING, AND SUPERVISION

How are mentors selected?

Selection of mentors is set minimally by state regulations and further developed by the district's mentoring plan. All mentors must apply for the position. The application should provide information on mentors' strengths and their desire for involvement in the mentoring program.

How are mentors and new teachers matched?

The principal assigns the novice to a mentor based on the minimum criteria in the regulations and additional criteria in the district's mentoring plan. The mentoring plan may incorporate a rubric to support the principal's selection.

Are mentors trained?

Mentors are required to undergo comprehensive mentor training. At a minimum, mentor training must incorporate basic roles and responsibilities, relationship building, adult learning theory, and an understanding of the professional standards for teachers. Mentor training can be developed in the district by district experts, or mentors can go to trainings provided by colleges, consultants, or education associations.

Who supervises the mentors?

The principal oversees the mentoring program in the school. Mentors can also be overseen by a mentor coordinator.

SUPPORTS FOR MENTORS

Is professional development available for mentors?

Mentors are expected to participate in learning connected to their role as a mentor and activities that support their needs for their classroom responsibilities. Mentors must undergo comprehensive mentor training per state regulation. Mentors must have basic support for their role.

Who provides this professional development?

Professional development for mentors can be provided by the district, district consortia, colleges, consultants, or education associations.

What resources are available for mentors?

Resources for mentoring are provided by the district.

PROGRAM COSTS AND FUNDING

What resources are required for the program?

All district plans must have a provision for comprehensive mentor training, and all resources for the mentoring program are the district's responsibility. Some of the costs include:

- Mentor training
- New-teacher orientation
- Materials
- Stipends for mentors
- Substitutes for released time
- The project director's salary, or the portion of it related to mentoring
- Hardware and audiovisual equipment

The 2009 state budget determined that the district is no longer permitted to spend monies on food for in-district workshops. Before this budget passed, providing food was a district decision.

What are the funding sources?

Districts fund the mentoring program from their Title II funds. Districts are expected to develop and implement a mentoring plan aligned to the professional standards for teachers, the regulations in New Jersey Administrative Code 6A:9-8.2, and the QSAC.

Who requests the funding?

NA

PROGRAM EVALUATION

How is the program evaluated?

The program is evaluated based on the district's mentoring plan. Several models are provided for district use in the *Mentoring for Quality Induction* toolkit.

Who sees the results of the evaluation?

Results must be reported to the local board of education on an annual basis. In addition, all districts are monitored every three years through the QSAC and must show evidence of their program evaluations in the personnel section. The QSAC monitoring tool can be accessed at www.state.nj.us/education/genfo/qsac/.

RECRUITMENT, HIRING, AND RETENTION OF NEW STAFF

How many new teachers are recruited and hired?

In 2007, 5,332 new teachers were enrolled in PTP; 1,311 of them entered through the alternate route.

Are there any data that correlate the mentoring program with the retention of new teachers?

The state does not collect complete data on the retention of new teachers at this time. However, this area is under exploration as part of a teacher database that has been recommended by a number of task forces. In addition, the QSAC district monitoring process looks at evidence of program effectiveness. The state is only in its second year of implementation of QSAC, a newly legislated process, and has no significant data on the process.

The New Jersey Education Association does an annual survey and disaggregation of data from the state-certified staff report that looks at the demographics and placements of new teachers and analyzes turnover and retention rates.

INDICATORS OF PROGRAM SUCCESS

What are the indicators of program success?

Through the QSAC monitoring process, districts are expected to show evidence and documentation of mentor and novice interactions, the topics discussed, evaluations, and the impact of novice and mentor teacher trainings and learning opportunities. The evidence must drive modifications or revisions to the mentoring plan to further enhance the retention of teachers. The evaluation of novice teachers (two formative and one summative evaluation completed by the principal of the school in which the novice works) provides direct evidence of successful completion of the first year of teaching. All districts use the *Mentoring for Quality Induction* toolkit to develop their mentoring program. The toolkit has been responsible for increased knowledge of effective mentoring practices and for providing additional support to local professional development committees, district administrators, and mentors. All districts meet the minimum requirements for mentoring. The PTP reports that over 95% of novice teachers successfully complete the provisional year and earn their standard certification.

6

Regional and National Efforts to Specifically Support New Mathematics and Science Teachers

The necessity of supporting mathematics and science teachers is well documented. Consider the following:

In far too many schools, new mathematic teachers receive challenging teaching assignments for which they are unprepared. These teachers, some of whom do not have strong backgrounds in mathematics content, are often isolated from professional involvement with colleagues. Frequently, they receive little content-specific professional development to support them in meeting the challenges that they face. As a result, their students may not be afforded the learning opportunities and quality instruction that the Council advocates as essential preparation for high-functioning adults in the workplace and everyday life. (National Council of Teachers of Mathematics, 2007, para. 2)

NCTM Position

States, provinces, school districts, and colleges and universities share responsibility for the continuing professional support of beginning teachers by providing them with a structured program of induction and mentoring. These programs should include opportunities for further development of mathematics content, pedagogy, and classroom management strategies. (National Council of Teachers of Mathematics, 2007)

Growing evidence suggests that new teachers of science who participate in comprehensive induction programs with a science-specific focus are more likely to remain in the teaching profession and continue to develop deeper pedagogical content knowledge and stronger abilities to enact standards-based science instruction (Smith and Ingersoll 2004; Lee et al.; Roehrig and Luft 2006). When these programs are coordinated with teacher preparation programs and mid-career professional development programs, teachers are likely to experience a continuum of professional development (Feinman-Nemser 1999). (National Science Teachers Association, 2007, Introduction section, para. 3)

The following descriptions have been written by the directors of the programs in conjunction with their colleagues and the author. Judgments about the programs are those of the program directors and their staff and not the opinion of the author. Unless stated otherwise, figures and information were true for the 2007–2008 school year.

MIDDLE SCHOOL SCIENCE MENTORING PROGRAM

Marian M. Pasquale, Co-principal Investigator
Middle Grades Science Mentoring Program
Education Development Center, Inc.
55 Chapel Street
Newton, MA 02458
617–618–2417
mpasquale@edc.org

The following information was obtained from telephone conversations and e-mail correspondence with Marian Pasquale.

Demographics

Since this is not a program of a particular district, many of the denominations in the chart below are not applicable.

Grade Levels	Middle school	Urban/Suburban/Rural	All
Student Population	NA	**Ethnic Makeup**	NA
Teacher Population	NA	**% New Teachers**	NA
		Per-Pupil Expenditure	NA

Program Highlights

Unique Feature of Program	Uses inquiry as the basis for mentoring	**Mentoring Is/Is Not Mandated for Certification/Licensing**	District dependent
Coaching Is/ Is Not a Component	Coaching is a component	**Mentors Do/Do Not Evaluate the New Teachers With Whom They Work**	It is strongly recommended that mentors not be given evaluation responsibilities
Cost of Program	Varies	**Funding**	District
Mentors Are Full-Time/Part-Time Teachers	Mentors may be full-time or part-time teachers	**Mentor Remuneration**	District dependent
How Long Program Has Been in Existence	Since 2002	**Duration of Program for New Teachers**	Suggested minimum of two years
Higher Education Affiliation	NA	**Program Coordinator**	District dependent

HISTORY

The Middle School Science Mentoring Program is based on a model developed by the Center for Science Education (CSE) at the Education Development Center (EDC) in Massachusetts between 2002 and 2005 with funding from the National Science Foundation (NSF). A group of 25 science teachers from across Massachusetts came together to work for three years with the EDC while developing the model for mentor professional development. Since then, the original model has been adapted in districts across the nation. In each case, the Middle Grades Science Mentoring Program is defined by core features that make it unique. It integrates science content, pedagogy, and mentoring skills in a seamless training approach and uses an inquiry focus for teacher learning and reflection as an underlying strategy in all its components.

In the program, teachers engage in science investigations using NSF-funded, inquiry-based curricula. Curricular topics are aligned to both national and state science standards for the middle grades. Teachers experience the science as adult learners and discuss the structure of the lessons and how the pedagogy supports students' development of the science concepts. These informal conversations lead to the more formal conferencing cycle (pre-observation conference, classroom observation, and post-observation conference) central to inquiry into best practices in the classroom.

Teachers gain experience with mentoring strategies and tools of goal setting, observation, and assessment in order to improve teaching practice and student learning. Video clips of pre- and post-observation conferences are used to provide teachers with examples. Teachers engage in activities such as viewing science classrooms and scripting and role playing how they would conduct a post-observation conference with a mentee.

The program responds to school districts' need for novice middle grades science teachers to develop their capacity to teach standards-based science. The underlying assumption of the mentoring program is that enhanced practice among mentors and mentees in turn helps their middle grades students better grasp science and scientific processes and develop a more sophisticated understanding of the world around them.

STATE MANDATES

Is mentoring mandated for new teachers?

NA

Is mentoring part of certification or licensure?

NA

Is funding provided to support the mandate?

NA

GOALS

Within this program, the goals are to:

- Increase mentors' content knowledge in life, physical, and earth sciences
- Enhance mentors' understanding and use of inquiry-based instructional strategies
- Improve mentors' familiarity with standards-based instructional materials and educational technologies
- Hone mentors' classroom practices and ability to model and articulate these practices
- Improve mentors' mentoring skills and strategies so that others can learn from them

PROGRAM DESIGN

What are the components and recommended schedule of the program?

The following components and recommended schedule are based on the original model, but have been adapted across the nation to the local needs of districts implementing the Middle Grades Science Mentoring Program.

Each year the program conducts at least two meetings for district administrators, curriculum staff, and/or principals. In year one, the purpose of these meetings is to:

- Familiarize administrators with standards-based, inquiry-oriented science instruction and its implications for teaching and learning
- Explore the mentoring role and essential support roles of district administrators and principals
- Develop ways to establish support and incentives that allow the program to flourish

The fall meeting provides an overview of the project and expectations for participation. In the spring, program staff assess progress and challenges and examine the support necessary for mentors and novices to thrive. Throughout the year, program staff continue to communicate with leadership team members and visit principals and, if appropriate, science coordinators during site visits. These contacts are invited to participate in all institutes, which helps to keep the lines of communication open.

In year two, the meetings are convened to continue communication about the program and support the work of mentors and the teaching practices of new teachers.

For mentors, the core program includes 10 institute days, observation and conferencing sessions with mentor colleagues and novices, and a bimonthly study group series.

Institutes

In year one, teachers begin their mentor training with five institutes that each last two days. The institutes weave science content, pedagogy, and mentoring strategies into a challenging experience for mentors. A key feature of the institute's design is mentoring strategies embedded in the inquiry experiences; they are not taught in an isolated manner. The most effective approach has been found to involve EDC staff and teachers' modeling and talking about both their inquiry-oriented teaching experiences and what they are thinking about as they plan and conduct each lesson. EDC provides mentors with a more concrete context for learning about mentoring strategies, such as pre- and post-observation conferences, and offers strategies for classroom observations. EDC also works with mentors to build skills, such as active listening, goal setting, building of relationships (among mentors and between mentors and novices), and problem solving and conflict resolution. Embedded in the institutes are opportunities for learning and trying out mentoring strategies with colleagues.

The institutes provide a comfortable environment for mentors to experience and struggle with the implications of standards-based teaching and learning by establishing a common language for talking about science teaching and classroom practice and by providing opportunities for participants to practice inquiry-oriented approaches to teaching. Teachers—working with EDC staff—engage in adult inquiry experiences tied to particular content areas of the National Science Education Standards as well as state science and technology standards. Over the course of the five institutes, EDC focuses on the scientific disciplines (physical science, life science, and earth science). As adult learners, teachers investigate phenomena or systems. This content is used to:

- Help participants gain a deeper understanding of phenomena in terms of specific scientific concepts, using a scientist as the content specialist
- Provide an example of a pedagogical approach to teaching science (guided inquiry, open inquiry)
- Isolate issues in the adaptation of curriculum and inquiry approaches to the mentor's classroom
- Develop a common understanding and vocabulary about inquiry
- Develop mentoring strategies to support novice teachers in their classrooms

EDC uses existing standards-based curriculum materials as a focus for its work, reflecting research that shows the value of combining content and pedagogy. The expectation is that mentors will use these (or other inquiry-based materials) in their classrooms. Some curriculum materials that have been used in the institutes include *Models in Technology and Science* (MITS), *Pond Study: An Extended Investigation of Macro-invertebrates*, and Project ARIES, all modules that provide extended, in-depth investigations to help master important skills and concepts, encouraging a progression from concrete, everyday acquaintance with phenomena to a more abstract, scientific understanding. EDC also makes available most of the research-based curriculum material supported by the National Science Foundation (NSF).

EDC works with teachers on how to adapt these materials in their classrooms, or, if necessary, on how to adapt materials from their own classrooms to reflect the types of experiences they are engaging in at the institute. Mentors put into practice some of the institute learnings, while they open their own classrooms to EDC staff for observations and begin to observe the classrooms of other mentors. Mentors gather to meet every other month in study groups to more closely examine instructional and mentoring issues that have been identified in an institute or that emanate from their work during the year.

A major part of follow-up of institutes during the school year focuses on classroom observations. In year one, mentors are paired to visit each other's classrooms to observe teaching of one of the lessons modeled during the institutes (for a total of four observations). This allows them to practice classroom observation skills and constructive feedback. It also gives them the perspective of the novice who will be expected to open his or her classroom to a mentor. EDC staff also visit mentors' classrooms twice during the school year, again providing an opportunity to reflect on issues of teaching and learning as well as modeling how to collect and share observation information. When possible, videotaping of the classes is arranged.

In year one, EDC organizes and facilitates bimonthly two-hour study groups with the mentors. These study groups are outgrowths of the experiences of mentors as they work in their own classrooms. Between study groups, mentors are involved in classroom observations by EDC staff or mentor colleagues. Therefore, teacher discussions are expected to be based on their own classroom videotapes as well as classroom vignettes EDC has collected. Mentors are expected to examine student work, thinking, and assessments to promote a better understanding of the impact of teaching strategies and materials.

In year two of this model program, mentors continue to attend institutes and study groups. Each mentor is assigned one novice teacher, and together they work out expectations for the year. Novices join the mentors for one of the mentor institutes. Throughout the year, mentors and novices observe each other's classrooms, reflect and conference about those experiences, and work together on issues of teaching and learning identified, in large part, by the novice teachers. The mentors continue to attend study groups, focusing increasingly on issues that emerge from the growing mentor–novice relationship. All resources of the CSE are available to the novices.

Are there any programs that complement the mentoring program?

Individual districts provide programs that complement the mentoring program.

Who designed the mentoring program?

The CSE at EDC designed the program.

Program Administration

Who coordinates the mentoring program?

EDC coordinates the program in conjunction with district or school administrators.

How is information communicated to shareholders?

Information is communicated through administrators' meetings and during institutes.

Who coordinates integration of the mentoring program with other professional development opportunities and requirements in the schools and district?

Integration of this program with professional development opportunities varies in each district.

PARTICIPANTS

Who is served?

The program serves middle grades science teachers, including those new to teaching, new to teaching science, and new to teaching middle grades science. The program has also been adapted for elementary-level teachers.

Is participation of new teachers voluntary or mandatory?

Participation is voluntary but recommended.

Who provides the mentoring/induction?

EDC project staff who have developed the program work with teachers from the district who become mentors.

What are the criteria for being a mentor?

The criteria for being a mentor are:

- A minimum of five years' science teaching experience
- Experience in inquiry instruction at the middle grades or use of research-informed curriculum programs that promote inquiry instruction
- Solid content knowledge
- Outstanding teaching skills and effectiveness in classroom management
- Experience working with colleagues through such means as professional development, analysis of student work, curriculum adoption committees, standards review, and development of assessments
- The ability to communicate well with students and colleagues
- Proven leadership in the profession
- Experience with, and openness to, collaborating with other teachers
- Flexibility, open-mindedness, and empathy
- Experience with diverse learners

MENTOR RESPONSIBILITIES AND REMUNERATION

What are the job responsibilities of mentors?

The mentor works with the teacher to establish a plan and set of expectations in regard to their work together. That plan includes setting goals for the teacher as well as the mentoring relationship, establishing a plan to gather data and assess progress toward those goals, and refining the goals and plans as needed. The mentor helps the teacher plan lessons, including setting goals for student learning. The mentor gathers data while observing the teacher and discusses the data as they relate to both the teacher's goals for her or his teaching and student learning. The mentor also offers support in terms of resources and other teaching-related needs.

Are mentors required to do peer observation and coaching?

Yes, mentors are required to do peer observation and coaching.

Do mentors have full-time classroom teaching responsibilities?

Typically, yes, mentors are full-time classroom teachers.

How are mentors available to participate in the program?

Mentors participate on Saturdays and through released time.

Do mentors evaluate new teachers?

No, mentors do not evaluate new teachers.

Is the mentor–new teacher relationship confidential?

Yes, the relationship is confidential.

Are mentors paid?

Mentor remuneration is a district decision.

MENTOR SELECTION, MATCHING, TRAINING, AND SUPERVISION

How are mentors selected?

Mentors are selected by their school or district administrator based on criteria.

How are mentors and new teachers matched?

Mentors and new teachers are matched in their districts. EDC recommends matching teachers at the same grade level.

Are mentors trained?

Yes, the project is a professional development program designed to prepare middle grades science teachers to be mentors.

Who supervises the mentors?

School and district administrators supervise the mentors.

SUPPORTS FOR MENTORS

Is professional development available for mentors?

This project is a professional development program designed to prepare middle grades science teachers to be mentors.

Who provides this professional development?

Program staff from the CSE at EDC provide the training for middle grades science teacher mentors.

What resources are available for mentors?

Curriculum materials and a toolkit of mentoring strategies are provided for mentors.

PROGRAM COSTS AND FUNDING

What resources are required for the program?

- Training facilitators
- Curriculum materials used in the training groups
- Stipends for teacher participation in Saturday institute sessions and afterschool study groups
- Substitutes to cover released time
- The project director's salary, or the portion of it related to mentoring

What are the funding sources?

Districts may use local or school-based professional development funds. In some cases, several districts may come together and pool their resources; in other cases, they solicit state funding (for example, Title IIB). In still other cases, they may include mentoring under the umbrella of a math and science partnership grant or solicit private or corporate funding for mentor training.

Who requests the funding?

This is dependent on the school district or districts. Funding can be requested by the principal, science coordinator, or professional development coordinator.

PROGRAM EVALUATION

How is the program evaluated?

The original model and its implementation were evaluated by WestEd.

When EDC works with districts to implement adaptations of the original model, EDC requests feedback from the mentor and teachers and encourages districts to gather more comprehensive data.

Who sees the results of the evaluation?

Appropriate CSE project staff and district staff see the evaluation results.

RECRUITMENT, HIRING, AND RETENTION OF NEW STAFF

How many new teachers are recruited and hired?

New teachers are recruited and hired by the districts.

Are there any data that correlate the mentoring program with the retention of new teachers?

No, EDC does not collect data on teacher retention in participating districts.

INDICATORS OF PROGRAM SUCCESS

What are the indicators of program success?

Most of the mentors from the model development are still mentoring. Mentees have reported increased awareness, understanding, and practice of inquiry-based instruction.

E-MENTORING FOR STUDENT SUCCESS

Lynn Kepp, Project Director
Alyson Mike, Associate Project Director
New Teacher Center
University of California, Santa Cruz
725 Front Street, Suite 400
Santa Cruz, CA 95060
831–459–4323
lkepp@ucsc.edu

The following information was obtained from telephone conversations and e-mail correspondence with Lynn Kepp and Alyson Mike.

Demographics

Grade Levels	6–12	Urban/Suburban/Rural	All
Student Population	NA	Ethnic Makeup	NA
Teacher Population	More than 300 teachers from 22 states	% New Teachers	NA
		Per-Pupil Expenditure	NA

Program Highlights

Unique Feature of Program	This is an entirely online program that is content specific, pairing mentors with beginning teacher partners who teach the same grade level and content area	Mentoring Is/Is Not Mandated for Certification/Licensing	Participants in the program are from many states, and the states have different requirements for certification and licensing
Coaching Is/Is Not a Component	Coaching is a component	Mentors Do/Do Not Evaluate the New Teachers With Whom They Work	Mentors do not evaluate
Cost of Program	$2,000 per beginning teacher; National Science Foundation funds offset the costs through 2008–2009	Funding	National Science Foundation, along with school districts, state departments of education, universities, and private funders
Mentors Are Full-Time/ Part-time Teachers	The majority of the mentors are full-time teachers; some are retired teachers or educational consultants who were formerly teachers	Mentor Remuneration	Mentors receive $1,800 per year for mentoring two beginning teachers; for each additional teacher they mentor, they receive an additional $400

How Long Program Has Been in Existence	Since 2002	Duration of Program for New Teachers	Up to three years
Higher Education Affiliation	University of California, Santa Cruz; Montana State University	Program Coordinators	Lynn Kepp, Alyson Mike

HISTORY

The inception of the e-Mentoring for Student Success (eMSS) program was a National Science Foundation (NSF) grant written by Gerry Wheeler from the National Science Teachers Association (NSTA), Ellen Moir from the New Teacher Center (NTC), and Elizabeth Swanson from Montana State University at Bozeman. The program began in Montana, a very large state whose population is dispersed throughout it.

STATE MANDATES

Is mentoring mandated for new teachers?

Mentoring mandates vary from state to state.

Is mentoring part of certification or licensure?

Certification and licensure requirements vary from state to state.

Is funding provided to support the mandate?

NA

GOALS

The eMSS program was developed to empower the next generation of science and mathematics teachers by providing content-focused mentoring through a national online network. The goals of the program are to:

- Support and extend mentoring for beginning science and math teachers
- Provide content-focused professional development through dialogue
- Facilitate the exchange of information, ideas, and experiences to advance high-quality science and math instruction for all students

PROGRAM DESIGN

What are the components and recommended schedule of the program?

There are four components of the program:

- Our Place is where beginning teachers work with their mentors to deal with pedagogical and content issues as well as day-to-day "being a teacher" issues.

- *Inquiries* are pedagogical and content curricula that last eight weeks. They are offered three times a year on a variety of topics, including managing student behavior, parent communication, diversity, communication in mathematics, and effective labs.
- *Content Areas* are facilitated online discussions in which beginning teachers and mentors engage in collaboration with teacher facilitators and university staff who are practicing scientists or mathematicians. Topics range from predetermined topics of the month revolving around standards to topics generated from questions from participants.
- *Dilemmas of Practice* are short, three-week case studies focusing on a pedagogical issue that many beginning teachers encounter. Mentors and mentees engage in discussion and problem-solve to provide strategies for the beginning teachers. Examples of issues that are addressed include how to prepare for a substitute, how to keep students engaged before a holiday and still cover curriculum, missing homework, and using YouTube in the classroom.

Are there any programs that complement the mentoring program?

The content-specific mentoring of eMSS complements on-site, face-to-face mentoring in the districts of the beginning teachers, if it occurs.

Who designed the mentoring program?

Gerry Wheeler from NSTA, Ellen Moir and Roberta Jaffe from the NTC, and Elizabeth Swanson from Montana State University at Bozeman developed the original program. Project staff have developed the program over the years based on continual review of participant feedback.

PROGRAM ADMINISTRATION

Who coordinates the mentoring program?

Lynn Kepp and Alyson Mike coordinate the eMSS program.

How is information communicated to shareholders?

For participants in the program, communication is done through the eMSS program. To communicate with the larger content-focused community about the program, Listservs of NSTA, Building a Presence for Science, and the National Council of Teachers of Mathematics (NCTM) are utilized. A variety of state-specific Listservs are also used to disseminate information. The Web sites of the aforementioned organizations also provided information about the program.

The program began in 2002 and was funded for five years. Now that NSF funding has ended, a marketing campaign is being launched, and the eMSS program will be communicated through brochures, flyers, presentations, Web sites, and mailings.

Who coordinates integration of the mentoring program with other professional development opportunities and requirements in the schools and district?

There is no explicit coordination between eMSS and the school districts of beginning teachers, but eMSS project staff are available to assist school districts with analysis of eMSS program activities and mentoring program requirements.

PARTICIPANTS

Who is served?

Beginning teachers of sixth- through twelfth-grade science or math in their first three years of teaching may participate in eMSS. This includes beginning science teachers who are part of the NSTA New Science Teacher Academy or beginning math and science teachers from one of the affiliates of the program. (An affiliate is a client who pays for beginning teachers to participate in the program. This could be a school district, state department of education, university, or private funder anywhere in the United States.)

Is participation of new teachers voluntary or mandatory?

Participation of new teachers is voluntary.

Who provides the mentoring/induction?

Mentoring and induction are provided by mentors, teacher facilitators, and university faculty. The university faculty have been recruited by the principal investigators of this program and have expertise in science or mathematics and experience working with teachers. Teacher facilitators are former mentors who have been selected based on their demonstration of high-quality online skills and trained to facilitate online discussions.

What are the criteria for being a mentor?

The criteria for being a mentor are:

- More than five years of teaching experience
- Strong content area knowledge in science or math

Other qualifications include:

- Involvement in mentoring programs
- National board certification
- Other evidence of exemplary teaching experience

MENTOR RESPONSIBILITIES AND REMUNERATION

What are the job responsibilities of mentors?

Mentors support their assigned beginning teachers. Mentors are expected to be online three to four times a week.

Are mentors required to do peer observation and coaching?

Peer observation is not a component of this program. In Inquiries, teachers engage in specific topics through cycles of "plan, practice, and reflect." Mentors coach beginning teachers online.

Do mentors have full-time classroom teaching responsibilities?

Most mentors are full-time classroom teachers. Some mentors are retired teachers or educational consultants.

How are mentors available to participate in the program?

Because this is an online, asynchronous program, mentors are available to participate at times that are convenient for them.

Do mentors evaluate new teachers?

Mentors do not evaluate new teachers.

Is the mentor–new teacher relationship confidential?

The relationship between mentors and new teachers is confidential.

Are mentors paid?

Mentors are paid $1,800 to support two beginning teachers and an additional $400 for each additional mentee.

MENTOR SELECTION, MATCHING, TRAINING, AND SUPERVISION

How are mentors selected?

In the past, affiliate coordinators selected mentors. For the 2008–2009 school year, eMSS program staff selected all mentors.

How are mentors and new teachers matched?

Mentors are matched by grade level and content, in state if possible, and then rural, urban, or suburban context.

Are mentors trained?

Mentors are trained for three weeks, online, during the summer. They spend 10 to 20 hours completing the training. Mentors must successfully complete the training to be placed in a pool of available mentors.

Who supervises the mentors?

During summer training, two facilitator coordinators provide the initial supervision of mentors. Small groups of mentors are overseen by a facilitator to ensure that mentors are actively engaged with their mentees. A protocol has been established for mentors who do not meet the expectations; they are followed up with by a program staff member. Mentors are removed from the program for inactivity and mentees reassigned.

SUPPORTS FOR MENTORS

Is professional development available for mentors?

After summer training, mentors receive ongoing professional development throughout the year. Many of the issues mentors encounter with their beginning teachers are addressed through facilitator-initiated discussion of the topic of the month. Topics follow the phases of first-year teacher development.

Who provides this professional development?

Teacher facilitators provide ongoing support of mentors based on a curriculum developed and made available by the program staff.

What resources are available for mentors?

During summer training and throughout the year, mentors receive and utilize many online text resources. Those resources and more are provided in a handbook designed to be used as a reference throughout the year. Concerns, problems, and challenges are addressed in the professional learning communities of mentors and facilitators.

PROGRAM COSTS AND FUNDING

What resources are required for the program?

The business model for the program is as follows:

- Fifty percent of program costs are stipends for mentors and compensation for content experts, facilitators, and lead facilitators.
- Fifty percent of program costs are technical costs and remuneration for program administration.
- The cost per mentee is $2,000.

What are the funding sources?

Originally, NSF funded the initiative. NSTA, Montana State University, and the NTC were the original recipients of the grant. NSTA has also partnered with Amgen and Agilent, pharmaceutical and technology companies, to create the New Science Teacher Academy. Fellows in that academy are beginning teachers from all over the country who have gone through a very competitive application process. One of the benefits of being a fellow is having an e-mentor provided through eMSS.

Payment of the fee can come from a variety of sources. In 2007, a Goldman Sachs grant to the NTC allowed funding of a pilot program in math. In addition, affiliates (school districts, states, or private funders) have paid for their new teachers to participate. The New Science Teacher Academy is funded through the corporate sponsors of Amgen and Agilent. Some states, such as Hawaii, pay for mentoring of their beginning teachers through a state department funding designation. Massachusetts has special grant funding that will pay for mentoring of some beginning teachers, and sometimes districts pay the fee.

Who requests the funding?

Now that the funding from NSF has ended, a comprehensive marketing plan is being developed to publicize the program to a variety of stakeholders, including potential funders who wish to support new teachers. The project is also seeking other avenues of funding to offset the cost of the program.

PROGRAM EVALUATION

How is the program evaluated?

An outside organization, Horizon Research, evaluated the program for the first five years, when NSF was providing funding. Now, an evaluation from the NTC is conducted annually. In addition, participant feedback is solicited periodically throughout the year.

Who sees the results of the evaluation?

Some of the Horizon research has been shared at conferences and is posted on NTC's Web site (www.newteachercenter.org/emss) and in project brochures.

RECRUITMENT, HIRING, AND RETENTION OF NEW STAFF

How many new teachers are recruited and hired?

A retention study is under way.

Are there any data that correlate the mentoring program with the retention of new teachers?

There are no student achievement data at this time.

INDICATORS OF PROGRAM SUCCESS

What are the indicators of program success?

Indicators of success include mentees who want to continue to participate; they are more empowered to teach their content and feel more confident in their classroom teaching as a result of the program. Horizon research and NTC surveys have revealed that participants report feeling better prepared to teach challenging curriculum. See below for excerpts from the 2007 Horizon evaluation.

Figures 2 and 3 clearly illustrate the preparedness to work with beginning teachers through pre and post survey results. The results show a significant preparedness to work with beginning teachers who teach challenging curriculum and the ability to be a content focused mentor. Participation in eMSS, through summer institutes, continued professional development, and engagement in the eMSS program contributed to those gains.

Mentor Composite: Perceived Preparedness to Work with Beginning Teachers in Various Areas (Year 2006–2007)

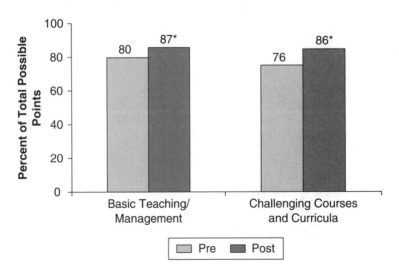

*There was a significant increase in composite scores from pre to post (one tailed paired samples *t*-test; $p < 0.05$).

Horizon Research 5 year Evaluation report (2007)

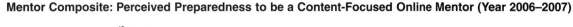

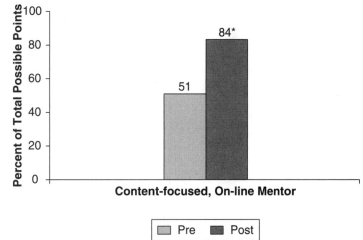

Mentor Composite: Perceived Preparedness to be a Content-Focused Online Mentor (Year 2006–2007)

Horizon Research 5 year Evaluation report (2007)

*There was a significant increase in composite scores from pre to post (one tailed paired samples t-test; $p < 0.05$)

The mentees also demonstrated gains because of their participation in eMSS. There was a significant increase in mentee reports of their preparedness in basic teaching and management skills after involvement in eMSS. Prior to their involvement in eMSS the mean composite score was 62 percent. After participation, the mean composite score increased to 70 percent (an effect size of 0.49 standard deviations).

SOURCE: From *Electronic Mentoring for Student Success Year Five Evaluation Report* by Joan D. Pasley and Lauren O. Madden, August 2007.

NORTHERN NEW ENGLAND COMENTORING NETWORK (NNECN) PROJECT AND NNECN CENTER

Page Keeley, Director
Maine Mathematics and Science Alliance
P.O. Box 5359
219 Capitol Street
Augusta, ME 04330
207–287–6646
pkeeley@mmsa.org
www.mmsa.org

The following information was obtained from telephone conversations and e-mail correspondence with Page Keeley.

Demographics

Grade Levels	K–12	Urban/Suburban/Rural	All
Student Population	NA	Ethnic Makeup	NA
Teacher Population	NA	% New Teachers	NA
		Per-Pupil Expenditure	NA

Program Highlights

Unique Feature of Program	Focus on content and instruction in science and mathematics	**Mentoring Is/Is Not Mandated for Certification/ Licensing**	NA
Coaching Is/Is Not a Component	Coaching is a component	**Mentors Do/Do Not Evaluate the New Teachers With Whom They Work**	Mentors do not evaluate
Cost of Program	$2,300,000 for three years	**Funding**	National Science Foundation
Mentors Are Full-Time/Part-Time Teachers	Mentors are full-time teachers	**Mentor Remuneration**	$1,000 per year for three years
How Long Program Has Been in Existence	The program was funded for three years and is now a content-based mentor training program	**Duration of Program for New Teachers**	One to three years
Higher Education Affiliation	None	**Program Coordinator**	Page Keeley

HISTORY

The Northern New England CoMentoring Network (NNECN) began in 2001 as a five-year tristate NSF-funded teacher enhancement project supporting middle and high school science and mathematics mentors and new teachers in Maine, New Hampshire, and Vermont. While a number of support systems in this tristate region had successfully addressed the "survival skills" needed by new teachers, they lacked expertise and had no capacity to address content and content-specific pedagogical issues to ensure that all students would learn science and mathematics successfully. NNECN's specific focus on the disciplines of science and mathematics ensured that the content and pedagogical needs of a new teacher were addressed by mentors with specific expertise in the discipline they taught.

NNECN's "co-mentoring" model developed reciprocal relationships among mentors, mentees, and colleagues that extended beyond traditional one-to-one mentoring and resulted in the establishment of learning communities that impacted entire school communities.

Several resources field-tested through the NNECN project are now widely used by math and science mentors, including *Science Curriculum Topic Study: Bridging the Gap Between Standards and Practice* by Page Keeley, *Mathematics Curriculum Topic Study: Bridging the Gap Between Standards and Practice* by Page Kelley and Cheryl M. Rose, *Uncovering Student Ideas in Science* (three volumes) by Page Keeley and others, and *Uncovering Student Thinking in Mathematics* by Cheryl M. Rose, Leslie Minton, and Carolyn B. Arline. These books have all been published by Corwin.

NSF funding for the NNECN project has ended. To sustain and continue the work in providing support to schools interested in science or mathematics mentoring, the Maine

Mathematics and Science Alliance has formed the NNECN Center to coordinate services and sponsor regional events (see www.nnecn.org).

STATE MANDATES

Is mentoring mandated for new teachers?

Mentoring mandates vary by state.

Is mentoring part of certification or licensure?

Requirements for certification and licensure vary by state.

Is funding provided to support the mandate?

Funding for mentoring programs varies by state.

GOALS

The overarching goal of NNECN was to support, nurture, guide, and retain new science and mathematics teachers while elevating the professional learning of experienced teachers for the purpose of improving the quality of all teachers. Specific desired outcomes for mentors, mentees, and schools were as follows.

Mentors would:

- Learn to understand and apply key research findings regarding curriculum, instruction, and assessment; professional development; adult learning; and the change process as they relate to mathematics or science education
- Gain deeper understanding of content and content pedagogical knowledge in math and science
- Develop knowledge and skills of formal mentoring and coaching practices
- Develop a personal and collegial relationship with a new teacher and support him or her through the induction process or his or her transition to teaching in a new content area
- Serve as district advisors for standards-based and research-informed practice in mathematics and science teaching and induction
- Move toward or assume new leadership roles and/or career pathways for supporting science or mathematics education

New teachers would:

- Gain confidence and expertise in standards-based and research-informed math or science content and pedagogy
- Successfully complete the induction period
- Form collegial relationships with other science and math teachers and gain linkages to important resources for improving science and mathematics teaching
- Remain in the teaching profession as highly qualified and highly effective science or mathematics teachers
- Provide opportunities for all students to learn science and math effectively
- Be contributing members of a professional learning community

Schools would:

- Increase the retention of new teachers of math and science
- Improve science and mathematics teaching among all teachers in a professional learning community
- Increase access to tools and resources for supporting standards-based and research-informed teaching and learning in science and mathematics
- Develop a sustainable, high-quality mentoring system that met the specific demands of science and mathematics, was compatible with local and state policies and general mentoring programs, and kept exemplary mentor teachers in the classroom
- Build learning communities within the school to provide continuous support for teachers at all levels of the teaching professional continuum in science and mathematics.

PROGRAM DESIGN

What are the components and recommended schedule of the program?

NNECN was a comprehensive three-year program for new teachers of science or mathematics throughout New England. Program components addressed mentoring and coaching, standards-based curriculum, standards-based and research-informed instruction, formative assessment, standards-based content, professional development, change process, technology, and leadership.

In year one, mentors participated in a weeklong summer professional development institute focused on developing formal mentoring and coaching skills. This intensive training helped mentors develop an understanding of the role of a mathematics or science mentor and provided them with tools, resources, and processes for leading content-focused mentoring.

In year two, mentors were trained to work with their mentees to examine and implement successful standards-based, research-informed strategies for curriculum, instruction, and assessment.

In year two, mentors helped create and lead learning communities within their schools or districts so that all teachers could benefit from NNECN tools, resources, and strategies to support high-quality teaching and learning and prevent the isolation that new teachers often experience.

In the final year, the goal was to have mentees emerge as "automentors" with an understanding of the use of NNECN tools and resources that would guide them in self-assessment of their teaching and help them identify their strengths and weaknesses. Mentees became active and knowledgeable participants in the school learning community and became anchored in lifelong professional growth and reflection.

Mentors began with one mentee in year one, then picked up another mentee in year two while entering a new phase of mentoring with the teacher from the previous year. In year three, mentors added a new mentee while gradually decreasing the dependence of the year one mentee. This phased mentoring approach built capacity for supporting new teachers while decreasing demands on mentors' time.

Mentors were accomplished science and/or mathematics middle or high school educators. They were paired with a "new" Grade 6–12 teacher from their school or district ("new" meaning new to the profession of teaching or new to teaching science or math after teaching other disciplines).

Are there any programs that complement the mentoring program?

NNECN mentors were able to earn graduate credit for their participation in the project. Participation in the NNECN program aided several teachers in their preparation for national board certification.

Who designed the mentoring program?

The NNECN project was designed by Page Keeley and Susan Mundry of WestEd as part of an NSF-funded program.

PROGRAM ADMINISTRATION

Who coordinates the mentoring program?

Page Keeley was the principal investigator of the NNECN project. Each of the three states had a state coordinator to manage and facilitate participant activities. Districts provided their own coordinator after funding ended.

Additionally, the Maine Mathematics and Science Alliance continues to provide technical assistance and consultation to schools and organizations interested in implementing the NNECN model or parts of it through its NNECN Center.

How is information communicated to shareholders?

Information about the NNECN project was communicated in a number of ways:

- Direct statewide mailings
- Listserv announcements
- Development of an NNECN Web site (www.nnecn.org)
- Presentations at numerous state, regional, and national conferences (including those of NSTA and the National Science Education Leadership Association and the New Teacher Center's Annual Induction Symposium in California)
- A published NNECN monograph available on the NNECN Web site

The Maine Mathematics and Science Alliance continues to disseminate information about the NNECN program and support services through its new NNECN Center Web site, www.nnecn.org.

Who coordinates integration of the mentoring program with other professional development opportunities and requirements in the schools and district?

As a condition of their participation, school superintendents and building principals of NNECN mentors were required to sign a contract outlining the commitments and responsibilities of the NNECN project. NNECN mentors, with support from these individuals, coordinated NNECN activities with those required by their schools and districts. NNECN was designed to enhance and complement programs already present in local systems.

PARTICIPANTS

Who is served?

The NNECN model served middle and high school science and mathematics teachers who were one of the following:

- A recent graduate of preservice programs
- A content major who had entered teaching through an alternative certification route
- An experienced teacher new to teaching science or mathematics
- An experienced teacher teaching new grade levels

Is participation of new teachers voluntary or mandatory?

Participation of new teachers in the NNECN project was voluntary. However, once a beginning teacher committed to participating, she or he was encouraged to participate fully in the local program's offerings.

Who provides the mentoring/induction?

Mentors were accomplished, trained middle and high school science and mathematics teachers with a minimum of six years of successful experience. Ninety-six teachers participated in the NSF-funded NNECN program.

What are the criteria for being a mentor?

The criteria for being a mentor were:

- A minimum of six years' experience in teaching math or science
- Certification in teaching mathematics or science at the secondary level (middle or high school)
- Strong interpersonal skills
- Leadership experience

Preference was given to accomplished teachers (for example, Presidential awardees, Milken Scholars, national board–certified teachers, teachers of the year, and teachers with previous mentoring experience).

MENTOR RESPONSIBILITIES AND REMUNERATION

What are the job responsibilities of mentors?

Mentor teachers agreed to:

- Participate fully in the NNECN project for three years. This included attendance at summer academies in years one and two and attendance at annual state spring meetings in years one, two, and three.
- Mentor three teachers over the course of the program. Each mentor added one new mentee each year.

- Provide a minimum of 80 hours of mentoring support to each new teacher over the course of three years.
- Actively participate in an electronic network with other mentor teachers.
- Submit monthly mentor reports, participate in evaluation and research studies, and communicate with their state coordinator.
- Lead science and/or mathematics study groups or other forms of embedded professional development in their schools or districts, beginning in year two. These learning communities met at least six times over the last two years of the project and included the mentees.

Are mentors required to do peer observation and coaching?

Peer observation and coaching were a key component of the NNECN project. Mentors and mentees observed one another or viewed a videotape of teaching to provide feedback on various aspects of instruction. Several formats, frameworks, and protocols were introduced to mentors and mentees for this purpose, including video demonstration lessons, Danielson's framework, the Vermont Classroom Observation Tool (VCOT), and collaborative peer coaching.

Do mentors have full-time classroom teaching responsibilities?

Virtually all mentors had full-time classroom responsibilities at the onset of the NNECN project. At the conclusion of the project, several mentors had transitioned into more formal mentoring and leadership positions in their districts (instructional math or science coaches). Districts using parts of the NNECN model are adapting it to fit their instructional coaching programs for science and mathematics specialists.

How are mentors available to participate in the program?

Mentors were available to participate in NNECN through project funding that covered the costs of conference expenses (meals, overnight accommodations, resources and materials, and some travel) for each participant. Twelve flexible days per mentor of substitute released time or paraprofessional support at $75 per day or $12 per hour were available.

Do mentors evaluate new teachers?

While "formal" evaluation of new teachers was not the intent of the NNECN project, some NNECN mentors who served as department chairs in their schools did evaluate new teachers following protocols outlined in their district's policy that were outside and separate from the NNECN project.

Is the mentor–new teacher relationship confidential?

Yes, the relationship was confidential.

Are mentors paid?

Mentors received a $1,000 stipend each year and stipends for attending summer institutes. NNECN provided the full $1,000 for mentors in year one, $800 in year two, and $600 in year three. The mentor's district contributed $200 in year two and $400 in year three.

MENTOR SELECTION, MATCHING, TRAINING, AND SUPERVISION

How are mentors selected?

Mentors applied to be NNECN participants and met specific criteria described by the program.

How are mentors and new teachers matched?

Mentors were matched with individuals in their schools who taught the same or similar subject matter and the same or a similar grade. Because NNECN participants often worked and resided in small, rural districts that might have only one or two science or mathematics teachers and thus lack mentor teachers, teachers were occasionally matched with mentors from adjacent districts.

Are mentors trained?

NNECN mentors received over a hundred hours of high-quality professional development as part of a carefully designed three-year curriculum of professional development skills and knowledge.

Who supervises the mentors?

Direct supervision happened within the districts. Coordination was provided by the NNECN program.

SUPPORTS FOR MENTORS

Is professional development available for mentors?

Professional development took place in a variety of formats and included offerings for both mentors and mentees. Weeklong tristate summer institutes, face-to-face state meetings, special focus or topic conferences (concentrating on, for example, formative assessment or new teachers), electronic forums, and a dedicated NNECN Listserv allowed all participants ongoing collaboration. Attending professional math and science conferences and participating in professional development opportunities as a mentor-mentee pair is one example of NNECN's "enhanced mentoring" strategies.

Who provides this professional development?

In addition to staff in the partnering tristate area, several nationally known presenters and researchers and/or their work were part of the professional development training for NNECN mentors and mentees. These included Kathy Dunne, director of professional development for learning innovations at WestEd, primary author of *Mentoring: A Resource and Training Guide for Educators*, and project director for the NSF-funded Teachers as Learners; Charlotte Danielson, author of *Enhancing Professional Practice: A Framework for Teaching* and co-developer of the Praxis assessments for beginning teachers; Bruce Wellman, nationally renowned facilitator of collaborative groups and coauthor of *Mentoring Matters: A Practical Guide to Learning-Focused Relationships*; Susan Mundry from WestEd, coauthor of *Designing Professional Development for Teachers of Science and Mathematics*; the staff of the American Association for the Advancement of Science's Project 2061; and Page Keeley, author of *Science Curriculum Topic Study: Bridging the Gap Between Standards and Practice* and primary author of *Mathematics Curriculum Topic Study: Bridging the Gap Between Standards and Practice*.

What resources are available for mentors?

Building a professional library for both mentors and mentees was a major feature of the NNECN model. By providing immediate access to high-quality science and mathematics professional literature and "experts at your fingertips" whenever needed, professional books extended the learning experiences of teachers in the NNECN project. Widely relevant professional publications were given to all participants, and mentors and mentees selected from a limited number of additional science or mathematics resources specific to their subject area and grade level (see Appendix D). They also had access to a lending library containing print and multimedia resources.

PROGRAM COSTS AND FUNDING

What resources are required for the program?

The cost of the program per mentor–mentee pair was:

- $500 to $1,000 per year for mentor stipends
- $300 for mentor and mentee professional materials
- $500 to $1,500 for shared attendance at a science or mathematics regional or national conference
- $200 to $500 for substitutes to cover released time for reciprocal observations
- $200 to $500 to support post-leaving certification courses
- Approximately $1,200 per day plus travel expenses for content-focused mentor training by the NNECN Center

Additionally, the program provided meeting space and refreshments for mentor–mentee professional learning communities.

The Maine Mathematics and Science Alliance now consults with districts interested in content-focused mentor training for mathematics and science teachers. Their rate is approximately $1,200 per day plus travel.

What are the funding sources?

NNECN was primarily supported by a five-year, $2,300,000 grant through NSF's Teacher Enhancement Program. Participants' school districts were asked to assume some of the costs of the program, including contributions to mentors' stipends; travel reimbursement; substitute costs for mentees; costs for administrators' optional attendance at summer institutes and state conferences; costs for mentors' and mentees' attendance at a local, state, regional, or national professional conference (aside from NNECN) at least once during the three years; mentor reimbursement for graduate credit as determined by district policy; and additional resources.

Who requests the funding?

Funding was requested by the grant writing partners.

PROGRAM EVALUATION

How is the program evaluated?

Because this was an NSF-funded project, an external evaluator was required. Components of the evaluation included:

- Teacher surveys
- Site visits

- Case studies
- Conference evaluations
- Monthly mentor reflections

Who sees the results?

Findings from the NNECN project were reviewed by the principal investigator, professional development providers, NNECN planning staff and partners, and NSF.

RECRUITMENT, HIRING, AND RETENTION OF NEW STAFF

How many new teachers are recruited and hired?

The number of new teachers hired varied by district.

Are there any data that correlate the mentoring program with the retention of new teachers?

Retention data would be at the district level, and no records are available regarding NNECN participants.

INDICATORS OF PROGRAM SUCCESS

What are the indicators of program success?

Results of an NSF-funded case study evaluation comparing new teachers from the NNECN program with new teachers from similar contexts who did not receive content-based mentoring revealed that NNECN-supported new teachers:

- are more likely to remain in the classroom;
- become confident teachers early in their careers;
- see teaching as a collegial enterprise rather than a solo enterprise; and
- see themselves as members of a specialized professional culture. (Bill Nave, Ed.D., Final Summative Evaluation Report, June 2006)

Surveys of NNECN teachers as well as case study interviews have consistently shown that the NNECN program had greater impact on science and mathematics mentors and mentees than a generic mentoring program would. Teachers valued having early mentoring focused not only on managing the classroom, but also on instruction in the content. As one mentor shared with program leaders, sometimes poor classroom management results from teachers' not knowing their content and pedagogy. By focusing early on substantive mentoring, new teachers gained help with instruction, not just management and survival skills.

7

District and University Programs That Support New Special Education Teachers

Consider this statement about the additional risks of teacher attrition for special education teachers:

> The magnitude of the additional demands placed on new special educators exacerbates the existing frustrations and stresses that all new teachers experience. These demands contribute to new special educators leaving their positions in special education. On average, an additional 7.4% of special educators move to general education classrooms annually. (Boyer & Gillespie, 2000, p. 10)

The following descriptions have been written by the directors of the programs in conjunction with their colleagues and the author. Judgments about the programs are those of the program directors and their staff and not the opinion of the author. Unless stated otherwise, figures and information were true for the 2007–2008 school year.

GREAT BEGINNINGS: BEGINNING TEACHER INDUCTION PROGRAM AND GREAT BEGINNINGS MENTOR PROGRAM

FAIRFAX COUNTY PUBLIC SCHOOLS

FAIRFAX, VIRGINIA

Richard Culp, Mentoring Program Manager
Great Beginnings
2334 Gallows Road
Dunn Loring, VA 22027
703–204–4009
richard.culp@fcps.edu

The following information was obtained from telephone conversations and e-mail correspondence with Richard Culp.

Demographics

Grade Levels	K–12	Urban/Suburban/Rural	Suburban
Student Population	138,000	**Ethnic Makeup**	African American 10.6% Asian 18.4% Caucasian 47.7% Hispanic 17.1% Multi-racial 5.7% Native American .3% Undesignated .2%
Teacher Population	Approximately 14,000 as of 2009	**% New Teachers**	10%; Great Beginnings serves 1,400 new teachers, of whom 300 are special education teachers
		Per-Pupil Expenditure	$13,407

Program Highlights

Unique Feature of Program	Voluntary afterschool induction program for beginning teachers, and experienced teachers new to Fairfax County, including special education teachers who work in grade level or subject area cohorts with coaches	Mentoring Is/Is Not Mandated for Certification/Licensing	Mentoring is not mandated
Coaching Is/Is Not a Component	Coaching is a component	**Mentors Evaluate/Do Not Evaluate the New Teachers With Whom They Work**	Mentors do not evaluate

Cost of Program	The budget for the combined Great Beginnings programs is approximately $1,000,000	**Funding**	FCPS budget and grant from the Commonwealth of Virginia
Mentors are Full-Time/ Part-Time Teachers	Mentors are full-time teachers; some are specialists working with students and/or have other responsibilities	**Mentor Remuneration**	Mentors are paid $450 for teachers new to the profession; coaches are paid according to the number of teachers they work with and the amount of teaching they do through the Fairfax County Academy ($2,100 for a two-credit, yearlong course)
How Long Program Has Been in Existence	Seven years	**Duration of Program for New Teachers**	Two years, the second at the general education level only (a second year for special education is being developed; an online component is also being developed for the first and second years)
Higher Education Affiliation	George Mason University, University of Virginia, George Washington University, Marymount University	**Program Coordinator**	Richard Culp

HISTORY

The Great Beginnings: Beginning Teacher Induction Program and the Great Beginnings Mentor Program began in 1995 to support new teachers in Fairfax County Public Schools (FCPS). Realizing that the needs of beginning teachers are unique, specialists and directors in the Office of Staff Development and Training created a program that would address those needs both inside and outside of the classroom. The program has expanded each year since then.

In its beginnings, the afterschool induction program served small cohorts of beginning elementary teachers who met with grade-level instructors and discussed classroom management, lesson planning, and reading strategies. After a couple of pilot years, secondary teachers were added to the group and met in subject-specific cohorts. The new millennium saw the addition of second- and even third-year teachers in cohort groups. Those programs, Continuing the Journey and Expanding Your Horizons, continue today with increased enrollment each year. In keeping with modern technological times, the secondary Continuing the Journey course for second-year teachers is conducted predominantly online, with quarterly face-to-face meetings.

A fairly recent addition is the Enriching the Experience group. As FCPS has seen a rise in the number of experienced teachers in the past few years, the need for support programs for them has become key. Enriching the Experience cohorts meet once a month to discuss FCPS policies and procedures and give new teachers a chance to discuss assessment and exceptional learners and participate in panel discussions related to advancement opportunities and meeting the needs of special education students.

Recent additions to the Great Beginnings program include special education–specific cohorts for both elementary and secondary teachers. These cohorts assist teachers of all special learners, including students with learning disabilities and emotional disturbances and children who are deaf, hard-of-hearing, and autistic. The cohorts are led by special education teachers and central office specialists so that they can help those teachers with not only the content knowledge, but also strategies for working with these very special learners.

Great Beginnings programs have served well over 10,000 FCPS teachers since their inception in 1995. Programs have been added, cohorts have been expanded, the office has become its own department and moved to a different location, and new staff have replaced former members who have moved on. But the mission of the programs has remained the same: to induct and retain high-quality instructional staff who ultimately contribute to increased student achievement.

STATE MANDATES

Is mentoring mandated for new teachers?

Yes, mentoring is mandated for new teachers.

Is mentoring part of certification or licensure?

No, mentoring is not part of certification or licensure.

Is funding provided to support the mandate?

Yes, funding is provided by the county and the Commonwealth of Virginia.

GOALS

FCPS is committed to promoting a high-performing workforce. That commitment starts from the very beginning. The Department of Professional Learning and Training welcomes teachers new to the system with a variety of system-wide and school-based programs to assist them in immediately becoming part of the Fairfax tradition of excellence.

PROGRAM DESIGN

What are the components and recommended schedule of the program?

Great Beginnings was developed for general education teachers as well as special education teachers. Elementary special education participants have cohorts dedicated to meeting their needs as teachers of special needs learners. The secondary model also has a specific special education cohort and keeps teachers of students with special needs in their subject area cohorts for the content portion (individual education plans [IEPs], learning disabilities, etc.). The secondary program integrates the teachers of special needs students with the regular education teachers. In so doing, it enhances general education teachers' understanding of the IEP process. For teachers of students with emotional disabilities, there are separate breakout sessions focusing on behavior plans, token economies, and so forth.

Teachers who volunteer to participate in the program do so one year at a time, opting for the second year after they've completed the first. The second-year program, Continuing the Journey, is less curriculum specific and does not offer special education–specific cohorts.

During 2007–2008, approximately 36 out of 300 special education teachers participated in the program. Teachers of students with learning and emotional disabilities participated in the general education sessions at the secondary level.

Beginning teachers are offered a three-day summer institute in August to help them kick off the school year. There is intensive bonding, and strategies for teaching are offered, including Rick Smith's *Conscious Classroom Management*, classrooms set up so teachers can see what a classroom should look like, instruction on ways to make materials, and learning-focused conversations.

Year One Components for Special Education Teachers

- At least 8 to 10 two-and-a-half-hour sessions are held for special education teachers. The curriculum for lower-incidence special education teachers is very different from that of regular education teachers and teachers of students with learning and emotional disabilities. Support sessions concentrate on the needs of the specific populations the teachers address.
- Coaches do on-site visitations within their own building to check use of materials and help teachers problem-solve regarding their work with low-incidence populations and students with moderate and severe disabilities. They observe lessons and help out. They also talk about schedules, lesson setup, and behavior issues.

Part of the Great Beginnings program is mentoring. Mentors are full-time teachers who are assigned to work one to one with new teachers at their school sites. Every new teacher, regardless of experience, gets a mentor at his or her school site, *or* a mentor is assigned from the central office if another teacher of the new teacher's content area is not available at his or her school. In these cases, the school assigns a "buddy," someone who can show the new teacher around the school and be a support for her or him in house. Mentors regularly meet with their new teachers and document what they do.

Mentor training is required before a teacher can become a mentor. The training consists of a course offered through the Fairfax County Academy periodically throughout the year and for five and a half days in the summer.

There is also a mentor resource teacher position, which requires training and carries the expectation that the mentor will work at least 10 hours a week, sometimes more. This part-time position is traditionally filled by teachers on maternity leave or retired teachers.

Teachers who work with new teachers in the afterschool induction program are referred to as coaches. They meet with the new teachers monthly in two-and-a-half–hour afterschool seminars, as well as for a week in late August for the Great Beginnings Summer Institute. Coaches also have the opportunity to visit the new teachers in their classrooms to see a lesson and offer feedback.

Are there any programs that complement the mentoring program?

There are also professional development internship programs with George Washington University, Marymount University, and George Mason University. Interns from these schools complete a yearlong program in a designated FCPS school team teaching alongside a classroom teacher. This includes working in centers for students with emotional disabilities.

Who designed the mentoring program?

The program was designed by the former Office of Staff Development and Training with Instructional Services at FCPS. It is now managed by the Department of Professional Learning and Training (PLT).

PROGRAM ADMINISTRATION

Who coordinates the mentoring program?

All new-teacher support is done under the umbrella of Great Beginnings. Coordinators of the departments meet with Sharon Mullen, director of professional practice and training. Richard Culp is a specialist with PLT and manages the mentoring program as well as the secondary Great Beginnings program. Ray Lonnett is the educational specialist for elementary Great Beginnings.

How is information communicated to shareholders?

Information is communicated through brochures for all the recruiters, the principals, and information on the FCPS Web site (www.fcps.edu/plt). Phone calls are made over the summer to remind principals about the Great Beginnings program and their role in encouraging new teachers to participate.

The Office of Human Resources communicates with PLT so that they have the names of the new teachers hired.

Who coordinates integration of the mentoring program with other professional development opportunities and requirements in the schools and district?

The Great Beginnings program is scheduled on Monday afternoons and Thursdays. Principals and other staff who coordinate professional development try not to schedule sessions on these two days. Department coordinators and the Instructional Services department work together to coordinate professional development opportunities.

PARTICIPANTS

Who is served?

Regular education and special education teachers participate in the Great Beginnings program.

Is participation of new teachers voluntary or mandatory?

Great Beginnings is voluntary, but principals strongly encourage teachers to participate.

Who provides the mentoring/induction?

Coaches and mentors provide the training, consultation, coaching, and support.

What are the criteria for being a mentor?

Mentors are selected by the principals and lead mentors at the school sites. Generally speaking, they are experienced teachers (those having taught three years or more) who are also leaders in their department or grade levels. They also must complete the required Mentoring Novice Teachers course offered by FCPS. This is a 15-hour course.

Coaches are selected by PLT program managers. They must complete an application, submit colleague and principal recommendations, and complete an interview process. They must also have a minimum of three years in the county and demonstrate evidence of leadership and expertise in their content areas and classroom management.

MENTOR RESPONSIBILITIES AND REMUNERATION

What are the job responsibilities of mentors?

As noted above, mentors provide in-house support for new teachers. They are selected based on similar subject areas and/or grade levels.

Coaches teach courses according to subject area and grade level. For example, there is a third-grade cohort and a foreign language cohort.

Are mentors required to do peer observation and coaching?

Observation is done informally by the coaches and also the mentors.

Do mentors have full-time classroom teaching responsibilities?

Yes, mentors and coaches have full-time teaching responsibilities.

Mentor resource teachers (20 for regular education and one for special education, with more coming in the future) are funded through Project Excel, which supports lower-achieving schools and has initially targeted first-year teachers in those schools. Mentor resource teachers are teachers who have retired or are on maternity leave. They work part time, and their only job is to support beginning teachers. They are required to be in class-rooms frequently (one time per week, minimally), and they write an IEP for their work with the teacher, documenting it each time they come.

How are mentors available to participate in the program?

School-based mentors are full-time teachers or curriculum specialists who meet an average of 20 to 30 minutes per day or three hours per week with beginning teachers in their schools. They visit the beginning teachers periodically in their classrooms. Coaches do the work after school and are given two days per year for classroom visits, which can be broken up into hours instead of days throughout the school year.

Do mentors evaluate new teachers?

No, mentors and coaches do not evaluate new teachers.

Is the mentor–new teacher relationship confidential?

Yes, the relationships between mentors and new teachers and coaches and new teachers are confidential.

Are mentors paid?

Mentors of teachers with no experience receive a $450 stipend for working with their mentees.

Coaches are paid $2,200 for teaching a two-credit class, less if they teach fewer credits.

MENTOR SELECTION, MATCHING, TRAINING, AND SUPERVISION

How are mentors selected?

School-based mentors are selected by their building principals based on their experience, how well their courses or subjects match those of mentees, and other criteria. In schools where there is no appropriate curriculum mentor, the central office assigns mentors from outside the school.

PLT staff interview and hire Great Beginnings coaches. Prospective coaches complete an application, submit recommendations from their principals and colleagues, come to an interview, and are observed in their classroom settings by a PLT specialist.

How are mentors and new teachers matched?

Building principals match mentors; coaches are divided by clusters at the elementary level and by subject at the secondary level. Special education teachers are divided as elementary or secondary.

Specialists from the Office of Instruction are matched with the general education teachers; the coaches are matched with the special education teachers.

Virginia state law requires that a special education teacher who is teaching on a provisional or conditional license be assigned a mentor who is certified in special education to obtain a collegiate professional license.

Are mentors trained?

Mentors are trained via the 15-hour Mentoring Novice Teachers course. They must complete this, or equivalent university coursework, to receive their mentor stipend. They also frequently attend training at their school sites with the lead mentor. Lead mentors currently attend two half-day workshops with the mentor program manager, Richard Culp, for program updates and staff development. They are then expected to do turnaround training for their mentors at their school sites.

Coaches are mandated to have five days of training every year. They consult with program specialists and others on topics such as how to work with adult learners and the needs of first-year teachers.

Who supervises the mentors?

Richard Culp manages the mentoring program at the central office level. Each school has a lead mentor assigned by the principal to manage the mentors at that school. Lead mentors report directly to Richard and their building principals.

SUPPORTS FOR MENTORS

Is professional development available for mentors?

Lead mentors and their administrators are expected to meet monthly with their mentor teachers for professional development.

Richard Culp provides twice-annual staff development for lead mentors, who do turnaround training with their school mentors and provide program updates and information.

Who provides this professional development?

PLT and Fairfax County Academy provide the training. Mentoring Novice Teachers is a one-credit course taught by experienced administrators and mentors.

What resources are available for mentors?

PLT is a resource for coaches and mentors. Specialists and coordinators do frequent school visits, especially when there are new lead mentors and/or coaches.

Each school has been provided with a copy of Paula Rutherford's *The 21st Century Mentor's Handbook*, compliments of PLT. Beginning teachers receive copies of Rick Smith's *Conscious Classroom Management*.

PROGRAM COSTS AND FUNDING

What resources are required for the program?

The cost of the program is approximately $1,000,000.

- Training for coaches and mentors
- New-teacher orientation
- Food for the summer institute
- Materials: Notebooks for the summer institute, copies of Rick Smith's *Conscious Classroom Management*, and resource notebooks with lots of ideas for the whole year
- Stipends for coaches and mentors
- Substitutes to cover released time

This includes compensation for mentors and coaches and substitute coverage allowing lead mentors to participate in professional development.

What are the funding sources?

The FCPS budget and grants for hard-to-staff schools from the Commonwealth of Virginia fund the Great Beginnings Program. Mentor resource teachers are funded through Title II monies.

Who requests the funding?

PLT requests funding for the programs.

PROGRAM EVALUATION

How is the program evaluated?

The Great Beginnings program is evaluated through a survey of new teachers. Mentor resource teachers write a narrative and document their work.

It is hoped that student achievement and teacher retention will be tracked in the future.

Who sees the results of the evaluation?

Instructional Services and the Department of Accountability see the results.

RECRUITMENT, HIRING, AND RETENTION OF NEW STAFF

How many new teachers are recruited and hired?

In 2008–2009, 1,397 new teachers received mentor support.

Are there any data that correlate the mentoring program with the retention of new teachers?

On average, FCPS retains 6 to 7 percent more teachers who complete the Great Beginnings program than those who do not. This statistic is generally above the national average for each of the first five years, the period for which data are available.

INDICATORS OF PROGRAM SUCCESS

What are the indicators of program success?

Indicators of program success include the retention data, testimonials from new teachers, national recognition in published articles, and the fact that the Great Beginnings programs offer one of three models that other county systems must use to qualify for state funding in Virginia.

ACADEMY I

SPECIAL SCHOOL DISTRICT

ST. LOUIS COUNTY, MISSOURI

Ros Van Hecke, Director of Learning and Assessment
Special School District
800 Maryville Center Drive
Town and Country, MO 63017
314–989–7804
rvanhecke@ssdmo.org

The following information was obtained from telephone conversations and e-mail correspondence with Ros Van Hecke.

Demographics

Grade Levels	PreK–12	**Urban/Suburban/Rural**	Suburban
Student Population	28,784	**Ethnic Makeup***	Caucasian 66 % Minorities 34%†
Teacher Population	2,761	**% New Teachers**	7–10%
		Per-Pupil Expenditure‡	$11,928

*This reflects the ethnic makeup of schools throughout the county.

†No information was provided on the breakdown of this percentage.

‡ SSD serves more than 25,000 students for whom it does not take attendance, and as such, expenditures per eligible pupil are not relevant. For the 2007–2008 budget, SSD calculated its per-pupil expenditures by using current expenditures divided by the total number of students receiving special education services from the district as of December 1, 2007. The budgeted amount for 2007–2008 was $11,928 per pupil.

Program Highlights

Unique Feature of Program	Induction and professional development are linked and planned for teachers' first five years	Mentoring Is/Is Not Mandated for Certification/Licensing	Mentoring is mandated
Coaching Is/Is Not a Component	Coaching is a component	**Mentors Do/Do Not Evaluate the New Teachers With Whom They Work**	Mentors do not evaluate
Cost of Program	$5,500 per teacher for two years (includes mentoring and specific professional development)	**Funding**	Districts
Mentors Are Full-Time/Part-Time Teachers	Site-based mentors are full-time teachers; instructional facilitators who provide instructional mentoring are full-time mentors/professional developers	**Mentor Remuneration**	Site-based mentors are paid $150 per year per new teacher; instructional facilitators are paid according to the district's teacher's salary
How Long Program Has Been in Existence	The current program is four years old; the original program started more than 10 years ago	**Duration of Program for New Teachers**	Three years plus two more years of professional development
Higher Education Affiliation	None	**Program Coordinator**	Ros Van Hecke

HISTORY

In December 1957, St. Louis County voters passed a referendum establishing a local public school district to support the educational needs of children with disabilities. That vote—which effectively established Special School District of St. Louis County (SSD)—was the net result of years of hard work and advocacy by parents of children whose educational needs were not being met by the existing public school system.

The district began humbly, with four teachers and a social worker serving 166 students in the fall of 1958.

The first students at SSD were taught in schools owned and operated by other school districts throughout the area. Soon, however, SSD began construction on several special education schools. The first of these, Ackerman School in Florissant, opened its doors to students in 1961. Today, SSD operates five special education schools—Ackerman, Litzsinger, Neuwoehner, Northview, and Southview.

The 1960s also saw SSD move into the area of technical education—a mission separate from the district's work in the special education field. SSD first began providing technical education in 1966. In the fall of 1967, the district opened South Technical High School. The following year, SSD opened North Technical High School in North St. Louis County.

Throughout the 1960s, SSD also built on its special education programs, providing newer and better forms of education for students with learning disabilities and behavioral problems.

In the 1970s, federal and state legislators began to take seriously the issue of special education. This culminated in the 1975 passage of the Education for All Handicapped Children Act, which eventually evolved into the Individuals with Disabilities Education Act (IDEA). The 1975 law mandates a free and appropriate public education for all students, regardless of their disabilities. These laws have helped form the basis of the special education services provided by SSD to the present day.

As legislators locally and nationally grappled with issues related to special education and disability, SSD strove to keep up with local demand for education services for children and young adults with disabilities. In 1974, the district began to serve students with more profound disabilities. As a result, many of these students, some with multiple disabilities or medical fragility, were now being served in a school setting for the first time.

SSD also began educating preschool-aged children in 1976. The students served at the outset of this early childhood program were deaf or had hearing or vision impairment. By the end of the decade, a federal grant enabled the district to expand its early childhood offerings to meet the needs of children with various disabilities.

The early 1980s were marked by rising costs and decreasing revenues for SSD. In April 1986, voters overwhelmingly approved a tax levy increase for the district, allowing SSD to continue to grow and expand its program offerings.

In 1996, the Missouri legislature passed into law a change to the district's governing structure, resulting in the creation of the Governing Council. This 23-member council, which includes a representative from each of the other St. Louis County public school districts, was established as an oversight committee to review and approve the district's budget and strategic plans. In 1998, the Governing Council's role expanded to include the election of the SSD Board of Education.

In November 2006, St. Louis County taxpayers voted to support Proposition S, a tax levy increase allowing SSD to continue growing its programs and services. In 2007, SSD celebrated both its 50th anniversary and the appointment of John C. Cary as its new superintendent of schools.

In 2008, SSD educated nearly 30,000 students with disabilities at sites throughout St. Louis County, including 265 public schools operated by the other 23 public school districts in St. Louis County. SSD also provides technical education to about 2,000 area high school students at the district's two technical high schools and at other satellite locations.

SSD has maintained a vigorous program for beginning teachers for more than 10 years. In the 2004–2005 school year, the teacher evaluation process was revised and a formalized professional development structure for all teachers was developed. SSD professional development is focused on specific skills and outcomes according to a teacher's years of SSD experience. The overall structure is shown in the following table, which delineates SSD's professional development strands.

Strand	Target Audience Teacher Group	Theme Area: Student Behavior, Quality Instruction, Student Performance/Literacy
Induction Program	All new hires	General information: Employment, orientation to the district's organization, expectations, procedures, and guidelines
Academy I	First- through third-year teachers	Fundamental skills across all three theme areas (prescribed by SSD)

Strand	Target Audience Teacher Group	Theme Area: Student Behavior, Quality Instruction, Student Performance/Literacy
Academy II	Fourth- through fifth-year teachers	Use of data to increase student achievement (prescribed by SSD with some latitude)
Research and Collaborative Learning	Sixth-year and beyond teachers	Collaborative work and research that supports SSD and partner district goals (self-directed with approval of supervisor)

The State of Missouri requires a mentoring program for beginning teachers. Certification requirements specify the number of professional development and mentoring hours needed for beginning teachers to reach their next level of certification. SSD has traditionally provided an induction program far beyond the minimum requirements. Its professional development for new teacher–level hires has always been rigorous, focusing on critical teaching behaviors, specific instructional strategies, and decision making based on student data. On-site support for teachers such as peer coaching has been used to provide feedback and guide teachers as they develop their skills. Since the program's inception more than 10 years ago, significant changes have been made that have strengthened and expanded the program. Major highlights are:

- All new teacher level staff (beginning and experienced) are now included in both the three-day induction program as well as Academy I.
- The content of Academy I is prescribed with specific skill sets correlated to the SSD teacher evaluation performance indicators.
- Academy I has been expanded from two years to three years for beginning teachers.

In addition to a school level mentor, beginning teachers now receive instructional mentoring from Academy I instructional facilitators. School level mentors support beginning teachers in a variety of areas (certification, building procedures, Encore, etc.), whereas instructional facilitators support beginning teachers as they implement, analyze, and reflect on the Academy I Classroom Supports for Instruction skill sets.

The Academy I skill sets serve as a framework for the course content. Academy I provides a solid foundation for newly hired teacher–level staff by inducting them into SSD procedures and expectations, providing specific skill development in quality instruction and universal classroom supports, and supporting them in their classrooms through mentoring and coaching. The Academy I program is differentiated for newly hired teacher–level staff based on their needs and their level of experience. Beginning teachers, those teachers hired by SSD with no prior experience, participate in Academy I for three years. Experienced teachers, those teachers hired by SSD with prior experience, participate in Academy I for two years. As a teacher completes the Academy I program, he or she develops a professional development plan for Academy II. The following table provides an overview of the current program for new teachers.

	First Year: Classroom Supports for Instruction (CSI)	Second Year: Effective Teaching (ET)	Third Year: Thoughtful Teaching (TT)
Instructional Days	3.5 per year	3 per year	3 per year
Skill Sets Focus Area	Student behavior Quality instruction	Quality instruction Student performance	Quality instruction Student performance
Instructional Focus	Classroom environment Universal supports Functional assessment	Quality instruction Reflection/evaluation	Quality instruction Reflection/evaluation
Mentoring/ Support	School-level mentor Instructional facilitator	Instructional facilitator Mentoring/coaching	Instructional facilitator Coaching

Many departments and individuals support newly hired teachers, depending on their certification and assignment. The Learning and Assessment department is directly responsible for the professional development and embedded support of the special education teachers who teach "school-age students" between the ages of 5 and 21 years of age. There are 11 instructional facilitators and one area coordinator whose primary role is to support these teachers.

STATE MANDATES

Is mentoring mandated for new teachers?

Two years of mentoring is required by the state for certification. SSD also mandates two years of mentoring. The first year of mentoring is delivered by the instructional facilitator, who provides instructional mentoring, in addition to the school-level mentor, who provides site-based support. The second year of mentoring is delivered by instructional facilitators, who provide instructional mentoring.

Is mentoring part of certification or licensure?

Yes, mentoring is part of certification and licensure.

Is funding provided to support the mandate?

Mentoring is funded through the school districts.

GOALS

The goal for Academy I is to develop and retain highly qualified teachers.

Academy I is divided into five areas based on the district's goals. These areas are:

- Student behavior
- Quality instruction
- Student performance in literacy and mathematics
- District expectations and procedures
- Professional growth

PROGRAM DESIGN

What are the components and recommended schedule of the program?

New beginning teacher–level staff participate in an instructional mentoring program. Every beginning teacher is paired with an instructional facilitator, who serves in the role of the mentor. New beginning teacher–level staff receive direct follow-up support from their instructional facilitator once or twice per month. Direct support could include coaching, consultation, and facilitation through site visits; e-mail communication; and/or phone conferencing. Classroom observations and feedback during site visits are other supports that may be provided.

Instructional mentoring allows beginning new-hire teachers to feel supported in their efforts to meet the high expectations of the district by implementing, analyzing, and reflecting on the Academy I year one skill sets.

Instructional mentoring provides ongoing guidance, support, and reinforcement to professionals new to the district through an organized, well-defined program that:

- Allows for greater retention of professional educators who provide a higher quality of instruction for students
- Increases mutual respect and collaboration among professional educators through collegial activities

In addition to the instructional mentoring program, first-year teachers with zero to one year of teaching experience are assigned a school-level mentor as another level of support. The assignment of a veteran teacher in the building assists beginning teachers with their questions. Topics covered by the teacher providing the school-level mentoring with new hires could include certification and mentoring program requirements, building procedures, resources and culture, special education procedures, how to develop and conduct IEP meetings, and scheduling. School-level mentors meet a minimum of seven hours with beginning teachers during the first semester (more frequently if needed) and a minimum of three and a half hours during the second semester. Beginning teachers also observe at least two veteran teachers (one of whom may or may not be the school-level mentor) throughout the school year. These contacts are logged by the school-level mentor.

Experienced teacher–level staff who are new to the district receive direct support from their SSD instructional facilitator during at least one opportunity following each day of the three days of professional development provided throughout the school year. Follow-up support may include individual and/or group coaching, consultation and facilitation through site visits, e-mail communication, and/or phone conferencing. Classroom observations and feedback during individual site visits reinforce skills learned and focus on classroom implementation. The purpose of follow-up support is to expand on the learning and application of the concepts presented during instructional days and to provide collaboration and reflection on teaching practices with fellow colleagues.

Each participant is required to maintain a portfolio throughout Academy I. The purpose of the portfolio is to gather artifacts containing a collection of the work of new teachers that will provide evidence of their knowledge, skills, and reflections as a learner. The portfolio also supports collaboration with fellow colleagues in the academy as well as with the area coordinator or principal.

Participants are required to attend all three days of professional development and to participate in mentoring and coaching support.

Are there any programs that complement the mentoring program?

The Academy I program includes professional development that provides skill development in the Academy I skill sets, as follows:

Student Behavior

- Using effective techniques to maintain positive behavior by recognizing and reinforcing appropriate behavior
- Using effective techniques to maintain positive behavior by making effective use of preventive strategies, including sensory supports
- Establishing, teaching, and maintaining rules, routines, attention signals, and schedules (universals)
- Using effective techniques to find and eliminate the causes of undesirable behavior
- Identifying the essential components of a functional assessment and resources to support the teacher in the team process
- Quality instruction
- Assessing student learning and using assessment results to plan, select learning experiences, deliver instruction, and reflect evidence of student learning
- Providing direct instruction in skills and strategies to ensure that students have access to and benefit from the general education curriculum, using the components of lesson design in the advance organizer, body, and post organizer
- Demonstrating techniques to promote maximum student involvement and learning
- Integrating basic technology into the learning environment
- Identifying cultural and diversity factors that contribute to student learning

Student Performance in Literacy and Mathematics

- Identifying multiple strategies and routines that address student needs in the component areas of literacy and mathematics
- Delivering instruction in strategies and routines, demonstrating the Academy I quality instruction skill set

SSD Expectations and Procedures

- Demonstrating knowledge of the IEP process and the legal issues relative to considering assistive technology and planning for transition
- Demonstrating basic technology skills to comply with district procedures, such as e-mail and Encore

Professional Growth

- Reflecting on teaching and learning through job-embedded staff development, self-reflection, and collecting teacher and student data

Academy I is for all new hires. Experienced teachers attend for two years and then go on to Academy II. Beginning teachers attend Academy I for three years and then go on to Academy II for years four and five. The Academy I program is a separate program from Academy II.

Who designed the mentoring program?

The mentoring program has evolved over the years and was developed by the Learning and Assessment professional development staff.

PROGRAM ADMINISTRATION

Who coordinates the mentoring program?

Learning and Assessment administration and the Academy I facilitators coordinate the mentoring program.

How is information communicated to shareholders?

Annual reports are presented to the board of education.

Who coordinates integration of the mentoring program with other professional development opportunities and requirements in the schools and district?

Learning and Assessment administrators and facilitators collaborate with other professional developers who provide professional development across the county.

PARTICIPANTS

Who is served?

All teachers new to SSD participate in the mentoring program.

Academy I is a two-year program for experienced new hires and a three-year program for beginning teachers who are new hires. The beginning teachers in Academy I are mentored for two years. The first year they are mentored by a school-based mentor and an instructional facilitator, who provides instructional mentoring. In the beginning teacher's second year, she or he attends professional development based on her or his needs and the skill sets and is mentored by one of the instructional facilitators, who provide instructional mentoring, peer coaching, and other types of individual support to implement the skills taught with fidelity. This same type of support and professional learning continues during the third year, but is less frequent and not termed "mentoring."

Is participation of new teachers voluntary or mandatory?

Participation of beginning teachers is mandatory.

Who provides the mentoring/induction?

Full-time facilitators provide instructional mentoring, and full-time teachers provide school-based mentoring in addition to their normal assigned duties.

What are the criteria for being a mentor?

Instructional mentors are hired as full-time facilitators. Job requirements include experience in professional development, coaching, and strong classroom experience.

School-level mentors should be:

- Successful teachers with three years of experience or more
- Willing to share time and materials with beginning teachers

- Well organized
- Complimentary of others
- Willing to coach (be a guide on the side)
- Respectful and responsible
- Effective teachers

MENTOR RESPONSIBILITIES AND REMUNERATION

What are the job responsibilities of mentors?

Instructional mentors are responsible for planning, implementing, and evaluating professional development based on effective, research-proven instructional practices. They are also responsible for providing a blend of coaching.

School-based mentors:

- Hold regularly scheduled meetings
- Complete all required paperwork and return it to Learning and Assessment by the required due dates
- Complete two observations of the beginning teacher using the observation format outlined in training
- Assist the beginning teacher in scheduling at least two classroom observations of experienced teachers (one of whom may or may not be the mentor)

Are mentors required to do peer observation and coaching?

Yes, peer observation and coaching are a requirement for instructional mentors.

Do mentors have full-time classroom teaching responsibilities?

Instructional mentors do not have classroom responsibilities. School-based mentors are full-time teachers.

How are mentors available to participate in the program?

Instructional mentors are employed as full-time staff developers. School-based mentors are given released time.

Do mentors evaluate new teachers?

No, neither instructional nor school-based mentors evaluate new teachers.

Is the mentor–new teacher relationship confidential?

Yes, the mentor–new teacher relationship is confidential. Administrators are given the syllabus and the names of the instructional mentors. At times, the instructional mentor and administrator may communicate, but specific performance information is not divulged by the mentor.

Are mentors paid?

School-based mentors are paid $150 per year per beginning teacher. Instructional mentors are paid a teacher's salary.

MENTOR SELECTION, MATCHING, TRAINING, AND SUPERVISION

How are mentors selected?

School-based mentors are selected by the beginning teacher's supervisor. Instructional mentors are hired and assigned by the Learning and Assessment administration based on their qualifications and expertise.

How are mentors and new teachers matched?

School-based mentors are matched by the beginning teachers' supervisors, and instructional mentors are matched by the Learning and Assessment administration.

Are mentors trained?

Instructional mentors are trained in the areas of professional development and cognitive coaching. Skills are reinforced through the structure of the entire department. School-based mentors are given a three-hour training session titled Foundations for School-Level Mentoring. The presentation explores topics such as adult learning principles and the needs of beginning teachers, the five phases of beginning teachers, observation strategies, strategies to support beginning teacher reflection, and the protocols associated with the mentoring process. All school-level mentors who didn't attend training in the 2006–2007 school year must attend updated training.

Who supervises the mentors?

Instructional mentors are supervised by the Learning and Assessment administration. School-based mentors are supervised by their assigned supervisor.

SUPPORTS FOR MENTORS

Is professional development available for mentors?

Professional development is ongoing. (See above.)

Who provides this professional development?

School-based mentors are provided professional development by the instructional mentors.

What resources are available for mentors?

Instructional mentors follow up with school-based mentors through e-mail and by phone throughout the school year to provide ongoing support. Site visits and consultation are available on request.

PROGRAM COSTS AND FUNDING

What resources are required for the program?

The cost for the program is approximately $5,500 per teacher, based on two years. This includes salaries for administration and facilitators, released time, materials, and stipends.

If readers would like more information about the costs of the program, the director or staff will provide it.

What are the funding sources?

The program is funded through district monies.

Who requests the funding?

The Learning and Assessment administration requests the funding.

PROGRAM EVALUATION

How is the program evaluated?

The program is internally evaluated by the professional development committee and included in its annual report and the board of education program evaluation.

Who sees the results of the evaluation?

The board, administrators, and stakeholders see the evaluation results. Program evaluation is available through SSD's Web site, www.ssd.k12.mo.us.

RECRUITMENT, HIRING, AND RETENTION OF NEW STAFF

How many new teachers are recruited and hired?

There were 349 new teachers in 2007–2008.

Are there any data that correlate the mentoring program with the retention of new teachers?

	1996–1997	2005–2006	2006–2007	2007–2008
Number of New Hires	134	275	255	349
Number of New Hires Who Resigned	35	26	32	18
Retention Rate of First-Year Hires	74%	90%	88%	95%

INDICATORS OF PROGRAM SUCCESS

What are the indicators of program success?

In addition to the data on teacher retention, the Professional Development Standard Program Evaluation, which was approved by the board on November 13, 2007, conducted extensive surveys and cited the following strengths:

- Beginning teachers are explicitly taught data collection skills as a component of the Academy I program.

- Analysis of student data, classroom observations, and survey results indicate that beginning teachers are using data to:
  - o Make decisions based on assessing student abilities and analyzing data
  - o Monitor student performance
  - o Adjust instruction

- Student survey data indicate positive perceptions of beginning teachers with regard to effective classroom supports and instructional practices.
- The Continuum of Skill Set Development indicates that beginning teachers are growing in their Academy I skill set development.
- Beginning teachers perceive the instructional mentoring component of Academy I as a positive support.
- Both beginning teachers and administrators noted Academy I professional development, support from instructional facilitators, support with problem solving and group coaching, and expectations of the supervisor as positive factors impacting teaching.

MENTORING UNIQUE SPECIAL EDUCATORS

Michelle Kama, Lead Mentor
University of Hawaii at Manoa
College of Education
Special Education Department
1776 University Avenue
Honolulu, HI 96822
808–956–0964
mkama@hawaii.edu

The following information was obtained from telephone conversations and e-mail correspondence with Michelle Kama as well as from the MUSE Web site (http://www.coe.hawaii.edu/sped/mentoring).

Demographics

Grade Levels	PreK–12	Urban/Suburban/Rural	All
Student Population	Students in 56 schools throughout Oahu as well as three neighboring islands (Moloka'i, Hawaii, Maui)	**Ethnic Makeup**	NA
Teacher Population	NA	**% New Teachers**	NA
		Per-Pupil Expenditure	NA

Program Highlights

Unique Feature of Program	An institute of higher education (IHE) program of support for special education teachers provided by full-time former special education teachers	**Mentoring Is/Is Not Mandated for Certification/Licensing**	Mentoring is not mandated
Coaching Is/Is Not a Component	Coaching is a component	**Mentors Do/Do Not Evaluate the New Teachers With Whom They Work**	Mentors do not evaluate
Cost of Program	$420,000	**Funding**	DOE
Mentors are Full-Time/Part-Time Teachers	Mentors are fully released from teaching	**Mentor Remuneration**	This is a salaried position on the University of Hawaii pay scale
How Long Program Has Been in Existence	Since 2003	**Duration of Program for New Teachers**	Mandatory two years; optional third year for graduates of program
Higher Education Affiliation	University of Hawaii at Manoa	**Program Coordinator**	None; Michelle Kama is the contact person

HISTORY

The Mentoring Unique Special Educators (MUSE) program began in 2003 with a partnership among the University of Hawaii at Manoa, the Hawaii State Department of Education, and the New Teacher Center at the University of California, Santa Cruz.

STATE MANDATES

Is mentoring mandated for new teachers?

The state superintendent wants all complexes to have mentoring, but it is not mandated for teachers. By 2010, it is anticipated that there will be some big changes in regard to induction and mentoring in Hawaii.

Is mentoring part of certification or licensure?

No, mentoring is not a requirement for certification or licensure.

Is funding provided to support the mandate?

There is no funding from the state to support mentoring.

GOALS

The vision statement of the program is to positively impact student achievement. Program staff at the University of Hawaii envision a collaborative program between the university and the Hawaii Department of Education (DOE) that facilitates the development and retention of knowledgeable, effective, and caring special education teachers.

PROGRAM DESIGN

What are the components and recommended schedule of the program?

MUSE is a three-year mentoring program.

Teachers are mentored for two years while they are in the program and teaching. Graduates have the option of continuing mentoring for one more year.

- New (first- and second-year) special education teachers are provided weekly one-to two-hour visits.
- Outer-island teachers are provided weekly contact via phone or e-mail and one face-to-face visit each month for a total of eight visits per year (the mentor flies to the island for one to two days each month to see the new teacher).
- Graduates are provided monthly visits or more if needed.

Are there any programs that complement the mentoring program?

The MUSE program complements the certification program of the University of Hawaii at Manoa (UHM), whose participants teach full time without having experience and go to school for a graduate degree in the evenings. The mentoring program provides the support to handle both responsibilities.

Who designed the mentoring program?

The program began in 2003. Three mentors along with a coordinator, Dr. Judy Coryell, designed the program in its first two years.

PROGRAM ADMINISTRATION

Who coordinates the mentoring program?

Coordination responsibilities are divided up by expertise and interest among mentors. There is no coordinator position; Michelle Kama is the contact person.

How is information communicated to shareholders?

Information is communicated in bimonthly, three-hour mentor meetings totaling six hours per month. These monthly mentor forums are professional development seminars designed to address mentors' need to learn the role of an effective mentor; develop high-caliber support and assessment skills; be on the cutting edge of school reform, curriculum development, instruction, and assessment; ensure consistency of program implementation; and emerge as professional leaders

Who coordinates integration of the mentoring program with other professional development opportunities and requirements in the schools and district?

Veteran mentors in MUSE coordinate the professional development opportunities in the schools and district with MUSE.

Various people are responsible to remain in contact with the department of education, department chair, school districts, and staff from the New Teacher Center (NTC), who update mentors on professional developments and other requirements.

PARTICIPANTS

Who is served?

All "in place" is for teachers who:

1. Are in the University of Hawaii's post-baccalaureate or M.Ed. program

2. Have taken a special education teaching position with the DOE

3. Are uncertified or unlicensed in special education

Is participation of new teachers voluntary or mandatory?

Participation of new teachers is mandatory.

Who provides the mentoring/induction?

Mentoring is provided by six full-time mentors who are former special education teachers with the DOE.

What are the criteria for being a mentor?

The criteria for being a mentor are:

- M.Ed. in special education
- Five years' Hawaii DOE teaching experience in special education
- Experience in leadership, presentations, and providing professional development

MENTOR RESPONSIBILITIES AND REMUNERATION

What are the job responsibilities of mentors?

Mentors provide support to caseload teachers once a week for one to two hours. Support is divided into three areas:

- Emotional
- Teaching
- UHM program

Are mentors required to do peer observation and coaching?

Yes, peer observation and coaching are required.

Do mentors have full-time classroom teaching responsibilities?

No, mentors have either taken leave or resigned from the DOE.

How are mentors available to participate in the program?

Mentors are full time in their role.

Do mentors evaluate new teachers?

No, this is a nonevaluative program. Teachers are already evaluated by special education faculty members for the field supervision course, including observation and evaluation of their lessons.

Is the mentor–new teacher relationship confidential?

Yes, mentors build a trusting relationship with their new-teacher partners that remains confidential.

Are mentors paid?

Mentors are paid on a university salary scale.

MENTOR SELECTION, MATCHING, TRAINING, AND SUPERVISION

How are mentors selected?

Mentors must apply to the University of Hawaii and go through the normal procedures of hiring, including providing a letter of application, curriculum vitae, and letters of recommendation as well as completing an interview by the committee, which includes special education faculty and mentors. The university hiring process concludes with an interview with three to four panel members, including a professor, faculty member, and mentor.

How are mentors and new teachers matched?

Matches are made based on the following:

- Mentor's expertise and experience with the teacher
- Geographic location of the school
- Equitable caseloads between mentors

Are mentors trained?

Yes, mentors are trained by the following:

- NTC training (Mentor Academies 1 through 6)
- If NTC trainings are not available, Hawaii DOE training is offered, which is a mixture of NTC and Pathwise/ETS.
- Veteran mentors in MUSE provide additional training via the Mentor Handbook

The MUSE mentor induction form specifies various things a new mentor must do:

- Shadow and observe another mentor (five shadow days)
- Read and reflect on three journal articles on induction or mentoring
- Meet with each mentor to review the five components of the Mentor Handbook (five meetings)
- Attend all specified trainings

Who supervises the mentors?

No one supervises the mentors presently. All mentors have been very hardworking, ethical, and responsible. However, as the program has grown, the need to have supervision or incorporate accountability measures is becoming apparent.

SUPPORTS FOR MENTORS

Is professional development available for mentors?

MUSE mentors participate in cognitive coaching trainings and NTC trainings. They participate in monthly forums with a lead mentor. Lead mentors ensure that the program provides quality mentoring and that all the components of an effective mentoring program are present.

Who provides this professional development?

Professional development is provided by DOE personnel, NTC staff, and various lead mentors.

What resources are available for mentors?

Mentors are supported by:

- Monthly mentor forums (based on a mentor needs assessment)
- Coaching partners established via mentor forums
- Professional development opportunities (NTC's annual symposium, special education conferences, cognitive coaching)

Resources for mentors include a MUSE resource library and resources via the university, Internet, and colleagues.

PROGRAM COSTS AND FUNDING

What resources are required for the program?

The cost of the program is $420,000. Resources for the program include a resource library, a place for mentors to meet, program forms for data collection, mileage reimbursements, and Formative Assessment System (from NTC).

- *Mentor training:* This consists of training by the NTC when they are already working in Hawaii, or training by the DOE
  - The Mentor Handbook is provided to new mentors, and all mentors participate in the training of new mentors by setting up meeting dates to review the handbook
  - New mentors are required to shadow each mentor for one to two visits

- *New-teacher orientation:* This is required by the university for new students. Mentors attend and then set up a social seminar for new "in place" teachers to attend.
- *Food for conferences and meeting:* A $100 food budget is provided for monthly teacher seminars.
- *Materials:* Mentors have personal resources as well as resources from the university and MUSE program.
- *Stipends for mentors:* University salary.

- *Substitutes for released time:* One third of teachers are given one full day of released time to observe a veteran teacher in another school.
- *Hardware/audiovisual equipment:* Funds to purchase needed equipment are available; university equipment can be used.

What are the funding sources?

Funding is from the DOE, also known as Felix Funds, and provided through an MOU (memorandum of understanding). Monies are allocated for "special needs." Mentoring is specifically for supporting teachers who serve students with disabilities.

Who requests the funding?

The Special Education Department in the College of Education requests the funding.

PROGRAM EVALUATION

How is the program evaluated?

The program is evaluated in the following ways:

- Teachers provide data four times a year.
- Pre-year, midyear, and post-year surveys are conducted.
- An annual online statewide survey is conducted.
- Mentors provide data on monthly contact logs, including the date, duration of visit, type of contact (face-to-face, e-mail, phone, or seminar), and type of support (emotional, teaching, or UHM program).

Who sees the results of the evaluation?

The following see the results of the evaluations:

- DOE
- Hawaii state school superintendent
- Special education department chair
- College of Education dean

RECRUITMENT, HIRING, AND RETENTION OF NEW STAFF

How many new teachers are recruited and hired?

Special education teachers that enter the program are mentored. Three to four other institutes of higher education offer similar programs, but this is the only program that provides mentoring. All other mentoring that may be provided to teachers is from the DOE. MUSE mentors are trained alongside DOE mentors, and some of its lead mentors have actually trained DOE mentors.

Are there any data that correlate the mentoring program with the retention of new teachers?

Yes, the retention rate (that is, teachers remaining in the field of special education) was 89 percent for 2007–2008.

INDICATORS OF PROGRAM SUCCESS

What are the indicators of program success?

- Teachers in the program have made word-of-mouth requests for a mentor even when they don't qualify for mentoring support.
- Participating teachers have positively evaluated the program.
- Ninety-seven percent of teachers indicated that they were satisfied with the support their mentor provides.
- After sixth months in the program, 56 percent of the participants viewed their role as that of an educator, compared to 20 percent six months earlier.
- Annual online surveys have returned positive evaluations.
- Efficacy of teachers is high.
- In August 2007, 37% of participants needed "very much" emotional support; in May 2008, the number of participants needing "very much" emotional support had decreased to 13 percent.
- According to collaborative logs and goal-setting systems, 86 percent of participants indicated that they felt they had accomplished their indicated goals. The help of others (mentor, colleagues, and professors) was the most frequent response (72 percent) to what contributed to these accomplishments.

8

Collaboration Among Three Institutions to Support New Teachers

T he following description has been written by the director of the program in conjunction with her colleagues and the author. Judgments about the programs are those of the program director and her staff and not the opinion of the author. Unless stated otherwise, figures and information were true for the 2007–2008 school year.

CROSS-CAREER LEARNING COMMUNITIES

ATLANTA, GEORGIA

Gwen Benson, Ph.D.
Office of the Dean
College of Education
Georgia State University
P.O. Box 3980
Atlanta, GA 30302–3980
404–413–8105
gbenson@gsu.edu

The following information was obtained from telephone conversations and e-mail correspondence with Dr. Gwen Benson.

Demographics

Grade Levels	K–12	Urban/Suburban/Rural	Metropolitan, high-needs
Student Population	12,632 (across four metropolitan school systems)	Ethnic Makeup*	African American 56% Asian 6% Caucasian 6% Hispanic 32%
Teacher Population	166 CCLC members in 2007–2008, 356 in 2008–2009	% New Teachers	28% in 2007–2008, 48% in 2008–2009
		Per-Pupil Expenditure	NA

* The statistics available from the district delineated the ethnic makeup as shown.

Program Highlights

Unique Feature of Program	Mentoring through learning communities that offer Critical Friends Group protocols, an online resource called the BRIDGE, and a professional growth plan	Mentoring Is/Is Not Mandated for Certification/Licensing	Mentoring is mandated in Georgia for certain types of alternative programs but not for traditional teacher preparation programs
Collaborative Coaching Is/Is Not a Component	Coaching is a component	Mentors Do/Do Not Evaluate the New Teachers With Whom They Work	Mentors do not evaluate
Cost of Program	Three-year grant for $750,000	Funding	Wachovia Foundation grant to Georgia State University and NCTAF
Mentors Are Full-Time/Part-Time Teachers	Mentors are full-time teachers	Mentor Remuneration	Stipends are paid for active facilitators only
How Long Program Has Been in Existence	Three years	Duration of Program for New Teachers	As long as new teachers want to participate
Higher Education Affiliation	Georgia State University	Program Coordinator	Dr. Gwen Benson

HISTORY

Georgia State University and the National Commission on Teaching and America's Future (NCTAF) cowrote an induction grant to the Wachovia Foundation. They received

$750,000 to be paid over a three-year period to set up Cross-Career Learning Communities (CCLCs) in 12 high-needs schools.

STATE MANDATES

Is mentoring mandated for new teachers?

Yes, mentoring is mandated by the State of Georgia for new teachers engaged in specific alternative route programs, such as the Georgia Teacher Alternative Preparation Program (GATAPP). Mentoring is a part of certification for teacher candidates in GATAPP.

Is mentoring part of certification or licensure?

Yes, mentoring is part of certification and licensure.

Is funding provided to support the mandate?

Funding is not provided by the State of Georgia.

GOALS

The goal of this project is to improve student achievement by addressing the high rates of teacher turnover that undermine teaching quality in low-income and minority schools in four districts in the Atlanta metropolitan area.

PROGRAM DESIGN

What are the components and recommended schedule of the program?

CCLCs have been established in 12 high-needs schools that have a professional development relationship with Georgia State University. The program includes the following:

- A Cross-Career Learning Community in each school with a Critical Friends Group that meets monthly and has a trained facilitator
- An online teacher resource called BRIDGE, available through the University of Georgia (www.teachersbridge.org)
- A professional growth plan (PGP) based on the *Georgia Framework for Accomplished Teaching*, which defines the realm of quality teaching in Georgia

Are there any programs that complement the mentor program?

No, this program of professional learning communities is not specifically connected to other programs in the districts.

Who designed the mentor program?

The CCLCs were designed through a collaborative effort among NCTAF, Georgia State University's College of Education, the University System of Georgia's Board of Regents, the University of Georgia, and PreK–12 partner schools.

PROGRAM ADMINISTRATION

Who coordinates the mentor program?

The program was coordinated by the induction grant manager, who no longer works with the project since funding has ceased. The program will be sustained and coordinated through the dean's office.

How is information communicated to shareholders?

Information is communicated through annual reports, advisory board meeting briefings, and national presentations.

Who coordinates integration of the mentor program with other professional development opportunities and requirements in the schools and district?

Coordination of the program with other professional development opportunities in the schools and district was handled by the different metro system's professional development directors and some school level principals. (The metro system includes school districts that border the City of Atlanta and Fulton County within a 50-mile radius.)

PARTICIPANTS

Who is served?

School facilitators were selected by each school principal; facilitators then created their own CCLC based on school requirements. Schools determine their own requirements, which typically relate to when teachers meet (during school or after school), how many teams are needed, modifications to learning community composition, and so forth. Some schools let the facilitators pick their own members; some schools asked the facilitators to include only new teachers.

Is participation of new teachers voluntary or mandatory?

Each school set its own requirements, but participation was generally voluntary.

Who provides the mentoring/induction?

Principals each selected a person to be trained to become a mentor and facilitator for the CCLC. The training of these facilitators was carried out by grant staff and Critical Friends Group trainers.

What are the criteria for being a mentor?

During the course of the project, no criteria were stipulated. However, it was recommended that criteria be established in the future.

MENTOR RESPONSIBILITIES AND REMUNERATION

What are the job responsibilities of mentors?

Each facilitator was advised to select his or her CCLC members, set up one meeting per month, and arrange meeting agendas and select correct protocols based on the work to be done by the group.

Are mentors required to do peer observation and coaching?

No. The only peer observation and coaching carried out was requested by members of the CCLCs.

Do mentors have full-time classroom teaching responsibilities?

Most CCLC members are teachers; some of the facilitators may not have had classroom duties, depending on the school.

How are mentors available to participate in the program?

CCLC members found time on their own unless they were lucky enough to have an administrator who provided time within the school schedule for them to meet during the day.

Do mentors evaluate new teachers?

No, facilitators do not evaluate new teachers.

Is the mentor–new teacher relationship confidential?

All CCLC members established norms for their group that usually included confidentiality.

Are mentors paid?

Grant stipends were awarded to active facilitators only.

MENTOR SELECTION, MATCHING, TRAINING, AND SUPERVISION

How are mentors selected?

Selection of facilitators was based on school administration recommendations.

How are mentors and new teachers matched?

Matches were made by the building administrators, depending on the administrative guidelines of the schools.

Are mentors trained?

Each facilitator attended a one-week training that included the use of Critical Friends Group protocols and the BRIDGE (teaching resources and an online meeting space) as well as writing a PGP.

Who supervises the mentors?

Facilitators were supervised by their school administration and were encouraged by the grant manager.

SUPPORTS FOR MENTORS

Is professional development available for mentors?

No professional development is provided for facilitators after the initial training.

Who provides this professional development?

NA

What resources are available for mentors?

Facilitators were provided with Critical Friends Group protocols and appropriate training.

PROGRAM COSTS AND FUNDING

What resources are required for the program?

The first three years of the program cost $750,000.

- Materials for a training session for 20 participants cost $200.
- Stipends for facilitators were administered by the districts and ranged from $100 to $200 dollars per day for five days.
- Substitutes were paid between $75 to 100 dollars per day, depending on the district. Teachers were offered one released day per year.
- The full-time project director's salary was $50,000.

What are the funding sources?

Wachovia Foundation funded the first three years, along with Georgia State University. In the fourth year, the funding for the CCLCs, including more facilitators, will be paid by funds from other foundations. The program director and staff at Georgia State University are encouraging the school districts to pay the stipends since Georgia State University will provide the training.

Who requests the funding?

Georgia State University's College of Education requested the new funding.

PROGRAM EVALUATION

How is the program evaluated?

The grant manager and the program evaluator evaluated the program based on self-designed surveys, Web site data, student test scores, principal interviews, anecdotal reports, and so forth.

Who sees the results of the evaluation?

Results were distributed to Georgia State University, NCTAF, the Wachovia Foundation, and anyone else who requested the information.

RECRUITMENT, HIRING, AND RETENTION OF NEW STAFF

How many new teachers are recruited and hired?

Recruitment and hiring are carried out by the school systems.

Are there any data that correlate the mentoring program with the retention of new teachers?

Teachers who have participated in CCLCs remain in teaching longer than those who have not participated.

INDICATORS OF PROGRAM SUCCESS

What are the indicators of program success?

The program's final report shows that the CCLCs are perceived as useful and helpful in creating a positive environment for teachers. The Critical Friends Group protocols are widely used and have been well received by teachers. The PGP, based on the Extended Georgia Framework for Teaching, Modified, is now accepted in a professionally printed format that has been used by many teachers in the Professional Development Schools (PDSs). (PDSs were already a part of a large federal grant to look at the impact of PDSs on student achievement and teacher retention. This is a network of four metro school districts and 15 high-needs schools.) The BRIDGE is becoming recognized not only as a source for teaching resources but also as a suitable space for CCLC meetings. CCLC members continue to feel that the CCLCs are contributing to a collegial and supportive environment.

Statewide testing data show statistically significant improvement in elementary treatment schools contrasted with comparison schools, continued superior achievement in middle schools, and increased achievement in high schools that is not statistically significant. Gains in achievement have traditionally been harder to obtain in upper grades than in lower grades. Whether the gains at the high school level could be retained or extended to the point that they are statistically significant requires further effort and research.

A seventh-grade math teacher summarized the feelings of many new teachers who are members of a CCLC. He wrote,

> My first year as a teacher has been enriched and improved through the many interactions I have had with other members. I have learned new strategies for teaching and classroom management. I have been exposed to new points of view and have had my awareness expanded. And, maybe most importantly, I have made life-long friends. I have often said that I cannot imagine teaching without access to today's technology and, now, I cannot imagine teaching without the support of my [CCLC] friends.

The following extract is taken from the Wachovia/NCTAF Progress Report, provided by the program director.

IMPACT OF CCLC PROJECT

Objectives

This progress report focuses on the implementation of the following long-term objectives:

1. Create learning communities and improve teacher satisfaction in high-needs schools;

2. Increase retention rate of teachers in high-need schools, especially of new teachers;

3. Improve quality of teacher skills in high-need schools; and, ultimately

4. Increase K–12 student achievement and school performance in high-needs schools.

KEY FINDINGS

Supportive Learning Communities

This objective is met through formation of Cross Career Learning Communities (CCLCs) composed of GSU student teachers, GSU new teachers, experienced teachers and GSU university faculty. CCLCs provided both face-to-face and online support to help new teachers and their colleagues enhance their knowledge and skills. Sixty-six CCLC facilitators were trained to support teachers. The 17 active CCLCs with 166 members included 28 new teachers who recently graduated from Georgia State University. Throughout the academic year, teachers consistently reported that CCLCs are collegial and supportive environments.

Increased Retention Rate of Teachers

The retention rate for new teachers who participated in the CCLC project was significantly higher than teachers in participating school districts.

Improved Quality of Teachers in High Needs Schools

Assessments of teacher portfolios using the Georgia Framework for Accomplished Teaching showed improvement of quality of instructional strategies used in high needs schools. Teachers' portfolio submissions far exceed teachers' submission from preceding years. Teachers submitted more differentiated samples of instructional plans, student work, and provided evidence of data-driven monitoring practices.

Significant Gains in Student Achievement

Analysis of treatment and comparison school test data revealed that treatment schools made more significant progress in student achievement based on gains in standardized test scores.

A Mentor's Season

We secure our tethers at temporary piers,

momentarily mooring our fortunes in port,

our preparation for the anticipated and unexpected vicissitudes of seas—

always in transition even as we steadily steer our course through uncertain waters,

seeking interlocutors to guide our travels.

The travails on landscapes take us from the snowy siege of winter

to the ever youthful activity of summer.

In fall we depart—

a dimly illuminated maple leaf,

so steady, so secure,

nurtured on the solid tree—

its attachment seemingly permanent and enduring.

Slowly it begins to be mentorly released,

the maple tree tugging as if to prevent it from taking that journey downward,

protecting it from a world unknown.

The vermillion leaf pirouettes,

exhilarated by the gentle wind wisps carrying it aloft,

frightened by the battering, blustering gusts

driving it groundward.

Resting among the varicolored maple, oak, and birch leaves,

its relatives and soulmates,

the leaf faces the azure sky,

severed from, yet still connected to, the tree,

yearning for regenerative recovery and discovery—

a springtime of renewal, hope, and new beginnings.

—David G. Hodgdon,
Assistant Superintendent of Curriculum and Instruction
Monadnock Regional School District, New Hampshire
Written for colleagues at the end of the summer professional
development about mentoring new teachers, July 10, 2003

PART III

Now What?

You know about the needs of new teachers and the ways that comprehensive mentoring supports them. You've familiarized yourself with the 18 different programs of mentoring and induction described in Part II. You are now ready to develop your own program or assess and revise an existing one.

9

Developing a Comprehensive Mentoring Program

While the number of mentoring programs has increased significantly in recent years, the challenge of creating sustainable comprehensive programs with such observable benefits as higher teacher retention, better instruction for all students, and cost savings for schools remains strong. In particular, our understanding of and expectations for mentoring need to expand to better address the crisis at hand. Susan Moore Johnson, who is doing a long-term, in-depth study of the next generation of teachers, writes of the importance of opportunities for new teachers to be observed and have conversations with colleagues about their practice:

> We found that, while almost all of our respondents had been assigned paid mentors, these pairings were often inappropriate (different subjects, grades, or even schools), personalities seldom clicked, and schedules rarely allowed for observing each other's classes (Kardos et al., 2001). (Johnson & Birkeland, 2002, pp. 43–44)

Mentoring that includes collaborative coaching addresses these issues. Furthermore, in my experience, mentoring with collaborative coaching not only benefits new teachers, but also has the potential to impact experienced staff and possibly the whole school or district.

If you are starting a new program, ideally you will have a year to:

- Form a steering committee to research and plan your program
- Collaborate with key shareholders
- Develop selection criteria for mentors and a matching process
- Plan professional development for mentors before they begin, as well as schedule ongoing support and follow-up sessions for them throughout the school year
- Create or adapt orientation materials for new teachers
- Plan how the program will be shared with the rest of the school community
- Decide how the program will be evaluated, formatively and summatively

However, "ideal" is often not within your grasp. Perhaps you don't believe you can wait a year to implement a program because you feel the urgency of doing something for the people you've just hired. Maybe others are waiting for a program to be established before they'll come on board. Perhaps you don't have the resources in time, personnel, or funds you need to do the job ideally. Get started somehow and plan on using your first year as a pilot, expecting that you'll be able to devote more time next year to researching and revising your plans.

GETTING STARTED

As you read about the programs in Part II, did you find yourself envisioning one of them in your district? Maybe some of the things you read sparked ideas you would like to explore. As you consider all of the information presented, think about what you want to achieve through your comprehensive mentoring program. Set the goals that you believe are important for your program. Think about the structures that you believe will have the most impact on the success of your new teachers, and then work to find ways to make them possible. Remember, what you are able to achieve is not necessarily a function of whether your state mandates and funds mentoring. State mandates address a variety of issues and state funding varies enormously. While you need to meet mandates, they may not be sufficient to meet your goals.

The graphic on page 192 portrays a comprehensive mentoring program that supports new teachers. Student learning and achievement are at the center, surrounded by curriculum, instruction, and assessment. The major inputs for a comprehensive mentoring program are school community support, mentoring and coaching, and content-specific professional development. Seven program components are shown:

1. Involvement of key shareholders and members of the school community

2. Administrator commitment and backing

3. Selection process and criteria for mentor teachers

4. New teacher and mentor matching method

5. Training and support of new teachers and their mentors

6. Sustaining policies and procedures

7. Mentoring program evaluation

BREADTH AND DEPTH

The following rubric (page 193) provides one way to assess the breadth and depth of your program. Use it to get ideas for your program or parts of it. You may have other things that you want to include in your comprehensive mentoring program as a result of reading about the programs in this book.

The Continuum of High-Quality Mentoring and Induction Practices has recently been released by the National Content Center for Teacher Quality (see Appendix F).

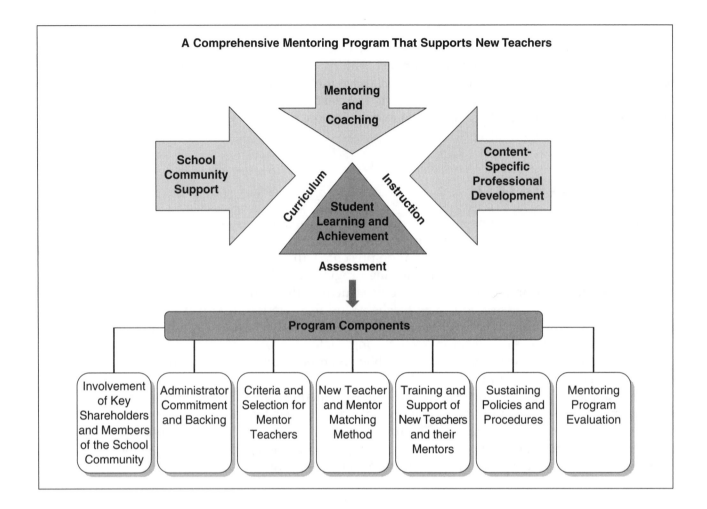

A Comprehensive Mentoring Program That Supports New Teachers

LOOKING AT AN EXISTING PROGRAM

Revising an existing program can be more complicated than starting anew. Existing practices, attitudes, and beliefs can be hard to examine objectively. You need to be clear about what is driving your review: a change in resources, concerns about program effectiveness, a desire to expand a good but limited program, a change in state mandates, or possibly something unique to your district. If possible, you should work with all shareholders to review and if necessary revise your goals, and then assess your existing practices in light of those goals. Achieving consensus at this stage will greatly enhance your chances of success further along.

Early in your review you will need to examine not only how you have defined mentoring, but also how you have actually practiced mentoring. As I have emphasized, mentoring with coaching is an essential component of a sustainable comprehensive mentoring program. This structured, definable practice may or may not be similar to the mentoring occurring in your district. Teachers or educators who have mentored in the past may well believe that they know the role. Nevertheless, you need to be assured that they have the capacity to participate as mentors in a comprehensive mentoring program. You could assess their skills, or ask them to do so anonymously, using the coaching rubric starting on page 198. Their knowledge and skills, and their ability to use them in a variety of situations, are crucial to the success of your program.

Developing Effective, Comprehensive Mentoring Programs

Criteria for Success	1 Emerging	2 Basic	3 Proficient	4 Sustainable
Involvement of Key Shareholders and Members of the School Community	A mentoring program is designed and planned by a few individuals; it could emerge from the "top down" or from the "bottom up." Teachers and other staff expect that new teachers will be assigned mentors, so no one else plans to help them.	Teachers and administrators work together to design the mentoring program. Teachers and other staff reach out to new teachers and respond to questions or requests for help.	Teachers and administrators representing all grade levels as well as school committee members are involved in designing and planning the mentoring program. Teachers and other staff collaborate with new teachers on curriculum and school-wide endeavors.	Teachers and administrators representing all grade levels as well as teachers' association and school committee members are involved in designing and planning the mentoring program. A multi-representative design team continually assesses the program, identifies what's working and not working, and makes changes along the way. Teachers and other staff meet regularly to do lesson study, work on common formative assessment, and analyze student work. New teachers are part of the groups of teachers and staff who meet, and their opinions are sought.
Administrator Support and Commitment	Principals show their support of new teachers by "walking them through" the new-teacher handbook and by providing an adequate classroom and appropriate furniture and supplies.	Principals show their support of new teachers by "walking them through" the new-teacher handbook and by providing an adequate classroom and appropriate furniture and supplies. Principals trust that the mentors will support the new teachers and honor confidentiality by not asking mentors how their new teacher is doing.	Principals show their support of new teachers by "walking them through" the new-teacher handbook and providing an adequate classroom and appropriate furniture and supplies. Principals trust that the mentors will support the new teachers and honor confidentiality by not asking mentors how their new teacher is doing. Principals refrain from assigning new teachers the most difficult class assignments and number of preparations and from asking them to lead extracurricular activities for their first few years. Principals schedule common preparation periods for new teachers and their mentors.	Principals show their support of new teachers by "walking them through" the new teacher handbook and providing an adequate classroom and appropriate furniture and supplies. Principals trust that the mentors will support the new teachers and honor confidentiality by not asking mentors how their new teacher is doing. Principals refrain from assigning new teachers the most difficult class assignments and number of preparations and from asking them to lead extracurricular activities for their first few years. Principals schedule common preparation periods for new teachers and their mentors. Principals meet regularly with new teachers, outside the times they formally evaluate them, to discuss school vision and major initiatives and to find out what the new teachers think

(Continued)

(Continued)

Criteria for Success	1 Emerging	2 Basic	3 Proficient	4 Sustainable
				about their work and need to be effective. Principals lessen the duties of new teachers and mentors so that they have time to meet each week. They provide coverage so that the new teachers can observe their mentors and other teachers and so that the mentors can observe the new teachers.
Selection Process and Criteria for Mentor Teachers	No criteria exist. Building principals handpick mentor teachers.	Mentors volunteer and are selected by a mentoring program committee. No criteria exist.	Criteria for selecting mentor teachers are identified. A mentoring program committee selects mentors, with input from the building principal, based on identified criteria.	Criteria for selecting mentor teachers are identified. A mentoring program committee selects mentors, with input from the building principal, based on identified criteria. Potential mentors complete an application and supply recommendations from colleagues.
New Teacher and Mentor Matches	Mentors and new teachers are matched without consideration of grade level, content area, or geographic location.	Mentors and new teachers are matched (to the degree possible) according to grade level and content area.	Mentors and new teachers are matched (to the degree possible) according to grade level and content area. Building principals contribute to the matching process by considering the compatibility of the individual styles of mentors and new teachers.	Mentors and new teachers are matched (to the degree possible) according to grade level and content area. Building principals contribute to the matching process by considering the compatibility of the individual styles of mentors and new teachers. A procedure exists such that, in the event that matches do not work, both parties are "held harmless" and a new match is made.
Professional Development and Training of New Teachers and Their Mentors	Mentor training consists of disseminating and "walking through" the new-teacher handbook.	An orientation session is held for mentors to outline roles and responsibilities. One or two days of mentor training are	An orientation session is held for mentors and new teachers to outline roles and responsibilities. Three to four days of mentor training are provided to all mentor teachers (one to two days prior to the start of the school year and two	An orientation session is held for mentors and new teachers to outline roles and responsibilities. New teachers participate, along with their mentors, in some of the mentor training that occurs before and throughout the school year. Three to four days of mentor training are provided to all mentor teachers

provided to all mentor teachers prior to the start of the school year. Training covers the qualities of effective mentors, needs of new teachers, communication and questioning skills, and a demonstration of collaborative coaching. Follow up mentor training sessions are not provided. New teachers are encouraged to participate in professional development opportunities, but those opportunities are idiosyncratic and not part of a comprehensive professional development plan.	to three days throughout the school year); training covers the qualities of effective mentors, needs of new teachers, active listening and questioning skills, collaborative coaching, and data collection techniques. New teachers and mentors are familiarized with technological resources that enhance their work together as well as their professional practice. New teachers are oriented to school-wide endeavors and supported with additional professional development that is part of a yearlong comprehensive professional development plan.	(one to two days prior to the start of the school year and two to three days throughout the school year); training covers the needs of new teachers, effective listening and questioning skills, collaborative coaching, data collection techniques, and working with teaching standards and curriculum frameworks to enhance ability to collaborate with new teachers. Mentor and new teacher pairs are provided with on-site coaching and continued training and support throughout the year. New teachers and mentors are familiarized with technological resources that enhance their work together as well as their professional practice, and they are provided with the hardware they need to utilize these resources. New teachers are oriented to school-wide endeavors and supported with additional professional development that is part of a three-year comprehensive professional development plan.

(Continued)

Criteria for Success	1 Emerging	2 Basic	3 Proficient	4 Sustainable
Supporting Policies and Procedures	There are no policies in place to support the mentoring program. However, the district has decided to implement a mentoring program of some sort.	A general set of guidelines is developed to support the mentoring program. Incentives are provided for mentor teachers. Mentors and new teachers have to "catch as catch can" regarding finding time to meet. Orientation materials are developed and dates for orientation of mentors and new teachers are scheduled. A basic curriculum for training mentor teachers is developed and the training is scheduled.	A specific set of guidelines is developed to support the mentoring program. Incentives are provided for mentor teachers. Structures are in place to provide mentors and new teachers with time during the school day to meet and visit each other's classroom. Orientation materials are developed, and dates for the orientation of mentors and new teachers are scheduled. A comprehensive curriculum for training mentors and new teachers is developed and the training is scheduled.	A specific set of guidelines is developed to support the mentoring program. Incentives are provided for mentor teachers. Structures are in place to provide mentors and new teachers with time during the school day to meet and visit each other's classroom. The school schedule provides regular professional development time during the school day for all teachers, allowing new teachers to link with and learn from other colleagues. New teachers, mentors, and all staff are encouraged to participate in local, regional, state, or nationwide professional organizations and programs through released time and travel reimbursement. Orientation materials are developed, and dates for the orientation of mentors and new teachers are scheduled. A comprehensive curriculum for training mentors and new teachers is developed and the training is scheduled.

Program Assessment and Evaluation	There is no evaluation of the mentoring program.	Evaluation of the mentoring program focuses only on participant satisfaction and enjoyment.	The impact of mentor training on supporting mentors to successfully fulfill their roles is assessed. A survey of new teachers' needs is conducted and used to evaluate how well the mentoring program serves those needs. Mentor teachers self-assess their performance as mentor teachers and coaches. Mentor teachers reflect on the impact of their mentoring on their own practice. A rubric identifying criteria for the success of a comprehensive mentoring program is used to assess the efficacy of the mentoring program. All of the data are analyzed and used to continually revise and improve the program.	The impact of mentor training on supporting mentors to successfully fulfill their roles is assessed. A survey of new teachers' needs is conducted and used to evaluate how well the mentoring program serves those needs. Mentor teachers self-assess their performance as mentor teachers and coaches. Mentor teachers reflect on the impact of their mentoring on their own practice. New teachers conduct self-assessment of their teaching against clearly defined teaching competencies. A rubric identifying criteria for success of a comprehensive mentoring program is used to assess the efficacy of the mentoring program. The mentoring program committee engages in an ongoing mentoring program evaluation process that provides opportunities to identify key program evaluation questions, data sources, baseline data requirements, and relevant evaluation strategies and tools.

SOURCE: Adapted from Dunne, K., & Villani, S. (2007). *Mentoring new teachers through collaborative coaching: Linking teacher and student learning.* Thousand Oaks, CA: Corwin.

Classroom Coaching Performance Rubric

	1 Emerging	2 Maintaining	3 Sustaining	4 Adaptive
Data Gathering and Coaching Observation	• Classroom data are subjective (i.e., based on the coach's judgment and inference).	• Classroom data are mostly objective (i.e., measurable and observable, though with some of the coach's judgment or inference included).	• Classroom data are objective (i.e., measurable and observable).	• Classroom data are objective (i.e., measured and observable) and include questions to elicit the teacher's intentions (at particular moments of the lesson) based upon the data gathered.
	• Classroom data are based on what the coach is interested in observing.	• Classroom data are mostly based on what was agreed upon between the coach and teacher during the planning conversation. Additional data are recorded by the coach based on the coach's opinion of what was important to gather.	• Classroom data are based on what was agreed upon between the coach and teacher during the planning conversation.	• Classroom data are based on what was agreed upon between the coach and teacher during the planning conversation and include additional data the coach is able to gather that pertain to issues that had been discussed and agreed to by the coach and the teacher during other planning/reflecting conversations.
	• Classroom data are not shared with the teacher.	• Classroom data are not shared with the teacher until the reflecting conversation.	• A written copy of the classroom data is provided to the teacher immediately following the coaching observation.	• A copy of the classroom data is provided in a variety of formats (e.g., written, audio, and/or video) to the teacher immediately following the coaching observation.

	1 Emerging	2 Maintaining	3 Sustaining	4 Adaptive
Questioning: The Reflecting Conversation	• Coach begins the reflecting conversation with her or his interpretation of what occurred during the coaching observation.	• Coach begins the reflecting conversation with a question that elicits the teacher's perspective of how the lesson went and then adds her or his opinion of how the lesson went.	• Coach begins the reflecting conversation with a question that elicits the teacher's perspective of how the lesson went.	• Teacher begins the reflecting conversation by reflecting on how she or he thought the lesson went.

	1 Emerging	2 Maintaining	3 Sustaining	4 Adaptive
	• Coach frames and poses questions that are based on the coach's beliefs and values about what happened or should have happened during the lesson.	• Coach frames and poses questions that prompt the teacher to examine the data and how they compare with what the teacher intended.	• Coach and teacher cocreate questions that prompt the teacher to examine the data and how they compare with what the teacher intended and to identify what she or he would do the same or differently next time and why.	• Teacher identifies and responds to questions that prompt her or him to examine the data and how they compare with what the teacher intended and to identify what she or he would do the same or differently next time and why.
	• Coach seldom asks questions that focus on student learning.	• Coach poses questions that ask the teacher to identify what the students learned.	• Coach and teacher cocreate questions that ask teacher to identify what students have learned and what evidence the teacher has of student learning.	• Teacher shares evidence that demonstrates student learning and any student misconceptions that may exist.
			• Coach asks questions that prompt the teacher to begin planning for the next lesson.	• Teacher identifies what she or he will do next with these students based on the classroom data and the teacher's own reflections.

	1 Emerging	2 Maintaining	3 Sustaining	4 Adaptive
Analysis of and Response to Teacher Reflection	• Coach assumes what teacher responses mean without checking assumptions or paraphrasing.	• Coach inconsistently applies the norms of pausing, paraphrasing, and probing when responding to the teacher's reflections.	• Coach consistently applies the norms of pausing, paraphrasing and probing when responding to the teacher's reflections.	• Coach consistently applies all seven norms of collaboration in conversations with the teacher.
	• Coach accepts vague responses without probing for specificity.	• Coach occasionally accepts vague responses without probing for specificity.	• Coach consistently probes for specificity around vague responses by the teacher.	• Coach consistently probes for specificity around vague responses by the teacher.

(Continued)

(Continued)

	1 Emerging	2 Maintaining	3 Sustaining	4 Adaptive
	• Coach advocates for her or his perspective without inquiring into teacher's perspective. • Coach uses only her or his preferred approach to coaching without consideration of the teacher's need for structure.	• Coach inconsistently engages in inquiry first and advocacy second when talking with teacher about how the teacher will apply learning from one lesson to the next. • Coach modifies coaching approach to match the teacher's need for structure some of the time.	• Coach consistently starts with inquiry first and advocacy second when talking with teacher about how the teacher will apply learnings from one lesson to the next. • Coach consistently modifies coaching approach to match the teacher's need for structure.	• Coach consistently uses inquiry when talking with teacher about how the teachers will apply learning from one lesson to the next. • Coach consistently modifies coaching approach to match the teacher's need for structure.
Engaging With Content	• Coach asks questions that elicit responses about the content goals of the lesson without reference to content/curriculum standards. • Coach references content-based tools and curriculum without using them with the teacher.	• Coach asks questions that elicit responses about the content goals of the lesson and about how those goals connect with content/curriculum standards. • Coach uses at least one content-based tool and one curriculum unit in coach's work with the teacher.	• Coach asks questions and provides examples of how to connect lesson/unit plans to content/curriculm standards. • Coach consistently uses most of the content-based tools and curriculum in the coach's work with the teacher.	• Coach conducts demonstration lessons that provide examples of content-specific instruction and assessment that connect to content/curriculum standards. • Coach consistently uses all of the content-based tools and curriculum in the coach's work with the teacher.

SOURCE: From *Mentoring New Teachers Through Collaborative Coaching: Facilitation and Training Guide*, 2007, by Kathy Dunne and Susan Villani. Reprinted with permission from WestEd.

The process of completing this rubric may alert mentors to things they had not previously considered. It may also highlight for them areas where they would benefit from additional professional development and support. The results of mentors' self-assessments can direct you as you plan professional development for current and future mentors.

21 STEPS TOWARD A COMPREHENSIVE MENTORING PROGRAM

The following 21 steps are offered whether you are establishing a new program or reviewing and revising an existing one. They summarize key actions needed in your quest to ever improve your support of new and experienced teachers.

1. Set goals for your comprehensive mentoring program. What do you want to accomplish?

2. Identify the new teachers who will be included in your program. Whom do you want to serve: beginning teachers; teachers new to your district; teachers who have changed grade level, subject area, or specialization; teachers returning to the profession after being absent for several or more years?

3. Identify your resources: money, other forms of compensation, and, most important, personnel.

4. Identify a coordinator or steering committee. Determine whether the committee is advisory or will have decision-making responsibilities.

5. Consider the models in Part II and determine if any of them address your goals in feasible ways. Continually research ways to provide professional development that supports new and experienced teachers.

6. Formulate a plan to pilot.

7. Establish a timeline for the implementation of your plan.

8. Meet with school administrators, teachers' association leadership, and the school committee or board to make the case for the program.

9. Revise your plan and timeline based on the input of the key shareholders, if necessary.

10. Communicate the beginning of your program with all school staff and the community, making sure they understand their roles in supporting new teachers.

11. Establish criteria and an application process for selecting mentors in the spring. Select extra mentors for unanticipated summer and last-minute hiring.

12. Create handbooks for mentors and new teachers that include the goals of the program, the expectations for participation by mentors and new teachers, and the schedule of meetings and professional development activities. Including other resource materials will increase the likelihood that it will be referred to throughout the school year.

13. Provide initial and ongoing professional development for mentors.

14. Plan and offer new-teacher orientation and ongoing professional development.

15. Form cohort groups of mentors and of new teachers and schedule periodic meetings for them throughout the school year.

16. Plan professional development for new teachers and mentors together.

17. Develop ways to evaluate your program. What will be your indicators of success? Do you have the capacity to track teacher hiring and retention? Do you have a way to assess professional development that transcends participant satisfaction? Is there any way you can assess whether the comprehensive mentoring results in heightened student achievement?

18. Begin collecting data when your program starts, and collect them periodically throughout the year. Determine who will analyze the data and how it will be communicated to the administration, staff, and larger school community.

19. Revise your program based on your analysis of the evaluations and your own perceptions.

20. Begin year two with increased confidence in the fit of your program to your school district's needs and resources.

21. Honor your mentors and the rest of the school community, who are passing the torch and welcoming new colleagues into the profession. Celebrate the induction of your new teachers into your school and district communities.

CELEBRATE

Charts and lists can be useful, but only in the service of something more. Your focus is the needs of your new teachers and how to best develop their skills, nourish their hopes, allay their fears, and expand their vision. So, amid all the hard work, remember to have some fun and celebrate what you're doing. After all, what could be more gratifying than ushering new teachers into the profession in ways that will heighten their effectiveness as teachers for the benefit of all students?

Appendices

Ways Principals Support New Teachers and Their Mentors

1. Working with others to develop and support a comprehensive mentoring program in the school or district

2. Encouraging master teachers to consider becoming mentors, understanding that there are criteria and process for mentor selection and training

3. Making sure that new teachers are not given the most difficult teaching assignments, the most challenging schedule, or many different class preparations

4. Supporting new teachers and mentors with:
   a. Common planning time
   b. Released time for observations and conferencing
   c. Remuneration for mentors

5. Matching mentors with partners as soon as possible

6. Involving the faculty and staff in supporting new teachers and understanding the comprehensive mentoring program in the district.

7. Encouraging new teachers to focus on teaching the first year or two and refrain from coaching and extracurricular activities

8. Respecting the confidentiality of the mentoring relationship

9. Anticipating the additional challenges faced by a diverse teaching staff and implementing supports

10. Involving families in supporting new teachers

11. Telling prospective teachers about the district's comprehensive mentoring program during interviews

12. Supporting mentors who want to advance their skills as teacher leaders

Map of State Induction Programs and Mentoring for New and Beginning Teachers

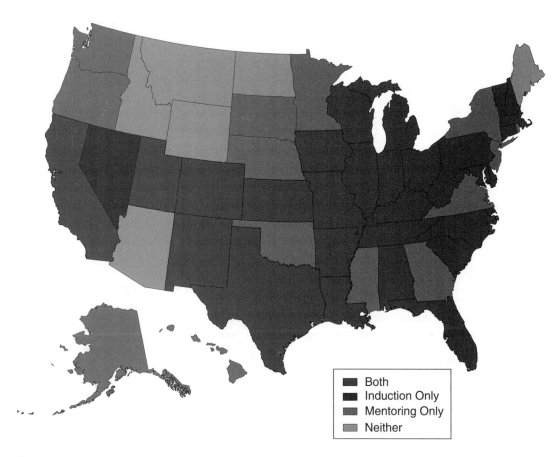

Both
Induction Only
Mentoring Only
Neither

Guam has both an Induction Program and Mentoring.
Puerto Rico has an Induction Program.
American Samoa and the Virgin Islands have neither Induction Programs nor Mentoring.

Note: There is no induction program for regularly licensed teachers in the state of Nevada, but there is a traning and orientation requirement for conditionally licensed teachers.

Copyright © by NCTAF. Used with permission.

Appendix C

Vicksburg Community Schools

Mentor Training Components and Expectations

Relating Year 1	Supporting Year 1	Assessing Years 2+3	Coaching/Guiding Years 2+3
Knowledge base Trust building Stages of concern Communication Personality styles	Knowledge base Induction strategies Resources Policies and regulations Professional development opportunities	Knowledge base Standards for new teachers Curriculum standards Data collection and analysis Learning styles Teacher development stages	Knowledge base Coaching/supervision models Problem solving Diversity Mentoring models Facilitation principles Curriculum Learning styles
Skills/application Empathy Time management Technology	Skills/application Networking Advocacy Celebration Sharing Collaboration	Skills/application Observations Change agentry Listening System expectations	Skills/application Observation Feedback Videotaping Goal setting Facilitation of self-assessment
Reflection topics Self-knowledge Beliefs/philosophy Relationship	Reflection topics Attitude and style Professionalism	Reflection topics Relevance of data Efficacy of analysis Decisions regarding modification and change	Reflection topics Evidence of growth Outcomes
Follow-through, year 1 Contact logs Six informal observations (keep a positive note and complete instructional skills/classroom management checklists for each) E-mails Journal entries Four days of training Five bimonthly mentor meetings		Follow-through, year 2 Contact logs Six formal observations with data, pre and post conferences Discussion outline: Curriculum, instruction skills, and cooperative learning classes Training day as needed Five bimonthly meetings	Follow-through, year 3 Contact logs Discussion outline: Classroom assessment data Six formal observations with data, pre and post conferences Training day as needed Five bimonthly meetings

Appendix D

NNECN Program Resources for Science and Mathematics Teachers

Science Resources Provided to Science Mentors and Mentees

Benchmarks for Science Literacy

How Students Learn: Science in the Classroom

National Science Education Standards

Science Curriculum Topic Study: Bridging the Gap Between Classroom and Practice

Science for All Americans

The Teaching Gap

Additional Science Resources Provided to Science Mentors

Atlas of Science Literacy

Classroom Assessment and the National Science Education Standards

How People Learn

Inquiry in the National Science Education Standards

Making Sense of Secondary Science

Science Matters: Achieving Science Literacy

Standards in the Classroom

Tips for the Science Teacher

Uncovering Student Ideas in Science

Weaving Continuous Assessment and Inquiry

Mathematics Resources Provided to Mathematics Mentors and Mentees

Benchmarks for Science Literacy

How Students Learn: Mathematics in the Classroom

Mathematics Curriculum Topic Study: Bridging the Gap Between Classroom and Practice

Principles and Standards for School Mathematics

Science for All Americans

The Teaching Gap

Additional Mathematics Resources Provided to Mathematics Mentors

Atlas of Science Literacy

Beyond Numeracy

How People Learn

NCTM Classroom Assessment Guide

NCTM Lessons Learned From Research

NCTM Research Ideas for the Classroom

A Research Companion to Principles and Standards

Standards in the Classroom

Tips for the Mathematics Teacher

General Resources Provided to Mentors

Classroom Instruction That Works

Enhancing Professional Practice: A Framework for Teaching

Mentoring Matters

Mentoring New Teachers

The Mentoring Year

Training Mentors Is Not Enough

General Resources Provided to Mentees

Classroom Instruction That Works

Enhancing Professional Practice: A Framework for Teaching

The First Days of School

Professional Development and Leadership Resources for Mentors

Designing Professional Development for Teachers of Science and Mathematics

Developing Teacher Leaders

Leading Every Day

Lesson Study: A Handbook of Teacher-Led Instructional Change

Mathematics Assessment: Cases and Discussion Questions (NCTM).

Professional Learning Communities at Work

Whole Faculty Study Groups

Windows on Mathematics Cases

Appendix E

PROGRAM DESCRIPTION TEMPLATE

Program name:
Director:
Mailing address:

Telephone number:
E-mail address:

Demographics

Grade Levels		Urban/Suburban/Rural	
Student Population		Ethnic Makeup	
Teacher Population		% New Teachers	
		Per-Pupil Expenditure	

Program Highlights

Unique Feature of Program		Mentoring Is/Is Not Mandated for Certification/Licensing	
Coaching Is/Is Not a Component		Mentors Do/Do Not Evaluate the New Teachers With Whom They Work	
Cost of Program		Funding	
Mentors Are Full-Time/Part-Time Teachers		Mentor Remuneration	
How Long Program Has Been in Existence		Duration of Program for New Teachers	
Higher Education Affiliation		Program Coordinator	

HISTORY

STATE MANDATES

Is mentoring mandated for new teachers?
Is mentoring part of certification or licensure?
Is funding provided to support the mandate?

GOALS

PROGRAM DESIGN

What are the components and recommended schedule of the program?

Are there any programs that complement the mentoring program?

Who designed the mentoring program?

PROGRAM ADMINISTRATION

Who coordinates the mentoring program?

How is information communicated to shareholders?

Who coordinates integration of the mentoring program with other professional development opportunities and requirements in the schools or district?

PARTICIPANTS

Who is served?

Is participation of new teachers voluntary or mandatory?

Who provides the mentoring/induction?

What are the criteria for being a mentor?

MENTOR RESPONSIBILITIES AND REMUNERATION

What are the job responsibilities of mentors?

Are mentors required to do peer observation and coaching?

Do mentors have full-time classroom teaching responsibilities?

How are mentors available to participate in the program?

Do mentors evaluate new teachers?

Is the mentor–new teacher relationship confidential?

Are mentors paid?

MENTOR SELECTION, MATCHING, TRAINING, AND SUPERVISION

How are mentors selected?

How are mentors and new teachers matched?

Are mentors trained?

Who supervises the mentors?

SUPPORTS FOR MENTORS

Is professional development available for mentors?

Who provides this professional development?

What resources are available for mentors?

PROGRAM COSTS AND FUNDING

What resources are required for the program?

- Mentor training?
- New-teacher orientation?
- Food for conferences and meetings?
- Materials?
- Stipends for mentors?
- Substitutes for released time?
- The project director's salary, or the portion related to mentoring?
- Hardware/audiovisual equipment?

What are the funding sources?

Who requests the funding?

PROGRAM EVALUATION

How is the program evaluated?

Who sees the results of the evaluation?

RECRUITMENT, HIRING, AND RETENTION OF NEW STAFF

How many new teachers are recruited and hired?

Are there any data that correlate the mentoring program with the retention of new teachers?

INDICATORS OF PROGRAM SUCCESS

What are the indicators of program success?

Continuum of High-Quality Mentoring and Induction Practices

National Content Center on Teacher Quality

INTRODUCTION

The Continuum of High-Quality Mentoring and Induction Practices is intended to help guide schools and districts in identifying the current level of practice of their induction and mentoring program as emerging, developing, or integrating. Identification of practices will inform the additional planning and design needed to strive toward implementing a high-quality mentoring and induction program.

This continuum is designed around nine specific elements identified by the Illinois Induction Policy Team (Illinois New Teacher Collaborative, 2008). Those elements were adapted with permission from the New Teacher Center (2007) as being essential for establishing a high-quality program that will support teacher retention, teacher development, and enhanced school improvement. This tool is intended to help initiate and support collaboration and conversation among administrators, beginning teachers, mentors, and other key stakeholders in assessing the components of a district induction program and in developing clearly articulated goals and a culture of shared responsibility around enhancing and developing a comprehensive, high-quality teacher induction program.

EMERGING PRACTICE

An induction program at the emerging level of practice provides limited support and training for new teachers and mentors. Although there is promise of growing the current program into something more robust, mentors, school administrators, and new teachers at this level receive only basic professional development on specific induction practices, often as a onetime event. The components of an emerging program exist as separate entities. At this stage, there is limited understanding and involvement by school administrators and limited buy-in from key stakeholders. Program feedback is not collected.

DEVELOPING PRACTICE

An induction program at the developing level of practice includes increased support and training for new teachers, mentors, and school administrators. Professional development at this stage is ongoing but still mainly considered "one size fits all." The separate components of a developing program are beginning to combine. At this level, there is support and buy-in of the induction program from all stakeholders, and some program improvements are made through limited data collection and evaluation.

INTEGRATING PRACTICE

An induction program at the integrating level of practice provides comprehensive and integrated training and support for new teachers, mentors, and school administrators. In its professional development for mentors and new teachers, this level of program includes ways of differentiating for different kinds of teachers new to the profession. An integrating program facilitates the complex incorporation of all of the components and engages in a cycle of continuous improvement based on data collection and evaluation. All stakeholders support the continuous professional growth and improved classroom practices of new teachers through robust advocacy for comprehensive induction and mentoring. An integrating program engages in a cycle of continuous improvement based on data collection and evaluation.

SUMMARY

1. Rigorous Mentor Selection
   - Specific criteria and standards for mentor selection are clearly articulated and followed.
   - Mentors are experienced teachers who have documented teaching and leadership skills and current knowledge of beginning teacher development.
   - Mentors are matched to new teachers based on location and grade-level or content-area expertise.

How does this contribute to a high-quality induction program?

A lack of strong criteria and a formal and rigorous selection process may lead to the risk of mentors selected based more on availability or seniority rather than their qualifications to engage in meaningful interactions with beginning teachers. When selecting mentors, criteria may include evidence of outstanding teaching practice, strong intra- and interpersonal skills, experience with adult learners, respect of peers, and knowledge of professional development.

2. Ongoing Professional Development and Support for Mentors
   - Mentors receive ongoing professional development and support.
   - Mentors participate in professional development around mentoring and induction requirements and participate in professional learning communities with other mentors.
   - Mentors in the district receive compensation and a reduced workload commensurate with their roles and responsibilities.

How does this contribute to a high-quality induction program?

Many mentors are also surprised to find that translating knowledge to students is not the same as translating knowledge about effective practice to a colleague who is new to the field. High-quality and ongoing training, as well as a strong professional learning community of other mentors and supportive staff, are needed to help mentors develop the skills to identify and translate the elements of effective teaching to beginning teachers.

3. Sanctioned Time for Mentor-Teacher Interactions
   - Mentor–new teacher interactions are regular and of a sufficient length.
   - Mentors and new teachers receive adequate release time for interaction and new teacher development.

How does this contribute to a high-quality induction program?

Mentors need sanctioned time to focus on beginning teacher development, and it is recommended that they spend 1.25 to 2.5 hours per week with new teachers to allow for the most rigorous mentoring activities. That time should be protected by all teachers and administrators.

   4. Multi-year Mentoring
      • The mentoring program has clearly defined and articulated long-term goals.
      • Mentoring and induction are such a deeply engrained part of the district and school culture that its requirements are fully integrated into other district/ school operations.
      • The mentoring program supports teachers through their first year and may continue up to year 5 of their teaching.

How does this contribute to a high-quality induction program?

Because the research suggests that the deepest learning about instruction (through mentoring) happens during the second and third years of teaching, mentoring should be intensive and ongoing (for at least two years) in order to improve teacher practice and consequently student achievement.

   5. Intensive and Specific Guidance Moving Teaching Practice Forward
      • Mentors provide new teachers with feedback on practice.
      • Mentors draw on professional teaching and content-area standards to provide new teachers with concrete next steps.
      • Mentors demonstrate effective teaching practices in their own practice.

How does this contribute to a high-quality induction program?

In order to focus on supporting instructional growth and improvements to practices, mentors need training and support to draw upon professional teaching standards and appropriate content-area standards. Rather than just providing emotional and logistical kinds of supports, the mentor provides deeper support around instruction and effective practice.

   6. Professional Teaching Standards and Data-Driven Conversations
      • Mentors use formative assessment tools to help new teachers improve practice.
      • These assessment tools are aligned to state professional standards.
      • Mentors observe new teachers and collect other artifacts demonstrating professional skills to help new teachers improve practice.
      • New teachers have the opportunity to observe experienced teachers and reflect on effective practice.

How does this contribute to a high-quality induction program?

As a parallel to student learning, new teacher learning should be data driven and standards based, and the feedback they receive must be grounded in evidence about their practice. This includes using data and information gathered through classroom observations and analysis of student work. Using professional teaching standards and data to guide the conversations between a mentor and new teacher about various components of classroom practice ensures a strong structure for focusing on continuous instructional growth.

7. Ongoing Beginning Teacher Professional Development
   - The district provides differentiated induction based on the background of new teachers (e.g., teachers new to the district, teachers new to the profession, teachers with alternate certification).
   - The district provides differentiated professional development opportunities.
   - Beginning teacher professional development aligns with professional teaching standards, content standards, and research.
   - Beginning teacher professional development addresses challenges common to the district/school/classroom context.
   - New teachers meet regularly to network, reflect, and collaborate.

How does this contribute to a high-quality induction program?

Because new teachers are in a unique developmental phase, "one-size-fits-all" workshops or trainings will not meet their needs as developing professionals. Beginning teachers benefit from being a part of a cohesive and sustained professional learning community that is guided by professional teaching standards and the appropriate content-area standards and is focused on teacher development, problem solving, and mutual support. Opportunities such as regularly scheduled networking meetings, workshops, and courses as well as the implementation of online learning communities provide a context for rich interactions, professional dialogue, and reflection, as well as combat isolation.

8. Clear Roles and Responsibilities for Administrators
   - The role of administrators in the mentoring program is clearly defined.
   - Administrators receive ongoing professional development in order to help them support new teachers.
   - Administrators work to implement strategies learned in professional development and may review school policies to help support the induction program.
   - Administrators support the induction and mentoring program and work to increase buy-in of other staff members in their schools.
   - Administrators support mentors and new teachers differently than other teachers in the school, helping them to complete their responsibilities.

How does this contribute to a high-quality induction program?

Administrators set the stage for beginning teacher and mentor success by creating time for induction activities and establishing a positive culture for teacher development in their building and within the larger school district. Administrators need their own professional development on how to set the stage for the success of new teachers, ensuring the programs and policies are aligned with new teacher needs and best practices of induction and mentoring. Ongoing communication with administrators about the needs of new teachers and the nature of the program ensures that they understand their role in fully supporting induction, so that they do not inadvertently undermine the prospects of beginning teacher success (e.g., assigning beginning teachers the most challenging classes, assigning additional responsibilities, or not anticipating their needs for basic resources).

9. Collaboration With All Stakeholders
   - There is school and district buy-in to the program.
   - Financing for the program is stable and used effectively.
   - Feedback is collected from participants and mentors.
   - Feedback is used to make program decisions and to improve the program's usefulness.

- All support for new teachers is coordinated and aligned so that the program feels seamless to new teachers.

How does this contribute to a high-quality induction program?

Without strong partnerships and alignment, instructional initiatives, such as mentoring and induction, can be undermined. For an induction program to be strong, new teachers must not receive mixed messages from their colleagues, administrators, or community, which can make new teachers feel overwhelmed, confused, and frustrated by all the different layers of information coming at them. Strong communication and collaboration among stakeholders, including administration, school boards, union/association leadership, and professional partners creates a culture of commitment and ensures success of the high-quality induction program.

10. Accountability and Standards-Based Induction
    - The induction program is aligned with state and national induction and professional standards.
    - The program includes measures for determining level of implementation.
    - District leadership uses data, including mentor and new-teacher feedback, to continually refine and improve the induction program.

How does this contribute to a high-quality induction program?

In order to create a program that has high standards for accountability, schools and districts must commit to using professional teaching standards and state induction program standards fully integrated into all aspects of their program. Without integrating appropriate program, professional, and content standards, programs lack quality and accountability and risk having little impact on beginning teacher and student performance. A commitment to being data driven through evaluation of the program will also continue to inform program development and its continuous improvement as well as inform policies at all levels.

Continuum of High-Quality Mentoring and Induction Practices

High-Quality Induction Practices	Emerging	Developing	Integrating
1. Rigorous mentor selection	There are no set criteria or standards used to select high-quality mentors. Mentors may have less than three years of teaching experience and little knowledge of new teacher development. Mentors are often selected on the basis of convenience, availability, or seniority.	General criteria and standards for high-quality mentor selection are present but are not articulated or followed. Mentors have at least three years of teaching experience and some knowledge of new teacher development. Mentors and new teachers are matched whenever possible by grade level, subject area, or location.	Specific criteria and standards for high-quality mentor selection are clearly articulated and rigorously followed. Mentors often have four or more years of teaching experience, documented teaching and leadership skills, and substantial knowledge of beginning teacher development. Mentors and new teachers are matched based on grade level, subject area, and location.
2. Ongoing professional development and support for mentors	Mentors receive little to no ongoing professional development training and support. Training on induction-program requirements, state standards for teacher knowledge, and assessment of new teacher practice may be offered; if so, it focuses on issues of compliance. Additional optional mentor professional development is not provided. Mentors are often not compensated or entitled to reduced workloads despite their additional mentorship responsibilities.	Mentors receive limited ongoing professional development training and support. Training on induction program requirements, state standards for teacher knowledge, or assessment of new teacher practice is required but focuses on issues of compliance. Additional optional mentor professional development is rarely provided. Mentors receive limited compensation and reduced workload for their additional roles and responsibilities.	Mentors receive significant ongoing professional development training and support. Training on induction program requirements, state standards for teacher knowledge, and assessment of new teacher practice is required and provides information beyond compliance. Mentors also participate in required professional learning communities of mentors. Mentors receive adequate compensation and reduced workload commensurate with their roles and responsibilities.
3. Sanctioned time for mentor–teacher interactions	Meetings between these two parties often occur informally or not at all. Sanctioned time for mentor meetings and interactions is nonexistent.	Mentor and new teacher interactions occur more frequently, but sanctioned time is elusive and often shorter than needed for rigorous interactions. Mentors and new teachers receive limited or infrequent release time.	Sanctioned time (1.2 to 2.5 hours per week) for interactions between the mentor and the new teacher is safeguarded by the school administrator. This time allows for rigorous interaction focused on new-teacher development.

4. Multi-year mentoring	The mentoring and induction program does not have any clear long-term goals or purposes. There is limited formal coordination of activities within the program beyond a partial-day orientation to the community, district, curriculum, and school. The mentoring support that is offered only lasts into the first year of a new teacher's career.	The purpose and goals of the mentoring and induction program are clear and long term but may not be clearly articulated. There is some coordination of activities into the first year; the induction program often consists of a one- to two-day orientation prior to the start of school that orients new teachers to the district or school and explains relevant policies and procedures and topics of high interest to beginning teachers. The mentoring support offered is extended to second-year teachers.	The program has clearly defined long-term goals that are articulated and that focus on improving new teacher practice throughout the school year. The mentoring program and induction practices have become "organic" or an integral part of school and district operations rather than occurring as a special or staged event. Finally, the support for new teachers extends through at least year 1 and up to year 5 of their teaching careers.
5. Intensive and specific guidance moving teaching practice forward	New teachers receive limited or nonspecific feedback on their teaching practice. Mentors often function primarily as "buddies" or "cheerleaders" for new teachers by providing mainly emotional support and do not draw on professional teaching or content-area standards. Mentors are often unable or unwilling to demonstrate effective teaching practices.	New teachers receive occasional and informal feedback from their mentors regarding their teaching practice. Mentors infrequently draw upon professional teaching or content-area standards and enact few concrete steps to help new teachers improve their practice. Mentors are either unable or unwilling to demonstrate effective teaching practices.	New teachers receive frequent and substantive feedback from peers and mentors. Mentors continuously draw upon professional teaching and content-area standards and tools to provide concrete steps to improve new teacher practice. They are able and willing to demonstrate effective teaching practice.
6. Professional teaching standards and data-driven conversations	No formative assessment tools for new teacher development based on data and professional teaching standards are currently used within the school or district. Professional teaching standards may be mentioned during orientation and may be the basis for certain district/school-based tools but are not incorporated into the induction program or mentoring conversations. Instead, undocumented conversations drive the interactions between beginning	There is some limited use of formative assessment tools (i.e., rubrics, protocols, checklists, observation schedules). Although used, these formative assessments are not closely aligned to state professional teaching standards, making the incorporation of the standards into the conversations general at best. New teachers are observed occasionally by mentors and begin to build and deepen their grade-level/subject-area expertise through feedback and discussion of the data and evidence collected during observation, which is generally	There is an established set of tools of formative or summative assessment that emphasizes the development of beginning teachers on a continuum of professional growth. Moreover, formative and summative performance assessments are closely aligned to state professional standards. Mentors and new teachers use these tools to document data about and evidence of teaching practice and individual growth through regular observations throughout the year. Evidence and data are collected from regular observations, individual growth plans, examinations and

(Continued)

(Continued)

High-Quality Induction Practices	Emerging	Developing	Integrating
	teachers and mentors. New teachers are not observed by their mentor. They also do not have an opportunity to observe experienced teachers.	documented. New teachers are able to observe an experienced teacher once or twice throughout the school year.	interpretations of student work, and beginning teacher portfolios. New teachers have the opportunity to regularly observe experienced teachers and have time to reflect on those observations with their mentor.
7. Ongoing beginning teacher professional development	No distinctions are made between the induction and professional development needs of traditionally certified teachers, alternatively certified teachers, new to the district, and new to the teaching field teachers, or new to the district teachers. Beginning teachers may be required to attend district-based professional development, but it is "one size fits all." These professional development offerings are not aligned to professional or content standards. Professional development is often disconnected from the district/school/classroom contexts of new teachers. New teacher networking is irregular and informal.	There is some differentiation within the required induction program and professional development offerings for traditionally certified, alternatively certified, new to the district, and new to the teaching field teachers. However, the support and training offered is still mainly considered "one size fits all." Professional development options are partially aligned with professional or content standards and sometimes address challenges common to the district/school/classroom context. New teachers meet periodically to network with peers or to participate in short inservice workshops; the networking is often geared toward emotional support, and the workshops are loosely supported by professional and content standards.	Different induction strands within one program exist for the variety of new teachers (i.e., alternatively certified, traditionally certified, new to the field, and new to the district). The professional development within the induction program distinguishes for the specific needs of these groups and may also distinguish for specific teaching areas (i.e., special education, English language learners, fine arts). The professional development offerings are aligned to professional teaching standards and content standards as well as to research on the needs of beginning teachers. The professional development also addresses challenges common to the teaching context of that district/school/classroom. Protégés meet regularly to network, problem-solve, reflect on their growth, and engage in professional dialogue with other new teachers.
8. Clear roles and responsibilities for administrators	The role of the school principal is not clearly defined or articulated as a component of the induction program. School administrators do not receive professional development focused on strategies to support beginning teacher and mentor success. Administrators do not know about or do not support	Some administrators take an active role in supporting new teachers as they acclimate to the school culture; however, these roles are not always clearly defined. School administrators receive professional development about supporting the professional dialogue between mentors and new teachers and begin to implement	There is a clearly articulated definition of the administrator's role in the induction program, and administrators actively fill that role. School administrators receive ongoing professional development about the needs of beginning teachers and strategies for supporting those needs. They implement those strategies by

	taking a proactive role in reducing the workload of new teachers. Administrators clearly articulate the goals of the induction program to all teachers in their school/district. They meet with beginning teachers regularly to support their development as professionals.	some specific strategies (i.e., protected time, mentor assignment, resource provision). Administrators are familiar with the district/school induction program but do not clearly articulate the goals to the staff at their school. Administrators meet with beginning teachers occasionally.	the induction program at their school/district. Administrators do not interact differently with beginning teachers as compared with other staff.
9. Collaboration with all stakeholders	There is strong buy-in and support at the district and school levels. Funding is adequate and specifically targeted for program components that need improvement. Program feedback is obtained through input from all stakeholders. Program evaluation data are acted upon for the continuous development of the program. The district aligns all of its initiatives and other supports for beginning teachers with the induction program so that the program feels seamless to those participating in it.	There is growing buy-in and support at the school and district levels. Schools and districts may have adequate financial resources, but they may be used inefficiently or ineffectively. Input and feedback about the program are collected, but this information is not acted upon. Other district initiatives or supports for beginning teachers begin to align collaboratively with the induction program.	There is little to no support or buy-in at the school and district levels. Likewise, there is limited time or financial resources committed to the development and continuation of the program. Program feedback is not collected from new teachers or mentors. The induction program is not aligned or coordinated with other district initiatives or beginning teacher supports.
10. Accountability and standards-based induction	The program is closely aligned with state and national induction or professional standards throughout every facet of the program. There are strong measures and comprehensive processes in place for determining levels of implementation and impact of the program. Multiple sources of data are used to substantially evaluate and continuously improve the induction and mentoring program.	The program aligns some of its components to state or national induction or professional standards. There are some baseline measures and emerging processes in place to determine levels of implementation and impact of the program. Program data are collected from either a single source or through a small set of sources, and, while reviewed, the data do not impact improvements to the program.	The program is not or is loosely based on state or national induction or professional standards. There are minimal or no measures and processes for determining levels of implementation and impact of the program. Program data are not collected or are only minimally collected through a single source but are not used to substantially evaluate and improve the induction program.

BIBLIOGRAPHY

Brewster, C., & Railsback, J. (2001). *Supporting beginning teachers: How administrators, teachers, and policymakers can help new teachers succeed*. Portland, OR: Northwest Regional Educational Library. Retrieved October 30, 2008, from http://www.nwrel.org/request/may01/Beginning Teachers.pdf

Bush, T., & Middlewood, D. (2005). *Leading and managing people in education*. Thousand Oaks, CA: Sage Publications.

Humphrey, D., Wechsler, M., Bosetti, K., Park, J., & Tiffany-Morales, J. (2008). *Teacher induction in Illinois and Ohio*. Menlo Park, CA: SRI International. Retrieved October 30, 2008, from http://policyweb.sri.com/cep/publications/JoyceTeacherInduction2008.pdf

Illinois New Teacher Collaborative. (2008). *Introduction and purpose for the Illinois standards of quality and effectiveness for beginning teacher induction programs*. Champaign, IL: Author. Retrieved October 30, 2008, from http://intc.ed.uiuc.edu/documents/pilots/ILInduc%20StdsDraftInductDrft .pdf

Ingersoll, R., & Kralik, J. M. (2004). *The impact of mentoring on teacher retention: What the research says*. Denver, CO: Education Commission of the States. Retrieved October 30, 2008, from http://www.ecs.org/clearinghouse/50/36/5036.pdf

Ingersoll, R., & Smith, T. (2004). Do teacher induction and mentoring matter? *NASSP Bulletin, 88*(638), 28–40.

Johnson, S. M., Birkeland, S. E., Donaldson, M. L., Kardos, S. M., Kauffman, D., Liu, E., et al. (2004). *Finders and keepers: Helping new teachers survive and thrive in our schools*. San Francisco: Jossey-Bass.

Kapadia, K., Coco, V., & Easton, J. Q. (2007). *Keeping new teachers: A first look at the influences of induction in the Chicago public schools*. Chicago, IL: Consortium of Chicago School Research at the University of Chicago. Retrieved October 30, 2008, from http://ccsr.uchicago.edu/publications/keeping_new_teachers012407.pdf

Learning First Alliance. (2005). *A shared responsibility: Staffing all high-poverty, low-performing schools with effective teachers and administrators. A framework for action*. Washington, DC: Author.

Moir, E. (2003). *Launching the next generation of teachers through quality induction*. Paper presented at the National Commission on Teaching and America's Future State Partners Symposium, Santa Cruz, CA.

Moir, E., & Gless, J. (n.d.). *Quality induction: An investment in teachers*. Santa Cruz, CA: New Teacher Center. Retrieved October 30, 2008, from http://www.newteachercenter.org/article1.php

New Teacher Center. (2007). *High quality mentoring & induction practices*. Santa Cruz, CA: Author. Retrieved October 30, 2008, from http://www.newteachercenter.org/pdfs/Cap_Hill_HQM_ final.pdf

Sweeney, B. W. (2007). *Leading the teacher induction and mentoring program* (2nd ed.). Thousand Oaks, CA: Corwin.

Wurtzel, J., & Curtis, R. (2008). *Human capital framework for K–12 urban education: Organizing for success*. Washington, DC: The Aspen Institute. Retrieved October 30, 2008, from http://www.aspeninstitute.org/atf/cf/%7Bdeb6f227–659b-4ec8–8f84–8df23ca704f5%7D/ED_ HCFRAMEWORK_2.PDF

References and Bibliography

Bartell, C. A. (2005). *Cultivating high-quality teaching through induction and mentoring.* Thousand Oaks, CA: Corwin.

Berry, B., Germuth, A., & Hirsch, E. (2003). *A report to Governor Mike Easley: Teacher working conditions survey follow up.* Chapel Hill, NC: Southeast Center for Teaching Quality.

Bey, T. M. (1995). Mentorships: Transferable transactions among teachers. *Education and Urban Society, 28*(1), 11–20.

Boe, E. E., Cook, L. G., Bobbitt, S. A., & Weber, A. L. (1995, May). *Retention, transfer, and attrition of special and general education teachers in national perspective.* Paper presented at the National Dissemination Forum on Issues Relating to Special Education Teacher Satisfaction, Retention, and Attrition, Washington, DC.

Boyd, D., Lankford, H., Love, S., & Wuckoff, J. (2005). Explaining the short careers of high-achieving teachers in schools with low-performing students. *American Economic Review, 95*(2), 166–171.

Boyer, L., & Gillespie, P. (2000). Keeping the committed: The importance of induction and support programs for new special educators. *TEACHING Exceptional Children, 33*(6), 10–15.

Brewster, C., & Railsback, J. (2001). Teacher mentoring programs. In *Supporting beginning teachers: How administrators, teachers, and policymakers can help new teachers succeed.* Retrieved January 15, 2009, from Northwest Regional Educational Laboratory Web site: http:www.nwrel.org/request/may01/mentoring.html

California BTSA: Beginning Teacher Support and Assessment. (n.d.). *BTSA—Basics.* Retrieved March 24, 2009, from http://www.btsa.ca.gov/BTSA_basics.html

Casey, J., & Claunch, A. (2005). The stages of mentor development. In H. Portner (Ed.), *Teacher mentoring and induction: The state of the art and beyond.* Thousand Oaks, CA: Corwin.

Center for Cognitive Coaching. (n.d.). *Overview of Cognitive Coaching^SM.* Retrieved January 17, 2009, from http://www.cognitivecoaching.com/overview.htm

Chaika, G. (2006). *Scrambling for staff: The teacher shortage in rural schools.* Retrieved April 8, 2009, from Education World Web site: http://www.educationworld.com/a_admin/admin/admin142.shtml

Commission on Teacher Credentialing. (2008). *Induction program standards.* Retrieved January 28, 2009, from http://www.ctc.ca.gov/educator-prep/standards/Induction-Program-Standards.pdf

Costa, A., & Garmston, R. (2002). *Cognitive coaching: A foundation for renaissance schools* (2nd ed.). Norwood, MA: Christopher Gordon.

Curran, B., & Abrahams, C. (n.d.). *Teacher supply and demand: Is there a shortage?* Retrieved January 19, 2009, from National Governors Association, Center for Best Practices Web site: http://www.nga.org/cda/files/000125TEACHERS.pdf

Danielson, C. (2007). *Enhancing professional practice: A framework for teaching* (2nd ed.). Alexandria, VA: Association for Supervision and Curriculum Development.

Darling-Hammond, L. (1999). *Teaching as the learning profession: Handbook of policy and practice.* San Francisco: Jossey-Bass.

Darling-Hammond, L. (2000). *Solving the dilemmas of teacher supply, quality, and demand.* Washington, DC: National Commission on Teaching and America's Future.

Darling-Hammond, L., & Sykes, G. (2003). Wanted: A national teacher supply policy for education: The right way to meet the "highly qualified teacher" challenge. *Education Policy Analysis Archives, 11*(33). Retrieved January 19, 2009, from epaa.asu.edu/epaa/v11n33

Dunne, K., & Villani, S. (2007). *Mentoring new teachers through collaborative coaching: Linking teacher and student learning.* Thousand Oaks, CA: Corwin.

Education Commission of the States. (2003). *Eight questions on teacher preparation: What does the research say? A summary of the findings.* Retrieved April 8, 2009, from ecs.org/html/educationIssues/teachingquality/tpreport/home/summary.pdf

Feiman-Nemser, S. (2001). From preparation to practice: Designing a continuum to strengthen and sustain teaching. *Teachers College Record, 103*(6), 1013–1055.

Fideler, E., & Haselkorn, D. (1999). *Learning the ropes: Urban teacher induction programs and practices in the United States.* Belmont, MA: Recruiting New Teachers.

Gardiner, M., Enomoto, E., & Grogan, M. (2000). *Coloring outside the lines: Mentoring women into school leadership.* Albany: State University of New York.

Garmston, R., & Wellman, B. (2009). *The adaptive school: A sourcebook for developing collaborative groups* (2nd ed.). Norton, MA: Christopher Gordon.

Gewertz, C. (2002, June 12). Qualifications of teachers falling short [Electronic version]. *Education Week.*

Gordon, S. P., & Maxey, S. (2000). *How to help beginning teachers succeed.* Alexandria, VA: Association for Supervision and Curriculum Development.

Harvard University Gazette. (2003, April 24). New research finds school hiring and support practices fall short in K–12 public schools: Thirty-three percent of new teachers are hired after school year has started. Retrieved April 14, 2009, from http://www.news.harvard.edu/gazette/2003/04.24/13-teachers.html

Hayes, M. F., & Zimmerman, I. K. (Eds.). (1999). *Teaching: A career, a profession.* Wellesley, MA: Massachusetts Association for Supervision and Curriculum Development.

Hull, J. W. (2004, Spring). Filling in the gaps. *Threshold.* Retrieved April 8, 2009, from www.ciconline.org

Ingersoll, R. M. (2001). Teacher turnover and teacher shortages: An organizational analysis. *American Educational Research Journal, 38*(3), 499–534.

Ingersoll, R. M. (2002). Holes in the teacher supply bucket. *School Administrator, 59*(3), 42–43.

Ingersoll, R. M. (2003). *Is there really a teacher shortage?* Retrieved January 19, 2009, from University of Pennsylvania, Center for the Study of Teaching and Policy Web site: http://depts.washington.edu/ctpmail/PDFs/Shortage-RI-09-2003.pdf

Ingersoll, R. M. (2006). *Teacher recruitment, retention, and shortages.* Unpublished manuscript, University of Pennsylvania and Consortium for Policy Research in Education.

Johnson, S. M., & Birkeland, S. E. (2002). *Pursuing "a sense of success": New teachers explain their career decisions.* Retrieved March 26, 2009, from http://www.gse.harvard.edu/~ngt/Johnson_Birkeland_Oct_2002.pdf

Johnson, S. M., & Birkeland, S. E. (2003). Pursuing a "sense of success": New teachers explain their career decisions. *American Educational Research Journal, 40*(3), 581–617.

Johnson, S. M., & Birkeland, S. E. (2003). The schools that teachers choose. *Educational Leadership, 60*(8), 20–25.

Joyce, B., & Showers, B. (2002). Student achievement through professional development. In B. Joyce & B. Showers (Eds.), *Designing training and peer coaching: Our need for learning.* Alexandria VA: Association for Supervision and Curriculum Development.

Kardos, S. M., Johnson, S. M., Peske, H. G., Kauffman, D., & Liu, E. (2001). Counting on colleagues: New teachers encounter the professional cultures of their schools. *Educational Administration Quarterly, 37*(2), 250–290.

Lee, E., Brown, M. N., Luft, J. A., & Roehrig, G. H. (2007). Assessing beginning secondary science teachers' PCK: Pilot year results. *School Science and Mathematics, 107*(2), 52.

Loucks-Horsley, S., Love, N., Stiles, K. E., & Mundry, S. E. (2003). *Designing professional development for teachers of science and mathematics* (2nd ed.). Thousand Oaks, CA: Corwin.

Luft, J. A., Roehrig, G. H., & Patterson, N. C. (2003). Contrasting landscapes: A comparison of the impact of different induction programs on beginning secondary science teachers' practices, beliefs, and experiences. *Journal of Research in Science Teaching, 40*(1), 77–97.

Meckel, A., & Rolland, L. (2000). BTSA models for support provision. *Thrust for Educational Leadership, 29*(3), 18–20.

Moir, E. (1999). The stages of a teacher's first year. In M. Scherer, *A better beginning: Supporting and mentoring new teachers* (pp. 19–23). Alexandria, VA: Association of Supervision and Curriculum Development.

National Center for Education Information. (n.d.). Alternative routes to teacher certification: And [sic] overview. Retrieved April 8, 2009, from http://www.ncei.com/Alt-Teacher-Cert.htm

National Center for Education Statistics. (2008). *Digest of education statistics: 2007* (NCES Publication No. 2008–022). Retrieved January 13, 2009 from http://nces.ed.gov/programs/digest/d07/

National Commission on Teaching and America's Future. (1996). *What matters most: Teaching for America's future.* New York: Author.

National Commission on Teaching and America's Future & NCTAF State Partners. (2002, August). *Unraveling the "teacher shortage" problem: Teacher retention is the key* [symposium]. Washington, DC. Retrieved April 8, 2009, from http://www.ncsu.edu/mentorjunction/text_files/teacher_retentionsymposium.pdf

National Conference of State Legislatures. (n.d.). *Teacher recruitment.* Retrieved April 8, 2009, from www.ncsl.org/programs/educ/TRecru.htm

National Council of Teachers of Mathematics. (2007). *Mentoring new teachers: A position of the National Council of Teachers of Mathematics.* Retrieved February 3, 2009, from http://nctm.org/about/content.aspx?id=12376

National Science Teachers Association. (2007). *NSTA position statement: Induction programs for the support and development of beginning teachers of science.* Retrieved February 3, 2009, from https://secure.nsta.org/about/positions/induction.aspx

Podsen, I. (2002). *Teacher retention: What is your weakest link?* Larchmont, NY: Eye on Education.

Portner, H. (Ed.). (2005). *Teacher mentoring and induction: The state of the art and beyond.* Thousand Oaks, CA: Corwin.

Public Education Network. (2004). *The voice of the new teacher.* Washington, DC: Author.

Reiman, A., & Thies-Sprinthall, L. (1998). *Mentoring and supervision of teacher development.* New York: Longman.

Roehrig, G. H., & Luft, J. A. (2006). Does one size fit all? The experiences of beginning teachers from different teacher preparation programs during an induction program. *Journal of Research in Science Teaching, 43*(9), 963–985.

Rothman, R. (2004, January/February). Landing the "highly qualified teacher": How administrators can hire—and keep—the best. *Harvard Education Letter.* Retrieved January 19, 2009, from http://www.edletter.org/past/issues/2004-jf/hiring.shtml

Sanders, W. K., & Rivers, J. C. (1996). *Cumulative and residual effects of teachers on future student academic achievement.* Knoxville: University of Tennessee, Value-Added Research and Assessment Center.

Saphier, J., Haley-Speca, M. A., & Gower, R. (2008). *The skillful teacher: Building your teaching skills* (6th ed.). Acton, MA: Research for Better Teaching.

Scherer, M. (Ed.). (1999). *A better beginning: Supporting and mentoring new teachers.* Alexandria, VA: Association for Supervision and Curriculum Development.

Smith, T. M., & Ingersoll, R. M. (2004). What are the effects of induction and mentoring on beginning teacher turnover? *American Educational Research Journal, 41*(3), 681–714.

Steffy, B. E., Wolfe, M., Preston, P., & Enz, B. (Eds.). (2000). *Life cycle of the career teacher.* Thousand Oaks, CA: Corwin.

Strong, M. (2006, January). *Does new teacher support affect student achievement?* (Research Brief No. 06-01). Santa Cruz: University of California, Santa Cruz, New Teacher Center.

Texas Center for Educational Research. (2000). *The cost of teacher turnover.* Austin, TX: Author.

Veenman, S. (1984). Perceived problems of beginning teachers. *Review of Educational Research, 54,* 143–178.

Villani, S. (1983). *Mentoring and sponsoring as ways to heighten women's career aspirations and achievement.* Unpublished doctoral dissertation, Northeastern University, Boston.

Villani, S. (1999). Mentoring new teachers: A good, strong anchor. In M. F. Hayes & I. K. Zimmerman (Eds.), *Teaching: A career, a profession* (pp. 19–25). Wellesley: Massachusetts Association for Supervision and Curriculum Development.

Villani, S. (2002). *Mentoring programs for new teachers: Models of induction and support.* Thousand Oaks, CA: Corwin.

Villar, A., & Strong, M. (2007, Summer). Is mentoring worth the money? A benefit-cost analysis and five-year rate of return of a comprehensive mentoring program for beginning teachers [Special reprint]. *ERS Spectrum, 25*(3).

Wong, H., & Wong, R. (2001). What successful new teachers are taught. *Teachers.Net Gazette, 2*(3). Retrieved April 8, 2009, from http://teachers.net/gazette/MAR01/wong.html

Zubrowski, B., Troei, V., & Pasquale, M. (2008). *Making science mentors: A 10-session guide for middle grades.* Arlington, VA: National Science Teachers Association.

The Corwin logo—a raven striding across an open book—represents the union of courage and learning. Corwin is committed to improving education for all learners by publishing books and other professional development resources for those serving the field of PreK–12 education. By providing practical, hands-on materials, Corwin continues to carry out the promise of its motto: **"Helping Educators Do Their Work Better."**

WestEd, a national nonpartisan, nonprofit research, development, and service agency, works with education and other communities to promote excellence, achieve equity, and improve learning for children, youth, and adults. WestEd has 16 offices nationwide, from Washington and Boston to Arizona and California. Its corporate headquarters are in San Francisco. More information about WestEd is available at WestEd.org.